# EVERTON

# SEASON 1888-89

## BY

## BILLY SMITH

First Published 2007 by Countyvise Limited,
14 Appin Road, Birkenhead, Wirral CH41 9HH.

British Library Cataloguing in Publication Data.
A catalogue record for this book is available from the British Library.

ISBN 978 1 901231 89 2

# *Introduction*

Football, the game as we now know it, has become the world's largest participant and spectator sport. The World Cup Finals is the world's biggest singular sporting event. The game is now defined as 'an industry', one, which is closely aligned to significant developments in modern culture, consumption, and specifically, the development of the television and telecommunications industries. Football has come an extremely long way, since its humble beginnings as a Victorian pastime, to the global phenomenon it is today.

The Victorian age was characterised by rapid change and advances in nearly every sphere, there were developments in medical, scientific and technological knowledge. Work and play expanded dramatically, communication and transport links encouraged travel and leisure opportunities for all, as Britain experienced changes in population growth and location. Visits to seaside resorts, race meetings and football matches could be enjoyed by a growing urban society. Improvements in literacy stimulated interest in popular journalism and literature. Victorian attitudes towards 'Cleanliness and Godliness' inspired a higher level of organised sporting activities (as was the case with St Domingo Methodist Church, from which Everton Football Club was formed), to siphon off the 'sinful' energies of the urban youth. It was within this crucible of change that modern football was born.

In 1885 professionalism was legalised under certain limitations and in March 1888 William McGregor, a Scottish Merchant and Director of Aston Villa Football Club, suggested a new system that would bring order to the chaotic structure that prevailed in the footballing world. As the urbanisation and industrialisation of football began to take full control, he proposed to bring an end to the difficultly facing *'football clubs of any standing to meet their friendly engagements and even arrange friendly matches'*, by introducing a structured league system that has remained largely intact today.  Everton Football Club, then as they are now, where able to boast regular attendances and good amenities; basic requirements of the 'new' league.

This book, which is the first of a series of season-by-season accounts of Everton Football Club's Victorian era, focuses on Everton's inaugural season in William McGregor's newly formed Football League.  It utilises unedited articles from contemporary newspapers, The Liverpool Courier, The Liverpool Mercury and The Liverpool Daily Post, to paint a portrait of a vibrant society and a national pastime in a state of ascendancy and transition.  It underpins the unique and continually evolving relationship that has existed between football and the media since its inception.  But more importantly it emphasises that even though the modern game itself is almost unrecognisable from its Victorian counterpart, the one thing that has remained constant in over a century's worth of football is the passion of the fans.

**William and Neil Smith**

# *Acknowledgements*

The Authors, wish to thank, David Prentice, Tony Onslow, Steve Milnes, Gavin Buckland, Vanessa Smith, James Smith, Chelsea Smith, April Smith, Maria Smith, Grace Smith, Henry and Iona Smith, and the Liverpool Record Office for their assistances.

# SEPTEMBER 1888

## START OF SEASON
*September 1, 1888. The Daily Post.*

Today inaugurates the season of football for 1888. When the
Association takes the field for an eight-month campaign. Perhaps
there has never been a period in its history when football-
that is the Association game-has excited so much interest and
attraction from the public, and this augers well for in its success
at the pay gates, a no slight consideration for management in
these days of large expenditure. Much legislation; - perhaps too
much for the football player himself, has been going on during
the summer, and a new venture has also been started under the
name of the Football League, which if importance of fixture and
combination go for anything should prove a great season.

As an instance of the feeling of interest in this neighborhood,
we may quote the scene which encurred a few Saturdays ago,
when it was whispered round that Everton were going to have
their first practice on a field off Belmont-road. Lookers on at
cricket and other games in Stanley Park, and else where at
once tipped off and by the time the men made their appearance,
2,000 or 3,000 people were present. Each new player, and there
are not a few-was critically scanned on his appearances in the
field. Some of the well-known men received a hearty welcome,
and the new captain, in the person of the celebrated N.J.Ross,
received quite an ovation. This augers well for the support the
club may expect to receive during the season. Many changes
have taken place in the executive as well, as the players since
last season. Mr. W.E.Barclay, the polite and energetic governor
of the Everton industrial School, has been installed as secretary,
and under his guidance the club should certainly not lose any
of its prestige. Early in the summer the wise precaution was
taken of getting tenders from practical men, to undertake the

apparently impossible task of making grass grow on what was then a bare brown patch of earth, but thanks to Messrs., Rowlands, of Green-lane, the skill and the fostering care of the groundsman, and above all the influence of St. Swithin, grass has grown in abundance, so that the novel sight has been witnessed of a mowing machine at work and sheep grazing. A formidable list of players has already being published, from which, the team will be chosen; in fact there are no less than three goalkeepers, four backs, and a host of half-backs. Still the front division is not all that could be desired, for amongst the forwards selected to do duty today against Padiham there are three of the old hands. On account of not having yet received his transfer from the Association, N.J.Ross will not wear the Everton colours to-day.

## EVERTON 4 PADIHAM 1

*September 3, 1888. The Liverpool Mercury.*

The Everton football Club opened their season on Saturday, and had, as their opponents, the once famous Padiham, who have been slightly strengthened since their last visit here. The home club tried all their new men, with the exception of Gillain who failed to turn up at the last minute, and they gave satisfaction to the 7,000 spectators, who lined the ropes. The ground, which was in good condition, reflects credit on the contractor, Mr Rollands, West Derby, the visitors were the first to appear, following closely by Ross and his men, amid ahearty round of applause. Winning the toss, Ross elected to play with a stiffish breeze in his favour. Craven kicked off, the ball travelling towards Dick, who planted it well up the field, and Farmer had hard luck in not scoring, the shot skimming the upright. Loftus starved off a dangerous rush from the home forwards, and Waugh tested Park, who had to concede a corner, but the wind carried Fleming's shot over the bar. A succession of corners caused the visitor's custodian some anxiety, but the defence was broken by Farmer, who scored with a nice shot five minutes from the start. Aided by Craven and O'Brien, Padiham got well down from the kick off, but Holt intercepted, and passed to his left wing pair, who dribbled well up, Chadwick finished with a screw shot, which Thompson in clearing, put through his own goal, thus registering the second point for Everton. Restarting, Chadwick, Farmer, and Warmby, treated the spectators to a nice bit of passing, Hudson causing the latter players to put wide his finishing shot. Waite, Waugh sorely taxed Parks who cleared at the expense of a corner, which, was got away, and play was taken to the other end, where Crears made a bad attempt to score. Again becoming aggressive, the homesters made many attempts to eject another downfall, but Parks and the backs defended nobly and succeeded in paying a visit to the home end, where Higgins was penalised for carrying the ball in clearing in a shot from Crears. Nothing resulting. Everton again had a succession of corners, and Ross sent in a scorcher to the visitors goalkeeper, which also was got away, half-time arriving with the score - Everton 2: Padiham 0. On changing ends, the home forwards soon bore down on the visitors, and Waugh, who had been playing a consistent game, enabled Farmer to head a third goal which, however, was disallowed for off-side. Nothing daunted the home forwards, again attacked and Farmer put a legitimate point on by scoring a third for his side from a pass by Holt. Waugh, and Costley having missed a chance from Waugh, owing to erratic shooting, the Pads paid another visit to the home-quarters, and Crears again muddled. Farmer got well down, but Hudson held him when dangerous, and from the free kick Birtwistle got nicely pass Ross finishing with a bad attempt. From now to the finish Everton continued to have all the play, and Chadwick scored a fourth goal from a pass by Waugh. Just on time Birtwistle got up and screwed across, Craven beating Higgins, for the first time, results Everton 4:

Padiham 1. For the winners, the backs half-backs, and wings were all that could be desired, and are sure to make their mark this season; for the losers Parks, McCrae and Hudson were the best of a medium lot. **Teams Everton: - Higgins goal, Dick and Ross (captain), backs, Holt, Dobson, and Warmby, half-backs, Fleming Waugh, Costley, Chadwick, and Farmer forwards. Padiham: - Parks, goal, McCrae and Hudson, backs, Luftus, Thompson and Sagar, half-backs, Crears, Birtwistle Craven, O'Brien and Waite, forward.**

## SALTNEY 1 EVERTON RESERVES 5
*September 3, 1888. The Liverpool Mercury.*

Played at Saltney on Saturday. The home teams were the first to score, through a misunderstanding between Joliffe and Chadwick. After 20 minutes play the superior skill of Everton began to tell, and Harper equalized. This was a supplemented by another goal-a spendid shot from Keys. In the second half Everton had matters all their own way, and eventually ran out easy winners by 5 goals to 1. The forwards played a splendid game. **Everton team: - C. Joliffe, goal, Hoaldsworth and Chadwick backs, Parry, H. Pollock, and W. Jones, half-backs J. Keys and W Briscoe, right wing, Harper, centre, Cookson and R. Falls, left wing.**

## EVERTON 1 BLACKBURN OLYMPIC 2
*September 4, 1888. The Liverpool Mercury.*

This match was played at Anfield last evening in the presence of a large number of spectators. Olympic won the toss and Waugh started for Everton, and Fleming ran up, and Wharmby shot, but the shot was repulsed. The visitors left now ran down pretty, but Ross in his own unique style, robbed them, and returned, Wharmby finishing with a bad shot. Everton still continued to pass, and Waugh playing strongly, secured a corner. Again Heyes and Dixon, by their pretty and unselfish passing troubled Ross, and, Dick and obtained a foul, but with no result. Loose play was now the order for some time, the Everton team becoming disorganised. At last Chadwick got a good shot, but Barrett cleared, and Strachan and Carlisle getting possession ran down, passing over Ross's head. Joliffe running out, and Heyes shooting. It appeared to every one present that the ball passed over the bar, but the referee gave his decision against Everton, and the visitors were award a goal, much to their surprise. Strachan and Carlisle again troubled Ross, who had his hands full, owing to the indifferent play of Warmby, but he was found to be all there. Chadwick obtaining possession, put in a good centre, which Fleming failed to utilize. Waugh repeated this unfortunate performance directly afterwards, from a good pass. The visitors by some strong and determined play forced a corner from Ross, and it being well placed, Heyes was enabled to defeat Joliffe a second time. Half-time was now called. Hothersall restarted and Everton pressed. Holt was applauded for the neat manner in which he robbed the visitors right. After a lot of give and take play, Keys mulled an easy chance from Fleming. The Everton forwards now completely fell off, but the Olympic improved, and pressed Ross, and Dick repeatedly. Their forwards were playing by a far more scientific game, and were supported by good back play. Ross here altered the team and going centre, and placing Dobson back, and Farmer half-backs, but although numerous chances were missed by Keys and others the change worked, and playing desperately, Chadwick scored a beauty. Everton now forced the game, but weak shooting applied all their efforts and eventually the Olympics won by 2 goals to 1. **Teams Olympic: - Barrett, goal, Davy, and Redhead backs, Starkie Sellars, and Gibson half-backs Strachan, Heyes, Carlisle, Hothersall, and Dixon forwards Everton: - C. Joliffe goal A. Dick, and NJ Ross (captain),** backs J. Holt, G. Dobson, and H. Warmby, half-backs G. Fleming, J. Keys, D. Waugh, E. Chadwick, and G. Farmer, forwards. H Brownlow Referee.

## BOOTLE RESERVES 0 EVERTON RESERVES 1
*September 5, 1888. The Liverpool Mercury.*

The first of a quartet of matches arranged between the above teams took place on the Bootle ground, last evening, and there being no counter attractions, a good proportion, for their respective supporters assembled to witness the contest. There being quite 2500, when McCowan opened the game on behalf of the home team. Some injudicious passing from the Bootle forwards, enabled the Everton forwards to assume an aggressive attitude, but Spencer, who was at the juncture exhibiting splendid form, defended his charge in fine style. A momentary visit to the Everton end, was nicely replied to by Higgins and once again the home team was called upon to save. The pressure was stubbornly maintained by the visitors, and from a tough scrimmage in front of goal, Briscoe draw "first blood" on behalf of Everton. Following this, Bootle, who had been playing, but an indifferent forward game, pulled themselves together, and Joliffe was repeatedly called upon to fist out some splendid shots from Fenn and Lewis. The visiting left were again prominent in an sudden spurt, and after a most stubborn defence, Falls put the leather through but the point was disallowed on the score of "off-side" Kicking out, Thompson sent in a clinking shot, and he experienced the disappointment of seeing it graze the crossbar. Later a corner secured to Everton, and Spencer averting danger. Thompson and Lewis contributed a splendid run down the home right, the latter leaving an easy opening for McCowan to equalise, however, was not put to the best advantage. This brought about the interval with Everton leading by one goal. Resuming the home team showed up to better advantage, but failed to make a breach in the visitors defence. Following this shot after shot was levelled at the Bootle citadel, but Newport displayed most excellent judgement in manipulating some really fine attempts from Harper and Briscoe. Spencer effected a speedy relief and the home forwards, getting well on the Everton line, tried hard to equalizes, but Joliffe was not to be beaten. The remainder of the match was most stubbornly, and evenly contested and as darkness was fast closing in, it became almost impossible to follow the progess of the game, but as no material point was added to the score the visitors retired victorious by one goal to nil. The home forwards proved to be the weak part of the team, while the backs played a sterling game conspicuous amongest them being Spencer, who played a faultless game throughout. Newport's performances in goal was a grand one, and should last night's display, he no exception. He will undoubtedly have a bright future before him. It will be remembered that the Reserves of Bootle have not been defeated since the season of 1885-86 and this reverse has somewhat nettled their most ardent followers; but it must also be remembered that while they were obliged to bid farewell to the backbone of their team, who were called upon to fill up the gap in the first eleven their opponents have, on the other hand, been considerably reinforced by players from their first eleven, and that on the whole their performance was rather a creditable one than otherwise. The constitution of the present Bootle Reserves must undoubtedly with practice prove to be a thoroughly reliable one, while the Everton executive can also congratulate themselves on being able to place a reserve team to this field which will stand the test with similar combinations. **Teams; Everton: - Joliffe, goal, A. Chadwick, and Higgins, backs Fayer, Jones and Pollock, half-backs, Falls Keys, Costley, Harper, and Briscoe forwards. Bootle: - Newport goal, Howarth, and Spencer, backs, Donaughine, McDonald and Dodd, half-backs Lewis, McCowan, Fenns, Barber, and Thompson, forwards.**

## EVERTON 2 HALLIWELL 1
*September 6, 1888. The Liverpool Mercury.*

This match the third engaged by Everton, within five days was
played last evening at Anfield, and excited much interests.
Halliwell who have always ensured a sterling game in their
visits to Liverpool, entered on their latest contest this season
with a couple of victories to their credit, they having overthrown
Burnley Union Star and Burslem Port Vale, whilst Everton,
against more serious opponents had been less fortunate. An
"accidental" reverse at the hands of Blackburn Olympic having
completely discounted their substantial win of 4 goals to 1 with
Padiham. The home team again underwent rearrangement in
order to recover some of their lost ground, and to be fully prepared
for the exciting encounter with Accrington-the opening League
fixture on Saturday. The weather however, interfered with both
good play, and the attendance's, though for such a slippery
ground a fair display was shown. Lewis of Bangor, displaced
Costley at centre, otherwise the names of the Everton team were
the same as announced. Hallwell were strongly represented. The
visitors at once had to clear a corner, when Mullen replied with
an off-side goal. Waugh assisted by Fleming gave trouble, Holt
finishing off the attack with a long shot which, was well taken
charge of by Bamber. Everton continued the pressure, and after
one or two near shaves of scoring, the home club obtained a
fine goal at the hands of Chadwick, who made a grand aim from
a Lewis pass. Another good shot was tried and then Hallwell
found their way down the hill, McGunness beating the defence
with a return. Farmer and Chadwick, at once replied with a
sharp run, but the former declined an easy opportunity. Lewis
and Waugh then put in a couple of ficklish shots. Dick came to
the rescue at an opportune moment and enabled the left wing
to get well up, to no purpose. Halliwell next made ground for a
corner, which, was immediately set of by Robbs rushing in, and

giving a corner. Everton in spoiling a splendid run by Chadwick and Farmer. Dick about this time resumed his place at back; Dobson going centre half-back and the interval arrived with the score a goal each. Everton having so far showed slightly superior tactics. On Lewis resuming, a strong kick, Lucas sent Everton backs, but the right wing easing. Fleming contributing one or two of his old style centre, the ball eventually rolling harmlessly away from Farmer's foot. The latter however, made amends by running well, scoring splendidly. He nearly repeated the movement a little later, but met a check. The game resulting in a 2 goals to 1 for Everton. **Everton: - Joliffe, goal, Ross (captain), and Dobson backs, Warmby, Holt, and Dick half-backs, Fleming, Waugh, W.Lewis, E. Chadwick and Farmer, forwards. Halliwell: - Bamber goal, Lucas, and Robbs, backs, K. Robinson, Crombie and McDougal, half-backs, Turner Hays, Mullen, Cross, and McGunness forwards, Referee J Rogers**

### EVERTON 2 ACCRINGTON 1 (Game 1)
*September 10, 1888. The Liverpool Mercury.*

A crowd of close on 12,000 turned up at the Anfield-road ground on Saturday, to witness the above encounter, which was the first of the series of fixtures arranged by the League. The Accrington team was the strongest they could put on the field, while the home club substituted R Jones at half-back instead of Warmby, and W.Lewis (Bangor) in Costley's place at centre forward, Smalley again taking his position between the posts. The weather was fine, with a strong sun and very little wind, and the ground was in good order. The visitors who turned up 20 minutes later, won the toss, and Lewis sent the ball rolling against the sun. Waugh was the first to be conspicuous by passing nicely to Fleming, who sent it to Farmer, and the latter put in a scorching shot. Horne clearing at the expense of a corner, which was badly taken. A goalkick to the visitors enabled Joe Lofthouse to get within shooting distance, but Dobson cleared nicely and gave Lewis's a chance. Stevenson robbing him, however, while in the act of testing Horne, from a throw in, Chadwick had a corner conceded to him, which Farmer put to the side. Aided by Dobson and Holt, the home right got away and Waugh sent in a low swift shot, which Pemberton negotiated, following by Chippendale being eased by Holt, who returned the leather well down, but Lewis found the defence impenetrable. An exciting bit of play now ensued. Howarth, in clearing a shot headed into Horne, who threw out in nice style, and Waugh rushing down, kicking on to the crossbar, the ball falling over. Dobson having had a trail for goal, the visiting forwards rushed up in a body, only to find Dick ready to meet them by planting to his right wing pair, and Waugh was loudly cheered for making a passage through the visitors and troubling Horne. Stevenson cleared off disaster, but Lewis eventually got cleverly away, and gave a long pass to Fleming, who could not get down, in time, and the ball rolled out. By means of a goal kick. Holden and Chippendale dribbled up, but the latter had his shot spoiled by Ross. Holt now got his hands in the way, and from the penalty, (Free-Kick) Howarth sent the ball spinning over Smalley's charge for the first time. R.Jones, who appeared to be lame, managed to beat Kirkham, and then the home left worked down, Farmer's attempt going wide, arousing themselves to the call of their captain to "play up Reds" Chippendale and Bonar each had shies, but Ross and Holt relieved and play was taken to the "Reds" end, where Lewis, Dobson and Chadwick had shots in rapid succession. Horne however, defended well, and managed to avert a downfall. Dobson, who had to keep watching Lofthouse enabled Joe to get freedom, that player giving Smalley his first handful with a stunner. Everton then had a couple of free kicks, from one of which, Lewis had hard luck in heading over the crossbar. Coming again, the home forward's swarmed around Horne, and

Stevenson managed to Spoil Waugh in a tricky run. Hands to the visitors in the home quarters gave the homester a chance, and Horne pushed Fleming, from a pass by Chadwick, off the ball, while in the act of shooting it through, half-time arriving with a clean sheet. On changing ends, Accrington became busy, but Dobson managed to clear, Ross having intercepted Chippendale who was playing a grand game in his new position, the home club took up the running, and literally swarmed Horne, who was in splendid form. Pressure was at length eased by Holden running to the other end, where Dick relieved and Dobson had the misfortune to foul Bonar. From the free kick Ross returned the ball, and Horne's charge was again in danger, the visitors conceding a corner. The kick was nicely taken, Dobson heading in, and McLallan and Stevenson preventing disaster. Another corner having been got rid of by the visitors. Dobson, who gave the pass to Waugh, who in turn gave to Farmer stopped Lofthouse in a run, and that player enabled Fleming to head the first goal. Striving hard to equalise, Bonar and Lofthouse was held, in check by Holt, but the visitors still kept in the home quarters, and Dick was the hero of the finest bit of back play seen on Everton ground for some considerable time, keeping his lines clear in grand style. Taking the play up the hill, Chadwick and Lewis looked dangerous, and the former sent in a low shot, when Horne, in clearing, fractured a rib, necessitating a stoppage of play. McLennan went in goal, and Howarth back. Resuming, Everton again became aggressive, and Fleming soon registered a second goal from a pass by Farmer.Accrington next had the best of the play, and after Holden had headed on to the bar and Kirkham had hard lines, a free kick was conceded them, from which Holden beat Smalley. Everton than had another try to score after which Holden severely tested the home custodian, but without effect, a strongly contested game thus ending with the result Everton two goals; Accrington one. **Teams; Everton:- Smalley, goal, Dick and Ross (captain), backs,**

Holt. R. Jones, and Dobson, half-backs, Fleming, Waugh, W. Lewis, Chadwick, and Farmer forwards. Umpire Berry, Accrington: - Horne, goal, Stewart, and McLennan backs Howarth, Wilkinson, and Pemberton, half-backs, Lofthouse, Bonar, E. Kirkham, Holden and Chippendale forwards, Umpire O. Oldham, referee J.J.Bentley.

**SPRING BRANCH ROVERS 1 EVERTON RESERVES 2**
*September 10, 1888. The Liverpool Mercury.*

Everton visited Ince on Saturday. Falls and Key were absentees, their places filled by Scott and Jones. Winning the toss the visitors took advantage of the wind, but good play was considerably interfered with by the state of the ground, the result being a win for Everton by 2 goals to 1. **Everton team: - Joliffe, goal, Ashcroft, and A. Chadwick, backs W.H. Jones, Pollock, and T.Fayer, half-backs Scott, Briscoe, Costley, Cookson and Jones forwards.**

**EVERTON REVIEW**
*September 10, 1888. The Liverpool Mercury.*

Everton's new govering body, taking up the enterprising lines of their prodecessors, have left no stone unturned to get their machinery in perfect order for the heavy programme, that has been mapped out. To justify their position as "one of the twelve" it has been neccassary to introduce new blood of the very first order, and which the valuable acquisitions of N.J Ross (of Preston North End), E.Chadwick (of Blackburn Rovers), W.Lewis (of Bangor), and Holt (of Bootle), together with Warmby and Keys, from Derby County, to reinforce Smalley, Dick, Dobson, R Jones, Farmer, Waugh, and Fleming, a team has been gathered together within the four corners of Anfield enclosure, that should and no doubt will improve capable of giving a good account of themselves against the powerful teams with which, they are to measure themselves. Such a team can only be maintained at an enormous expense, but the executive can rest assured that the public will gladly assist them in their ambition to possess Liverpool of champion exponents of the game. The opening contest on the first was judiciously arranged, for the Padiham they met one of their weakest, but at the same time most popular opponents. Of course Everton won and that substantially by 4 goals to 1. The play, however, cannot be called brilliant, the balance of strength not being sufficiently true to test the powers of the home representatives. Behind, Everton were all that could be desired, but the combination of the forwards was lacking, Costley at centre being a vertable fish out of water in such company right and left. On Monday Blackburn Olympic came, saw, and conquered, a new formation was tried. Costley stood down, Waugh went centre, and Keys was tried with Fleming but the move proved a failure. The vistors soon received a lead with a very doubtful goal, and this whim of fate, no doubt, had a good deal to do with the demoralisation that set in along the front line, Half-time came, Hayes improved the chance of Olympic by successfully flourishing off a corner. Key next mulled badly, with matters looking serious, and time and light becoming less, Ross reformed, going centre himself to rush the game, and by this means, as he has done on previous occasions, received some of the lost ground; but there was only time for a solitary goal, so there was nothing for it but to accept a defeat of 2 to 1. The losers only consolation being that the winners besides playing a surprisingly neat game, had all the luck. For the third engagement of the season, against Halliwell on Wednesday evening, the one great desideration was supplied-a centre forward up to the standard of the powerful wings. W Lewis of Bangor, of well-known Welsh international fame, was at last requisitioned, and proved an unmistakable success, the five forwards working as solidly as though they had long been associated. The back division also was as safe as ever, the least conspicuous being Warmby; whilst Holt was hardly so much at home as when frisking with his old Bootle colleagues. Altogether Everton played a sterling game against the strong Halliwellians, among when McGuinness was always a (bete noir) to the home defence, the result of 2 goals to 1. In no way helping the respective tactics. The last of the Anfielders Preliminary journeys was by far the best, and from which, they emerged with evidence for the more serious business of League engagement, for the first of which, the supporters of Everton turned up at Anfield to something like the number of 12,000-this was perhaps the largest attendance at any of the League matches-the bulk of whom were thoroughly satisfield with the display of their pets. Everton with the exception of R.Jones, whose leg again gave way, and caused him to be of little service, played a hard and fast game, although at times not a combined one. Smalley was safe in goal, keeping his head cool, and baffling Holden time after time. Dick and Ross were in splendid form, especially the former, who fairly excelled himself, and indeed, may be reckoned one of the finest backs in the country. At half-back, Dobson, and Holt worked hard, it not always judicious in their kicks; while the forward rank maintained the improvement, observable in the Halliwell contest. Practice alone being requisite to develop sound combination, the visitors all round veined great determination to win, and never relaxed their efforts one moment to secure victory. Unfortunately Horne their custodian, received an injury in clearing a shot from Chadwick, which of course placed Accrington at a disadvantage.

**EVERTON 5 STANLEY 0**
*September 14, 1888. The Liverpool Mercury.*

The first encounter between the above locals took place last evening before about 2,500 spectators. Everton played the same teams as on Saturday with the exception of McKinnon, a "Stranger" from Edinburgh, while Stanley were reinforced by the services of Quine (Press Guards), Stevens (Police Athletic), and Griffiths (Press Guard). Everton won the toss, and elected to defend the Anfield road goal. Within 30 sec, from the start, Everton scored from a foul in front of Stanley's goal. Following this, the home team pressed the visitors pretty severely, Fleming ultimately shooting wide. Threllfall and Stevens effected relief, with a neat run down the right, but failed to escape the vigilance of Ross and Dick. Holt despoiled Quina, and parted nicely to Farmer, who badly misjudged his kick. "Hands" in front of goal looked ominous for Stanley, but Wilson cleared, following which Roberts saved at the expense of a corner from which, Farmer registered the second goal. The home forwards were now having all their own way, but the shooting was very erratic. The visitors for the next quarter of an hour were playing an entirely defensive game, Chadwick finally beating the Stanley custodian with a clinking shot. Half time soon arrived with the home team leading by three goals. Resuming, Everton at once pressed, Holt giving a good chance to score, which was not put to the best advantage. Immediately afterwards Ross had a "shy" that did not make allowance for the wind, and a foul a yard in front of the Stanley goal did not prove of any advantage to the homesters. Roberts cleared some fine shots from Farmer and Chadwick, when Pickstaff, taking up the running levelled the first shot at the Everton citadel, which passed rather wide. The visitors now showed up the better advantage, but Dick and McKinnon were ever watchful. At length Everton again came to the attack, and after a tough scrimmage in front of the Stanley goal, Farmer notched the fourth goal. The light was now very bad the progess of the play being simply marked by the movement of the players. After two or three momentary spurts down the visitors left, Ross caused great anxiety to the Stanley defence, finally adding the fifth goal. Shortly after this the game ended, leaving Everton winners of a one-sided game by five goals to nil. **Teams. Everton:- Joliffe goal, Dick and McKinnon backs, Warmby, Dobson, and Holt half-backs, Farmer, Chadwick, Ross (captain), Waugh and Fleming, forwards. Stanley: - Roberts, goal, Griffiths, and W. Wilson, backs, Roberts, Martin, and J. Wilson, half-backs Threllfall, Pickstaff, Stevens, Brown, and Quine, forwards.**

## EVERTON 2 NOTTS COUNTY 1 (Game 2)
*September 17, 1888. The Liverpool Mercury.*

The league fixture, the second engaged in by the home club was played on Saturday. At Anfield Road, before 9,000 spectators. Notts, who had not previously taken part in any match this season, were without Jackson, Daft, and Gunn-the two latter playing in the North v South cricket match-but their places were ably filled, and the teams showed to greater advantage than they did in the two encounters last season. The home team was the same as that last Saturday with the exception of McKinnon late of Hearts of Midlothians", who temporally took up his position at center-half-back. The rain which fell previous to the starting of the game caused the ground to be a little treacherous, and may account for the few mishaps which occurred. Winning the toss Ross took the advantage of a slight breeze, but had the hill against him. Jardine put the ball in motion, and Fleming, nicely eluding Shelton and Guttridge ran up and centered, Chadwick finished with a wide shot. Moore and Wardle got away from the goal kick, and looked like scoring Ross giving a corner to save. After that had been cleared, Chadwick and Farmer worked up to within shooting distance, only to be spoiled by McLean returning the ball well down, when Hodder finished up by sending high over the crossbar. The visitors again got down on the left wing, but Dick intercepted, and sent to Farmer, that player looking dangerous, when McLean tackled and got the ball away. After

McKinnon had put in some tricky play, Dick got possession and sent in a long shot, Chadwick charging Holland as the ball rolled between the posts, thus securing the initial point for Everton, amidst great cheering. With this reversal the County worked hard and made incursions to the home quarters, but found no opening. Harker and Hodder, who were warmly cheered for their short and speedily passing, made a strong chance but, did not score and Ross had to concede another corner to get rid of a hard shot from Shelton, which, however, came to nothing. Hands against Warburton was ominous for Notts, as from the free kick, Fleming headed nicely into goal and McLean was lucky in saving his side from again being lowered. From a throw in Dobson tested Holland with a stinger, and then play was worked to the other end, where Smalley had a handful from Harker and Guttridge, from a corner, was high with his shot. Arousing themselves, the homesters worked hard and well all round, and kept up a persistent attack on Holland's charge for some considerable time. Pressure being eased by the ball going over the line, the Notts left pair again got away, and Harker screwed across the goalmouth, but Jardine failed to get up, thus enabling Waugh to get possession, and the latter dashing up the field, passed neatly to Chadwick, who could not get the upper hand of Holland. The home team aided by their half-backs, continued to play up and found the visitors back division plenty to do. Ross lobbed into the Notts goalkeepers who seemed to be impenetrable and managed to defy all efforts of the Everton lot to augment their score. Guthridge having staved off Fleming, and Dick prevented Jardine from having a try at goal. Lewis missed an easy chance, Half-time arriving with the score Everton 1: Notts County 0. On changing ends, Holland was heartily cheered by the big crowd for his remarkable saves in goal. Resuming after the interval the game soon became fast, and Everton were the first to attack, Farmer and Chadwick aided by Holt and McKinnon, getting into the Notts quarters, but Brown, who had been playing consistently checked the raid, and Hodder unfortunately got offside a few yards from Smalley. Moore and Wardle having been pulled up in a dangerous rush by Ross, Hodder tested the home custodian with a clever shot which, he manipulated in good fashion. From the goal kick the Visiting left again got up but, Dick impeded their progess and enabled his right wing pair to get near Holland, where a couple of fouls to Everton, from one of which Ross notched a second point for his side with a swift shot. Arousing themselves, Notts continued to play hard, but Holt and Dobson staved them off time after time. Fleming got away in a grand run and centre, Lewis finishing up with an erratic shot, the ball going over the bar, Moore tested Smalley and Ross eased Jardine by dribbling through to Fleming, who found Guttridge in readiness by planting the ball at the other end where Ross kicked out. After Lewis and Warburton had collided a corner fell to Notts which, was nicely cleared by Smalley. Holt was here seen to lie down in midfield owing to an accidental kick in the ankle, which necessitated his removal from the field. Chadwick went half-back, and play continued fast and furious, each goal being visited in turn, when at length from a throw in, Moore was allowed to score for Notts, the home captain thinking the ball was going to the outside of the upright, calling to his men to let it ran. Chadwick then had a trial for goal, but Holland threw out, and after a fast game, Everton won cleverly their second league match by 2 goals to 1. The losers played a sterling game throughout, and their back play was greatly admired. Shelton was most conspicuous of the halves, while the left wing pair were the best of a good lot. The home team are getting stronger in their play every week, and no doubt, when McKinnon gets fixed as centre-forward, will be able to show still better combination. They played to win and succeeded in their object. **Teams; Notts County: - Holland, goal, J.McLead, and F. Guttridge, backs, G.H. Brown, Warburton, and A. Shelton, half-backs, F. Wardle,**

A. Moore, T. Jardine, W. Hodder, and Harker, forwards.
Umpire Browne, Everton:- Smalley, goal, Dick and Ross
(captain), backs, Holt, Mckinnon, and Dobson, half-backs,
Fleming, Waugh, Lewis, Chadwick, and Farmer forwards.
Umpire F Perry, Referee W.H.Jope

## AINTREE CHURCH 4 EVERTON RESERVES 8
*September 17, 1888. The Liverpool Mercury.*

These teams met at Walton on Saturday afternoon in dull and
threatening weather, and in the presence of a few hundred
spectators. Owing to the late arrival of the Everton team, a start
was not made until 3-00. Aintree was successful in the toss, and
decided to kick uphill. Costley started and some spirited play
on the part of Everton won a corner, but A.Jones placed a good
shot out of danger for the home team. Then the home forwards
showed a bit of grand play, and was rewarded with a goal from
the toe of Cornock within, five minutes from the start. Everton
now pressed very much, but the Aintree men were equal to the
work, and certainly had the best of the game for some time.
Joliffe having to fist out a beauty. Again the Everton custodian
had to fist out, a corner resulting for the home club, with no
result. Some very good all round play on the part of Aintree
resulted in a second goal for their club, to the credit of Shaw and
Roberts. This seemed to wake up the visitors, who for a time did
very good work, but their opponents were more than a match for
them, and some steady unselfish play in the part of the homesters
right wing was rewarded by a third goal from S.Shaw. Everton
now had a good chance, but Falls made a wretched shot. Nidd
then showed very prominently, and made good attempts, but
the posts were in the way. Everton again played with a will and
some good passing on the part of Falls and Cookson in the first
goal for Everton, kicked by Briscoe. Aintree still kept the upper
hands, in the play and had "hard lines" in front of the goal.

Great pressure was now the order with the Evertonians, and a bit of grand passing on the part of Cookson and Falls ended in a second goal for the visiting team. Shortly afterwards the whistle announced. Half-time with the score- Aintree Church 3 goals, Everton two. For a short time after restarting Aintree showed the best form, but very soon fell away. Good play by Keys and Briscoe, and a timely pass to Costley who scored, resulted in even goals. From this time to the finish of the game, the Evertonians had all the best of the play. Keys and Briscoe especially distinguishing themselves, with an occasional bit of good back play on the part of Pollock and Fayer. Keys had the honour of scoring the fourth; fifth and sixth goals; his shooting and the general play of the visiting team received some applause from the spectators. Pollock was the next to take down the home club's colours. Getting past Barton in fine style. Towards the finish, Aintree made a determined effort to score, and were successful, although with little credit to themselves, as Joliffe was almost useless, having received a severe injury to his arm. A few minutes before the call of time, Cookson sent in a beauty past Barton, making the eight goals for his side, and the whistle blew with the score Aintree Church 4 goals Everton 8. While in the first half Everton team disappointed their friends, in the second half their all-round play was very good. For Aintree Jess Taylor played splendidly at back. **Teams: - Everton Reserves: - Joliffe, goal, Ashcroft, and Fryer, backs, W.H.Jones, Pollock, and Harbour, half-backs, Keys Briscoe, Costley, Cookson, and Falls, forwards. Aintree Church: - R. Barton, goal, R. Jones, and J.Taylor, backs, A. Ray, A. Jones, and F. Nidd, half-backs, C. Meakins, S. Shaw, G. Curnock, H. Roberts, J. Jones, forwards.**

## EVERTON REVIEW
*September 17, 1888. The Liverpool Review.*

Everton having on Thursday severely beat a team under the title of Stanley by 5 goals to 0, entered on their second League engagement on Saturday which was with Notts County. The visitors, who had not before played this season, brought a strong team though without Gunn, Daft, Jackson, and W Shelton the two former not having yet abandoned cricket. Taken all round, however, Everton's latest opponents proved a good lot, and with more practice will hold their own. The home team were strengthened by the help of McKinnon late of Hearts of Midlothian, who played centre half-back, but is destined for centre forward. The game was very fast, each goal being reached in turn, but Dick scored the only goal of the opening half. Chadwick attending to the goalkeeper whilst the long shot passed through. Ross followed with a second goal from a foul close in, and thus it happened that the home full backs shared the scoring. Holt soon after met with an injury to his foot, which unfortunately means his absence from the field for a few weeks, and when rendered short-handed, the Everton defence was beaten, Moore turning a throw in to account, Ross thinking the shot was wide of the mark. Shouting to his men to let it go. Everton however, prevented further disaster, and won their second League engagement by 2 goals to 1. The Anfieldites are to be congratulated on such a promising commencement, and they should face Aston Villa next Saturday at Perry Barr with confidence. The Notts custodian delighted the spectators with his dexterity in goal, and on changing over he received a hearty cheer; whilst the home team, though still lacking in combination displayed improvement, notwithstanding that Waugh was suffering from an injured ankle. On Thursday next R Anderson, the old and popular Bootle forward, takes his benefit at Hawthorne road when Bootle and Everton combined will try conclusions with a lancashire team.

## EVERTON 6 DERBY MIDLAND 0
*September 20, 1888. The Liverpool Mercury.*

The latter paid their first visit to Liverpool last evening, opposing Everton at Anfield enclosure and between 3,000 and 4,000 persons assembled to witness the play. Everton lost the toss, and kicked off against the wind. A visit to the Midland goal was repelled by Smith, and the visitors left was just pulled up in time by Dick. A corner was cleared by Dick, Bailey and Daft however, returned. Everton were only playing ten men, Farmer getting his leg slightly hurt. This of course weakened the left wing considerably. A run by Waugh placed the Derby citadel in danger, the ball, however, being shot high over the bar. Play was even and exciting, both goals being assailed in turn. Keys sent in a hot shot at the Midland goal, Gibbert repelling in capital style. A free kick to Derby in the Everton half was taken by Smith. The ball was landed well in goal, but Dick kicked away to the centre, Chadwick put in a capital dribble, the sphere landing in the mouth of goal. Stones headed out Wharmby however, returning and passing to Waugh the latter transferred to Watson, who at the second attempt dashed the ball past Storer. This success stimulated the home team to greater energy, and in a minute they almost scored again. A throw in by Smith (who was working extreme hard) caused the Midland to attack. Daft shot finely, causing Smalley to fist out. Derby returned, the ball, however, rolling harmlessly over the line. At the other end Waugh and Wharmby sent in capital shots, and then Chadwick scored a second time. Everton were now showing fine form and the Midland and citadel was again in danger of being captured till Gilbert, with a huge kick landed the ball to the centre. Ross returned and for a time Storer was hotly pressed. A corner kick to the homesters was well placed by Farmer. Wharmby just kicking over the bar, from the kick out of goal the visitors forward reached the centre of the field,

Chadwick robbed Smith in fine style, and along with Farmer ran past the visitors half-backs. The Derby backs, however, played a sturdy game and Steven stopped the rush. The Everton goal was next the scene of hostilities, and Midland claimed for a "foul" for hands? but were overruled. Ross took a free kick at the Derby goal, Wharmby sending a low shot, which W. Ross intercepted. The visitors were hard pressed and Storer had all his work cut out to keep the ball from going through goal. Dick shot finely from half-back the visitors custodian placing the ball over the bar. From the resulting corner Waugh added the third point to the home score. This reverse aroused the Midland men, who attacked pretty strongly until the ball was placed the wrong side of the posts from Ross's kick out. Watson shot weakly at the Derby goal, Gilbert clearing with ease. The visitor's backs showed a sturdy defence and often kept the home forwards from adding to their total. "Hands" to Everton was given in the centre. But no advantage resulted as the whistle was blown for half-time. Everton leading by 3 goals to nil. Evans restarted the ball on behalf of the visitors who in an endeavour to break away were stopped by Weir. A long kick by Dobson sent the ball to Chadwick who centred grandly right in front of goal. Storer fumbled the ball, and it seemed likely that Everton would score but the Derby custodian recovering himself, and just threw out in time. The homesters returned and in succession Waugh and Wharmby cleared the bar on an attempt to score. The Midland forwards now dashed off, and Dick missing his kick, which, let in Evans, who tricked Ross and had the goal at his mercy. His shot however, landed in Smalley's hands, the home custodian throwing well out of danger. Watson and Waugh put in good play, and Farmer rushed down the Everton left only to be brought to a standstill by Gilbert. The Derby backs defended capitally, but Ross sending in a long shot caused the visitors quarters to be invaded, Watson shot, the ball missing its intended mark by only a few inches. Dick dribbled the ball, his shot however, failing.

Everton were having slightly the best of the play, and Waugh pouncing smartly on the ball, ran into Midland quarters - Stones kicking away, however, in good style. After a dribble by Daft, Bailey and Shannon into the Everton half Ross from the centre, sent in a clinking swift shot which completely beat Storer. From the centre kick Derby had a chance, the ball however, going into touch, Watson, Waugh, and Weir here showed splendid passing, and Storer was almost beaten - just clearing in time. Chadwick shot prominently, the leather shaving the posts. The Midland players next invaded the Everton quarters, a palpable foul by Ross however, relieving the presure. The ball was worked nicely down the centre to the visitors lines, Gilbert kicking out to save. From the throw in, Jack Ross showed tricky play, and, kicking well, gave Watson a chance, of which he was not slow to avail himself, for, with a capital attempt he registered a fifth goal. From the re-start, Everton were again found at their opponents goal, Chadwick shooting into Storer's hands. The visitors custodian cleared and although the Derby forwards made repeated efforts to break away they were always pulled up by Ross and Dick. The left wing were the most prominent, but it was without avail. A long kick however, by Ross then placed the ball in the Everton half, Weir stopping the visitors forwards in an attempt to score. Hands of Wharmby was the next item, Derby however, spoiling their chances by giving Everton a similar claim. Midland then pulled themselves together and Daft sent in a stinging shot which, Smalley repulsed in a clever manner. Waugh now dashed off down the Everton right, and parting with the ball at the right moment enabled Keys to shoot, Storer calmly fisting out. With the light failing considerably Everton assumed a strictly aggressive attitude. Repeated shots were aimed at the Derby goal, which was at last reduced by Keys. This was the last point scored. Everton thus winning easily by 6 goals to nil. **Teams:- Everton:- Smalley goal, Dick and Ross (captain), backs, Wharmby, Dobson and Weir, half-backs,**

**Farmer, Watson, Keys, Waugh, and Chadwick forwards. Derby Midland: - Storer, goal, Gilbert, and W. Stone, backs, W. Ross, J. Flowers, and Smith half-backs, Bailey, T. Daft, G. Evans, J. Shannon and G. Smith, forwards.**

## BOOTLE AND EVERTON 2 LANCASHIRE TEAM 2
*September 21, 1888. The Liverpool Mercury.*

The above fixture was arranged for the benefit of E Anderson, who has now entered the Bootle veteran list. The attendance was rather below the average, the number not exceeding 2,500; but it must be remembered that the football public has been overdosed with football during the week, this being the third match. Hay opened the game on behalf of the Lancashire team, and passing nicely to Morris the latter parted to Wood, who raced nicely down the right only to be pulled up by Veitch. Fleming followed up with a neat run, and putting in a good centre to Farmer, the latter player notched the first goal to the Liverpool teams credit. Restarting Briscoe, and Fleming were soon away, but Robertson repelled strongly calling upon Dick to reply who caused much amusement to the spectator by dribbling round the opposing forwards and leveling a shot to Jackson. From the throw in close to the visitors line Wood and Morris got away, but on Campbell replying. Briscoe and Fleming were again causing anxiety to Jackson. Kicking off, the Lancashire forwards executed some very brilliant passing, but the final attempts to score were extremely weak. During the next few minutes the home forwards, Hasting, Farmer, and Fleming sending in hot shots kept up a strong fusillade, which Jackson cleverly manipulated. On Robinson relieving, Brogan and Wood worked nicely down the right, and the after player wheeling round, Veitch sent in a beauty which, Dick timely cleared. The play now waged very evenly when Wood getting away sent in a ground shot which, however grazed the crossbar.

Following this Anderson had the goal at his mercy, but was as usual, "bowled" over before the attempt could be made. The interval now arrived with the Everton and Bootle team leading by a goal. Resuming, both ends were quickly visited, and a little more excitement prevailed than in the first half. A corner to the home team was of no advantage, for Wood and Brogan were again busy in taxing the home defence. Dick cleared well and had a shy at goal, from the centre of the field a grand one which, Jackson fisted out. Shortly afterwards a corner accured to the Lancashire team, who experienced hard lines in not scoring, the leather shaving the crossbar. Hasting contributed a neat run, and sent in a stinger which Jackson cleared, and Wood taking the running, spurted down the right finally parting to Morris, who equalized with a clinking shot. The home defence was now heavily pressed, Roberts especially causing great trouble. After a couple of erratic shots from Anderson and Farmer, the latter managed to again beat Jackson. The remainder of the game was well contested, McFarlane equalizing on the call of time. **Teams Bootle and Everton: - Griffith goal, Veitch, and Dicks backs, Higgins, Allsop, and F. Wood, half-backs Hasting, Farmer, Anderson, Briscoe, and Fleming forwards. Lancashire team; Jackson, goal, Robinson (Bolton Wanderera), and Lucas (Halliwell) backs, McFarlane, Woods (Bootle) and Roberts (Wanders) half-backs, Brogan (Wolverhampton) Wood (Bootle), Hay (Halliwell), Fenn and Morris (Bootle) forwards.**

### ASTON VILLA 2 EVERTON 1 (Game 3)
*September 24, 1888. The Liverpool Mercury.*

Everton journeyed to Perry Bar Birmingham on Saturday to play their League match with Aston Villa. The weather was fine, but the ground rather hard. Warmer was the only absentee from the Villa team, his place being filled by Ashmore; while the Evertonians were heavily-handicapped through having to fill up three gaps. Dobson, Holt and Lewis being substituted by Wharmby, Higgins and Keys. There were 5,000 spectators present who behaved themselves in a obnoxious manner to the visitors throughout the entire game by hissing and hooting. The Villa won the toss, and Keys kicked off with the sun in his face. Play soon became fast, and after Dick had cleared a dangerous rush by the home right and centre. Waugh sped nicely to the other end and screwed across the goal mouth, but Cox managed to put the ball to Brown who ran along the right wing, and passed to Hodgetts, that player beating Smalley four minutes from the start. A claim was made that the ball was over the line before Hodgetts got it but it came to nothing. Restarting Dixon was nicely brought up by Ross, and then Chadwick was seen in a tricky run down the left, Dixon going to the aid of Coulton and preventing the visitors from scoring. Aided by the shouts of their supporters. Aston paid another visit to the visiting end, but Hunter was very erratic in his shot the ball going yards over the crossbar. Everton now pressed, and Farmer, Waugh, and Watson gave the backs plenty to do, a foul against Cox in the goal mouth being got away with some difficulty. Continuing to work hard Ross, Weir, and Chadwick each had shies Coulton rebirthing to the kicking out principle to save his side from being lowered. A foul was then given against Brown in front of Smalley, and from the kick, Chadwick again raced down, and had hard luck in not scoring, the ball just shaving the upright. Waugh next paid a visit to Ashmore, but Cox transferred to Brown, and that player placed the ball to Hodgetts who headed, what appeared to be an off-side goal but the referee gave his decision in favour of the home club. Striving hard to score Everton continued to work hard, and had a succession of corners and fouls awarded them, but failed to register a point, half-time soon after arriving with the score:- Villa 2 goals Everton 0. On changing over Everton with the sun in their favour, soon took up the running, and kept plugging away, Cox, Coulton, and Green having to work hard to avert a downfall. Hands having been given against Allen, Dixon had to clear a concerned run by the Everton forwards and Hunter was nicely pulled up by Weir, who was playing a grand game, but Hodgetts evaded Warmby and Smalley was seen at his best keeping out three shots in gallant style. The game after this was very rough on the part of the Villa and the referee custioned Brown and Hodgetts, resuming Waugh soon tested Ashmore and Watson was tripped up, as he was in the act of shooting for goal. Continuing the pressure Everton completely hemmed the Villains, and, after many repeated attempts to score Watson beat Ashmore with a scorcher in dead silence. Called on by Ross to play up, the visitors kept hovering around the homesters quarters and had the worst of luck, but failed to break through, and the whistle blew just as Waugh shot in, a very unpleasant and rough game on the part of Aston Villa resulting in their favour by 2 goals to 1. For the Villa, their backs played an erratic game, the ball seldom going where they intended; Dixon and Yates were the best of the half-backs and resorted to dirty tactics; while forward Green and Allen were decent in their work, although the same cannot be said of Hodgetts, who seemed determined to leave his mark on the visitors. Everton back division played a good and clever game throughout; which however, does not apply to the half-backs. Weir being the only one to show up while Warmby was an entire failure forward. All with the exception of Keys worked well but had no luck. **Teams Aston Villa: - Ashmore, goal, Coulton, and Cox, backs, Yates, Devey, and Dixon half-backs, Brown Green, Hunter, Allen and Hodgetts, Everton: - Smalley goal, Dick, and Ross (Captain), backs, Weir, Warmby, and Higgins, half-backs Waugh, Watson, Keys, Chadwick and Farmer, forwards. Umpire E Berry Referee Fitzroy Norris.**

## EVERTON RESERVES 3 BORTH ATHLETIC 0
*September 24, 1888. The Liverpool Mercury*

The Everton Reserves appeared for the first time at the home ground this season on Saturday, and fully 2,000 spectators turned up to show their appreciation of the recent victories of this unbeaten reserves. The teams faced each other and H Pollock, captain and Gibson lost the toss Milward from Great Marlow who was tried in the centre. Costley placed kick off for Everton. The Athletic rushed off, at once, but was stopped by Pollock, who obtained possession and passed to Briscoe, who in turn passed to McKinnon, and this extremely cool player, with splendid judgement shot right in the visitors goal, Fyfe, the custodian, who was a worthy successor to the "Prince of Goalkeepers" cleared with apparent ease. Briscoe and McKinnon by most judicious passing, and peppering at the opponents goal, but could not find an opening. After Fall had unfortunately missed a pass from Milward, McKinnon immediately scored for Everton. Although upto half-time the Reserves pressed continuously they failed, partly through some excellent goalkeeping and partly through bad shooting, to add to their score. Upon restarting Cookson, whose knee had been injured at the start of the game, now broke down altogether and did not take part any further part in the game. This accident of course benefited the Athletic and, showing improved form, they for a while pressed Everton, but this did not last long, and again the Reserves were the aggressive, and from a well placed corner kick, Pollock, whose judicious play reminds one of Gibson, headed a beauty. The game now slowed down, and after a good run by Falls to centre, Milward, who improved towards the end of the game scored again for Everton, and at this, the game entertained, for Everton, Chadwick and the three halfs-backs played with their skill, and forward, although two strangers were included the combination was at times very good.

On the opposing side Fife was the shining player (although Clarke and Murdock worked hard). **Teams; Atletic: - T. Fyfe goal, Thompson and Cotton backs, Fergun, Stewart, and Withers, half-backs, Graham, Murdoch, Harper, Clarke, and Harper, forwards; Everton: - Joliffe (c) goal, Chadwick (a), and N. Ashcroft, backs, F.Parry, H. Pollock (captain) and WH.Jones, half-backs, R. Fell, T. Cookson, A. Milward, McKinnon, and W. Briscow forwards.**

**EVERTON 2 DERBY JUNCTION 1**
*September 27, 1888. The Liverpool Mercury.*

Derby Junction who effected such a surprise in beating Blackburn Rovers and attaining semi-final status in last season's National cup competition visited Anfield last evening. About 3,000 spectators were present. Everton gave a trial to Pollock and Milward of the Reserves, while the Derby visitors, besides being otherwise well represented, were assisted by Plackett and W.Smith from Long Eaton Rangers. Derby Junction kicked off, and Everton made ground on the left, but in a moment Hopkins and Radford eased and racing strongly, the former evaded the home defence, and scored an easy goal. Everton next attacked a centre by Farmer being mulled, and the visitors replied with another burst on the right, but found Ross this time impassable. The invaders were not yet beaten off, however, giving trouble at the right corner again and then attacking from the centre . Joliffe having to handle sharply Smith winding up a further onslaught with a fine attempt the ball going just outside. Pollock sent up well, but Farmer failed to turn the chance to advantage, and then Dick, Weir, Watson and Waugh improved the outlook for Everton. Morley however, cleverly beat the attackers, and the Junction once became tantalizing in some clean strong kicking. Joliffe narrowly clearing a shot near the post. Relief coming from a kick behind. Chadwick ran himself over, and in reply

Derby went rapidly down forcing a futile corner. When half-time was announced shortly after play was just inside the visitors quarters. Crossing over with a goal to nothing against them, Everton at once forced a corner from which a hot tussle in the goalmouth was intiated, and a goal from a foul scored. Bromage soon had to clear a fast shot from Farmer and on Derby Junction closing up, Plackett lifted over the bar. Watson next shot hard, Bromage giving another corner, placed by Farmer, a simlilar point being risked to clear; but the siege was renewed and Pollock gave Everton the lead in a nice shy the ball striking the bar and dropping through. The home team just now had fairly taken the measure of their opponents, Farmer and Waugh each making good bids for goal, the former causing Hind to head behind and the latter shooting over near the left post. Another severe tussle ensued from hands against Derby close in, which was renewed when Ross kicked up splendidly twice despite a nasty knock on the leg just previously. Morley, however, cleared with effectively and Joliffe touched the ball in the first time since the interval. A short attack followed by the visitors, which, on Farmer being pulled up in a sparkling run was taken up again, the ball going over twice or thrice. Farmer next missed the chance he had at a favorable moment and taking advantage of the mistake, Hopkins from a pass shot through, but just as he was kicking the whistle blew for off side, and the point was lost. In the fading light Everton got down to goal, and forced two corners whilst Farmer shot too high in a long kick. Waugh passed over splendidly to the left. Hind intercepting and then Waugh tried a shot himself only to be well met. Both sides then indulged in spurts the closing item being a corner to Everton. This was well got away, and a hard and even contest terminated in favor of the home team by 2 goals to 1. The visitors though beaten, played the most finished game. Their kicking was very neat and generally well injudged; whilst Everton were weakest forward, the combination being poor and the passing erratic

Farmer especially spoiling chances. **Teams- Everton:- Joliffe, goal, Ross (captain), and Dick backs, Higgins Pollock and Weir half-backs Farmer, Chadwick, Milward, Waugh, and Watson forwards. Derby Junction:- Bromage, goal, Hind and Morley backs, Walker, Plackett, and Snelson half-backs, Kinberley, Smith, Housley, Hopkins, and Radford, forwards.**

# OCTOBER 1888

## BOLTON WANDERERS 6 EVERTON 2 (Game 4)
*October 1, 1888. The Liverpool Mercury.*

Everton journeyed to Bolton on Saturday to play their League fixture with the Wanderers. The Liverpool club was heavily handicapped through five of their players suffering from recent injuries. Pollock took Holt's place in the half-back division and Chadwick changed position with Lewis. The day was a bad one for football, a small drizzling rain falling during the whole game, and saturating the players, while the ground was in a wretched condition, the grass being to long and spoiling the visitors in their passing game. There was nearly 5,000 spectators present including a large following of the Liverpool club. Everton won the toss, and elected to play with a strong wind at their backs. Barbour kicked off, and he ran down Dobson had the misfortune to give hands, from the free kick, which was taken by D.Weir. Davenport ran along the wing and beat Smalley with an easy shot a minute from the start. Everton from the kick-off went down the right, and had a corner, Simmers clearing and passing the leather to Barbour who carried play to the visiting quarters and the Wanderers registered another point, this time by Tyrer. A protest that the ball had not gone though was not sustained although the referee acknowledged his mistake after he had given his decision. Arousing themselves the visitors kept sprinting away, and Harrison had a busy time having to keep out a succession of shots from the opposing forwards. Three corners to Everton being cleared, Lewis managed to break through the defence and scored the first goal for Everton, with a speedy shot. Encouraged by this success, Everton was seen in the best pass of the game, all the forwards going up the field in a line and Watson equalised with a scorcher, amidst the greatest excitement. Restarting, luck was again with the Wanderers and Tyrer rushed through a third goal for his side. Striving to equalise, the visitors made many attempts to score, and had hands in goalmouth which however, cleared and Barbour was pulled up by Ross when dangerous J.Weir gave Chadwick a chance close in, but the shot was wide. Working hard, Everton again hovered around the Wanderers quarters and Brogan was lucky to spoil Lewis in his shot for goal half-time thus arriving with the score- Wanderers 3, Everton 2. Up to this stage of the game Everton had the best of the play, put were unfortunate in their final attempts. On changing ends Watson and Waugh were soon busy and hands near in, but Barbour got the ball away and D.Weir finished with a weak shot. Tyrer falling on the leather another free kick was given to Everton, and then Pollock was cheered for rousing the enemy when dangerous. The homesters were again on the ball, and Milne beat Smalley for the fourth time. Everton then put on a spurt, and rained in a lot of shots put failed to augment their score. Brogan was here seen at the best running up the field and screwing across to Rennie who failed to take the opening and the ball rolled harmlessly out. Give and take play ensued for some considerable time, and Dobson made the mistake of heading the wrong way, Smalley having difficulty in clearing, J. Weir who was playing a good game intercepted Tyrer and Roberts pulled up Waugh and Watson. Everton now showed signs of weakness, owing to their injured players breaking down and the Wanderers succeeded in adding a fifth point Davenport putting the ball through from a scrimmage. This followed by Milne beating Smalley with a sixth goal, an evenly contested game thus ending in favour of the Wanderers by 6 goals to 2. The winners showed a great deal of their old form and could do nothing wrong in front of goal; while the reverse was with Everton the visitors experienced the hardest of luck in their shots. Ross had to play back himself. Dick being unfit to play a remark which applies to Smalley, Dobson, and Watson, while the Everton executive had to rearrange their forwards, which may account somewhat for the defeat. **Teams: - Wanderers, Harrison goal, Jones, and Robinson backs R. Weir, Simmers, and Roberts, half-backs, Davenport, Brogan, Barbour Milne, and Tyrer, forwards Umpire Parkinson, Everton: - Smalley, goal, Dick and Ross (captain), backs, J. Weir, Dobson and Pollock, half-backs, Waugh, Watson, Chadwick Lewis, and Farmer forwards. Umpire, E.Berry, Referee T.Helme.**

### EVERTON RESERVES 4 TURTON 2
*October 1, 1888. The Liverpool Mercury.*

Lancashire senior cup-first round.
The visitors arrived behind time and forfeited the tie, about 2,000 spectators were present, and a friendly game was played, which proved even in the first half, two goals each side being scored. The latter part of the play was more of less in favour of Everton, who won by 4 goals to 2. **Teams; Everton Reserves: - Joliffe goal, N. Ashmore, and A. Chadwick, backs, W.H. Jones, T. Hayes, and Harbour (w), half-backs, W. Briscoe, G. Fleming, J. Whittle, D. Berry and J. Costley forwards. Turton: - Watson, goal, Wallwork, and W. Mulliday backs, T. Key, J. Simmers, and Corden half-backs Smith Estwistle, T. Trainer, J. Stenson, and G. Haughton forwards.**

### EVERTON REVIEW
*October 1, 1888. The Liverpool Mercury.*

Everton, for the wind up of their evening engagement, on Wednesday were visited with another Derby club. This was the Junction, the despoilers of Blackburn Rovers intention in connection with the English cup, and a much better team they proved than their Midland neighbors. Instead of Everton attaining a 6 goal victory they were if anything a bit fortunate in obtaining a win by a bare margin of 2 goals to 1. The home team it must at once be conceded was not fully represented seeing that Higgins Milward, and Pollock were included, with the consequence that the essential combination were entirely absent. Dick and Ross, of course greatly helped keep the scoring down, and Pollock and Weir were effective, but the forwards were all sixes and sevens. Farmer had some splendid chances and did some strong running but he was particularly wanting in tact, at a critical moment, either losing opportunities through dallying too long, or shooting wildly Chadwick and Milward were tame; Watson was suffering from lameness and Waugh, from his henchman's inability to render his usual efficient support, had little chance to delight the spectators with the grand passing runs of the previous Wednesday's match. The visitors from Derby were a broad bottomed team, and if none were especially clever they played with a thorough understanding of each other. At times they went away in formation and the feature of their play was the quality and cleanest with which, the ball was sent from one to another with accuracy. Harden Morley late of Derby County was left full back facing Weir, Watson, and Waugh. He accordingly found a tremendous lot of work to negotiate, and he acquitted himself of the heavy task with perfecttion, establishing a claim to be as equal at least of any back on the field. Of the other members of the team, Bromage the custodians and Snelson, Hopkins, Radford, Plackett and W Smith made their pressure the more recognizable the last two being requisitioned for the occasion from Long Eaton Rangers. Everton like their Bootle neighbours experienced great inconvenience owing to several men being on the wicked list. These extra matches have done considerable harm to players, and it is with facing of relief, now that the evening exhibitions are at an end that undivided attention can be given to the important Saturday's business. Everton suffered a second reverse in their League engagement on Saturday. Bolton Wanderers giving further proof of increased strength by overthrowing the Anfieldites in a decisive manner of 6 goals to 2. The game, however, was much more even than the score indicates, as the visitors attacked almost as often as the home team. At half-time the record stood 3 to 2, and this was a better index of the respective merits of the opposing sides than the monopoly of scoring attained by the winners in the second half. The losers were handicapped, in not being in a position to put their full strength on the field, and some of those that did play were not in good heart, Dick, Smalley, Dobson and Watson all being indisposed from various causes. Compared with Aston Villa experience the match was pleasantly conducted, though hard, as all tussles between rivals have ever proved. But the tactics on either side were of the rushing order rather than that of scientific combination. Throughout the game rain fell heavily, rendering the ground which was so lumpy, very treacherous, and the long grass was a source of considerable embarrassment to the players, especially to the visitors, who found it rather different work running on the trim turf at home. The home team all played well, Davenport and Brogan, if anything being the more prominent of the forwards, and D.Weir the most brilliant of the back division. The hero of the visiting team was J.Weir, who was equal if not superior, to his namesake of Bolton. Ross also did well, but Dick and Dobson, though doing as well as could be expected under adverse conditions, were only moderate. Everton's front men again underwent transposition. Chadwick was tried at centre, Lewis partnering Farmer, but its latest phase was no improvement on what has gone before, and the disorganization, perhaps was rather intensitied than cured. It seems that the evil will not be remedied until a centre forward can be secured that will command the confidence of the wings and one who would effectually stop the semblance even of selfish play.

## EVERTON 2 ASTON VILLA 0 (Game 5)
*October 8, 1888. The Liverpool Mercury.*

This return League match was played at Anfield Road ground
on Saturday in the presence of 12,000 spectators. The visitors
team was the same, with two exceptions, which played at
Birmingham a fortnight ago. Warmer taking up his place in goal
and Dawson substituting Dixon at half-back. The home club
was greatly strengthened. Sugg, Holt, and McKinnon playing
instead of Keys, Warmby and Higgins. Everton, who were not
satisfied with their two previous defeats were under the care
of Fred Willis during the week, and entered the enclosure
strong, and in good trim. Holt and Sugg got hearty reception on
making their appearance, and a similar compliment was paid to
the Aston lot. Previous to starting the game, Hodgetts, against
whom hard things had been said, openly apologized to Dick for
the treatment that player was subjected to at Birmingham, and
said he was sorry for what he had done. The ground was in true
order, but the sun slightly interfered with the play. Everton won
the toss, and Archie Hunter kicked off with the wind at his back.
Everton were the first to show, and McKinnon receiving the
ball from Ross, soon tested Warmer with a warm handful; but
that player was cool, and threw out. Getting again into Aston
quarters Everton had a free kick, which was nicely taken and
Warmer had some difficulty in clearing his lines. Working well
down, Hodgett shot across, and Dick in negotiating, kicked the
wrong way nearly letting in Brown, who slightly injured himself
in charging Smalley, and the ball went over. Aided by Dick,
Waugh ran nicely up, and screwed across the goal mouth, but
Sugg failed to get up, and Cox transferred play to the other end,
where Devey sent over. Watson having tested Warner. Brown
sped along the right, and cross to Hodgetts, who headed wide.
A pretty bit of passing by Watson and McKinnon was spoiled
by Cox near in, and Hunter was easily robbed by Holt. Green

and Brown having been successfully tackled by Ross, Watson again tried Warmer who kicked clear, and Green gave Hodgetts another chance without any effect. A tricky bit of play by Waugh and Chadwick caused the Aston custodian to conceded a corner, the ball twisting in his hands and going to the side of the upright. Continuing aggressive play Everton had the hardest of luck, shot after shot being rained in quick succession, but Warmer nullified all their attempts to score. At length the Villa got away, and after Ross had spoiled Hodgetts. Allen had the misfortune to get his hands in the way near Smalley's charge. From the free kick the homesters again hovered round the visitors quarter and Warmer had a lively time of it. But had to succumb to Waugh, who from a pass by Watson, registered the first goal for Everton amidst loud cheers. Resuming the home club, encouraged by this success made tracks to the Aston end, and Cox was compelled to give a corner to prevent another downfall which, however, was cleared. A free kick being headed over the bar by Waugh, half-time arrived with Everton pressing, and the score –Everton 1, Villa 0. On changing ends, the large crowd gave vent to their feeling by loudly cheering Warner for his excellent defence. Kicking off Sugg passed the ball down, but Coulton returned to Green and that player got near in, only to find Ross in readiness, by planting well down when Hunter was seen to be erratic in his play. Brown having shot wide, Chadwick and McKinnon each had shies and after Warmer had cleared, Waugh and Watson were both very near augmenting the home score by sending in two scorchers. At the stage of the game Waugh received an accidental kick in the leg from Coulton, and Brown overreached himself. Necessitating their withdrawal from the field. With ten men on either side play was resumed, and the home team again took up the reins, and were soon awarded a free kick, which came to nothing. The Villa made a momentary visit to the Everton quarters by the pass by Hodgetts, who found Dick hard to beat, and Cox had to give another corner to prevent a dangerous raid taking effect. The kick was nicely placed, but the ball was eventually worked clear, and Allen and Hodgetts wended their way to Smalley's end where Ross was in waiting, and Farmer soon after beat Warner with a good shot, the Villa custodian looking after the home centre while the ball rolled past him. After this play continued fast, each side paying respective visits by nice passing, but no further point was gained. Everton thus reversing their previous meeting with a well earned victory of 2 goals to nil. For the losers Warner in goal played a champion game, and is undoubtedly the best custodian the Everton men have ever had against them. Devey was the pick of the defence, while all the forwards are of the best class, and played a good game, their passing at times being brilliant. For the winners, Smalley had little to do, the ball seldom passing Dick and Ross, the latter of whom was seen in his old form; the half-backs were the best trio that have done duty for the home club this season. Farmer giving the greatest satisfaction to the large crowd; and the forward rank worked well, and will be very hard to beat when they have a little more practice. **Teams; Everton:- Smalley goal, Dick and Ross (captain) backs, Weir, Holt, and Farmer, half-backs, McKinnon, Watson, Sugg, Chadwick, and Waugh forwards. Umpire Berry (e), Aston Villa: - Warner, goal, Coulton, and Cox, backs, Yates, Devey, and Dawson, half-backs Brown, Green, Hunter (captain), Allen, and Hodgett forwards, Umpire G. Ramsey, referee Mr, McIntyre (Manchester).**

**CREWE STEAM SHEDS 1 EVERTON RESERVES 5**
*October 8, 1888. The Liverpool courier.*

Played on Saturday at Crewe, Steam kicked off against the wind. Everton pressed for some time and Crewe had somewhat hard lines, Everton by obtaining a fast and exciting goal was placed to the credit of the Evertonians, who kept the ball, dangerously near their opponent's goal almost the whole of the first half. Score at half time 2-0 for Everton result Everton beat Crewe by 5 goals to 1.

**EVERTON REVIEW**
*October 8, 1888. The Liverpool Mercury.*

Everton, since they met Aston Villa at Birmingham a fortnight ago, have undergone a great change, and not a stone has been left unturned to wipe out the 2 to 1 defeat they then received. During the week the executive of the club met and decided that the team should train more than they had done, and the players taking the hint put themselves under their trainer with the result that they came out of the contest on Saturday with flying colours, beating the ex-cup holders pointless and filling the hearts of their supporters with great hopes of the future. Everything was in favour of a good game, and Hunter kicked off in their presence of a tremendous crowd, which contrasted itself very much with that at PerryBarr. During the earlier stages of the game the home team was seen to the best advantage, with the result that Warner-who, by the way, was an absentee in the first League encounter-had a busy time of it, but did his work in a masterly way, and, 40 minutes had elapsed before Waugh managed to beat him. The visitors who at times were very brilliant in their pass, seldom got beyond the home defence, who prevented Smalley from having much to do, and half-time arrived with Everton in command with 1 goal to nil. On restarting both sides warmed to their work. Green failed to avail himself of a chance offered him, and then Waugh and Brown simultaneously withdrew from the field owing to injuries, thus leaving the respective wing weak. Each club continued to play hard, and again the visiting goalkeeper had plenty to do, McKinnon, Watson, Sugg and Chadwick each trying to increase the lead, but it was not until within ten minutes of the finish that

Farmer sent one through from the side of the mid-field line; Everton avenged their previous reverse by achieving a brilliant victory of 2 goals to nil. Everton, in their new formation, had Farmer at half-back, showing that the committee was wise in giving him a trial there. Sugg did creditably at centre forward for a first appreance, and, no doubt after their success of Saturday the cause team will be entrusted to carry the club through their future exacting engagement.

**BURNLEY 3 EVERTON 0**
*October 9 1888. The Liverpool Courier.*

The first of the two extra matches between the above clubs took place at Turf Moor Burnley, yesterday in very dull weather. The victory of Everton over Aston Villa made the fixture very attractive, fully four thousand spectators being present including a contingent from Liverpool, who accompanied the team. Burnley played their full strength, but the visiting team was considerably weakened by the absence of Weir and Waugh, who through indisposition were unable to play, and Higgins and Chadwick of the Reserves had to fill the vacancies. Dick was suffering from lameness, and to make matters worse, Ross received a nasty kick on the knee cap which rendered him almost useless for the remainder of the game. Ross having won the toss, Rolland kicked off downhill. The Burnley forwards got well down the centre, the ball going over. From the kick-off Everton took up the attack, McKinnon striking the upright the ball going over. A foul against Kennan was well placed by Holt to McKinnon who struck the cross-bar with a magnificent shot. By good passing the Burnley forwards worked the sphere to the other end Brady experiencing hard lines in not scoring. Again Burnley pressed and Dick had to concede a corner. Nothing tangible resulting, the Everton forwards left took up the running. Lang having to kick out in order to save. Burnley now played up remarkably well, but Ross And Dick were hard to pass, and Smalley's charge remained impregnable, an overhead kick by Tait going outside. A grand run by McKinnon and Watson gave Everton a chance, when Keenan with a good punt removed the danger. Burnley now raced down the right Ross putting an end to the invasion by some excellent tackling. A good shot from Friel was well fisted out by Smalley, and this brought half-time, with no goals having been scored by either side. After the usual interval, Sugg kicked off downhill, Kennan, with a long kick getting the ball well in front, Gallacher however, shooting over. Everton increasing the pace gave the backs some trouble. Kennan saving in the goalmouth, Everton still kept up the pressure and Kay had to throw behind. Another corner now fell to Everton. McKinnon again being unfortunate in not scoring. The Burnley van, getting into line, rushed up the field, and passing the half-backs Gallacher with a low shot, scored the first goal for Burnley. From the kick-off, the Burnley forwards again pressed and Gallacher scored another goal after an accurate pass from Brady. Everton now dribbled down the right, and Sugg passed to Chadwick who shot in, but Kay again cleared. A foul in the Everton goal mouth was well placed by Kennan, and Lang getting possession scored with a screw shot. From the kick-out Dick dribbled down the field, his shot going wide, and from then to the finish Everton pressed hard, but could not break through the powerful defence of the Burnley back division. The game throughout was of a very pleasant character, the Everton forwards being very unfortunate in failing to score. Final result-Burnley three goals, Everton nil. **Teams:- Everton: - Smalley, goal, Ross (captain) and Dick backs A. Chadwick, Holt, and Farmer half-backs Higgins, E. Chadwick, Sugg, Watson, and McKinnon, forward. Burnley:- Kay, goal, Berry, and Lang backs, Keenan, Friel and Abrams, half-backs Brady, Tait Gallacher, Roland and Yates forwards.**

## NOTTS COUNTY 3 EVERTON 1 (Game 6)
*October 15, 1888. The Liverpool Mercury.*

Everton travelled to Nottingham on Saturday to play their
return League fixture with Notts County, arriving in the town
about noon, and this having ample time for rest, after three
hours, jolting in the railway saloon carriage. The match was
set down for three o'clock, and punctually to time Everton
entered the well arranged and leveled enclosure, meeting with
a cheer of welcome by the 4,000 spectators that had assembled
at Trent Bridge ground. A few minutes later Notts appeared on
the scene. They applauded and then operations commenced, the
only alteration in the announced teams being that Watson vice
Fleming. The weather was delightfully fine, with perhaps a little
too much wind, which blew from goal to goal, and against which
the visitors kicked off. Notts at once went off in a rush and taking
Everton some what by surprise were very near effecting a goal
a fine shot from the left striking the bar. Dick cleared another
attack but Notts were not to be stalled off, and in a moment
Daft and Jardine broke through, the latter sending past Smalley
very easily, a feat so early in the game that was greeted with an
unmistakable hilarious shout. Everton plucked up considerably
on restarting, and got well within Notts quarters, but only a goal
kick came of the run on the right. Farmer gave his forwards an
opportunity of moving again towards goal, Briscoe running on,
and from a free kick well taken by Farmer, the ball was headed
behind. Jardine relieved, beating Dick, and forcing a corner which
was cleared out, though Dick interposed as a critical moment
on the left, the home forwards came with renewed energy, a
really clever shot from Daft fairly nonplusing Smalley for the
second time. Weir next came out well in staying an exciting
rush, but the ball was immediately impelled towards Everton's
goal, Smalley this time saving brilliantly shot from Hodder and
Allen being also rendered harmless. A short respite now fell to

the visitors defending line, Holt getting far enough down to test Holland, who easily checked and cleared, Moore replying with an indifferent shot. A free kick again fell to Everton, entrusted to Farmer, Dick putting over, and Cursham risked a corner, from which Allen and Daft went of pretty style, as far as Ross, who discounted the effort with a characteristic kick. However, it was Farmer who throughout had played with splendid judgement that effectual beat off the attack and in turn enabled Everton to force play round about Notts goal, the visitors tactics in front being a great improvement on what had hitherto been shown. There were no flaws to be found in the home defence though, and after Holt had received a jeer from the partial onlookers for the way in which he floored an opponent, Jardine had hard luck in a keen oblique shot. The home forwards, who had so far maintained a tremendous speed, now began to tame down, and Everton corresponding gathered energy, the latter attacking rather strongly, the best effort being Watson's from McKinnon's pass the ball being a little to high. The goalkick was availed of by Notts for a sharp run, and Smalley, fumbling with the ball, seemed to put it through, giving the home team a lead off 3 goals to none, an accident which brought on the interval. The outlook thus looking serious for Everton, Ross tried a re-arrangement, himself going centre-forward, Sugg half-back and Holt in partnership with Dick, and certainly a change for the better became observable in the attack, which had been of only milk and water quality during the first half. Ross on Allen restarting was at once in command, and was disappointed in a hot shot, a well-sustained assault following, but Cursham and Guttridge were always in the way. Moore caused a momentary diversion and then Ross was foiled in a shot. Everton by means of a nice piece of passing at close quarters again gave trouble, and a terrific tussle ensued right in the goalmouth. Holland saving miraculously, he falling with the ball in his arms, and then scrambling through the chargers and chucking clear. It was a clever performance, and met with proper recognition from the spectators. Notts next got well away, Guttridge kicking accurately, but the movement proved expensive as Ross wound up a powerful run by scoring a splendid goal, a significant silence being evinced by those who saw this lowering the chocolate and blue colours. Chadwick followed with a good shot, the ball grazing the bar, and immediately after Everton came out with a grand passing movement. Farmer, Briscoe, Watson and McKinnon being the chief actors, and it fairly delighted the hitherto partial spectators, the performance eliciting the remark, and this from an "enemy" that they deserved a win by play like that. Uttridge, however, was relentless in beating McKinnon, and at all this fine display went for nothing. Notts then had a share of attacking, Smalley clearing twice, Everton battling against the invaders amidst discouraging hooting of the "Lambs" which only ceased when their pets were in troubled waters. Dick had given mortal offence for resorting in the excitement to his old doubtful tactics of giving a knee, and after this he experienced the utmost discourtesy. The game continued with great spirit, the Anfieldites having far the best of play, but never being lucky enough to get another goal, and so Notts, by 3 goals to one, scored their first success in the League engagement. **Teams; Everton: - Smalley, goal, Dick and Ross (captain) backs, Weir, Holt, Farmer, half-backs, Watson, McKinnon, Sugg, Briscoe, and Chadwick, forwards. Notts: - Holland, goal, Cursham, and Guttridge backs, Brown, A. Shelton, and Hall, half-backs Hodder, Moore, Allen, Daft, and Jardine, forwards. Referee Mr Meon.**

**EVERTON RESERVES 11 EARLESTOWN 1**
*October 15, 1888. The Liverpool Mercury.*

This game was played at Anfield on Saturday before fully 3,000 spectators, and the splendid performance of their Everton

Reserves richly deserved such support. The teams which faced each other about four p.m. were: -Earlestown: - Weir goal, Tyrer, and Johnson backs, Harrison, Bowker, and Anderton half-backs, D. Jones, Conway, J. Jones, Lerus, and Siddeley, forwards. Everton:- Joliffe, goal, Chadwick and Ashcroft, backs, Fayer, Pollock (captain), and Jones, half-backs, Keys, Berry Milward Costley, and Falls forwards. Pollock won the toss, and Earlestown started, and at once, very pretty passing attacked Joliffe's charge, and Siddeley, centering with accuracy enabled Lerus the Earlestown centre to scored for the visitors. Two minutes after the kick off. This was most unexpected, and several of the Everton spectators like "Jobs" comforters could prophecy nothing but defeat; but here they were great mistaken for the Reserves team somehow never seen to play with any fire until their opponents scored. Upon restarting Earlestown still continued to press the vireo of very good passing, but they had shot their bolt after a quarter of an hour's play, for the Everton forwards commenced a bombardment which grew furious at the game went on. First Berry and then Keys, Pollock and Costley scored and this brought half-time. The combined play of the forwards was now excellent, and with help of the half-backs, they began to "pile on the front" adding seven goals to their edit, Pollock taking effect two minutes from the start, then Key scored from a pass by Costley, Costley placed another goal to the Everton total, Milward ran up the centre, Bowler clearing, but Falls and Costley again placed the Earlestown citadel in danger. The backs defend well until Berry received from Falls, who again scored. Immediately afterwards Milward scored with a low shot and later on Falls scored during a scrimmage and Everton winning an easily by 11 goals to 1.

## EVERTON REVIEW
*October 15, 1888. The Liverpool Mercury.*

Everton departing from "the noiseless tenor of their way" experimented with a mid week match away from home on Monday, and the result has not been such as will encourage further exploit of a like "exhibition" caliber. They were induced to run over to Turf Moor, to play a match with Burnley, and at the game time, in the shape of a good "gate" that would ensure, gave their co-leaguers a timely financial impetus. This latter benevolent object was attained, for a big company gathered themselves together; but the game was not so pleasing in its result from an Evertonians point of view, as the visitors were 3 goals to nil, behind the home eleven at the finish. However, the disaster need not be considered of much, as Everton had not got their full team in hand, and the true relative status of the two clubs will be shown in their home and home League games on Nov 17 and 24. In the meantime, taking up the threads from Aston Villa noble victory, Everton on Saturday pitched their tent on the historic ground of Notts County on the banks of the silvery Trent, in order if possible, to repeat the success of three weeks ago. A big but painfully one sided crowd assembled round the excellent field of play. The weather was neither too hot nor too cold, for football, and with the sunshining, everything promised a pleasant afternoon amusement. This roseate fore assault, and, after being subjected to what was nothing less than insolence almost throughout the proceeding an attempt was made to mob the Everton players, which was in a measure prevented, though Dick brought back visible proof of the severity of a blow with a stick. It must be admitted that Dick did one or two shady and unnecessary pieces of work, some people alleging that he struck Hodder, but he certainly did not deserve the maltreatment meted out to him, and the Nottingham ensuing papers are strong in denouncing the conduct of the spectators towards the visitors. On the game itself Notts County were not three goals to one, as the scorer would seen to indicate better than Everton for, balancing the early with the later stage of play, the form displayed was about even. Two at least of the Notts goals were lucky ones, which does not say much for Smalley by the aye whilst towards the finish the Anfieldites had to contend against both good defence and better goalkeeping and luck. Waugh is still incapacitated from the kick in the Aston Villa match and he was sorely missed, especially in the first half, when the forwards line was hardly ever seen in combination. With Ross at centre after the interval, the passing and formation was excellent, the captain making a striking contrast with Sugg who resumed his proper place at half-backs, whilst Holt was put in Ross's position at back. Smalley shaped very indifferently at the start, and to this fact must mainly be attributed Everton's defeat. Dick was not well, but still he played a safe game though unhappily marred by an indulgence in an old weakness of going for his man, after the ball had been dispatched clear away. Weir and Farmer were both correct, but the latter outshone his colleague, and playing throughout with coolness and good judgement, seemed to be always too clever for Hodder and Moore was the best half-back on the field. Of the forwards, next to Ross comes Chadwick, whilst Briscoe did some excellent dribbling at times. Notts were happy in five consistent forwards, who thoroughly understood each other, the two outsides men, Jardine and Hodder, qualifying for special commendation, the former at the context being far too dashing and tricky for Dick to cope with. The half backs and backs were reliable, if not super excellent, but Holland in goal proved ever wily and cool. Meanwhile Everton have been draw against Padiham in the Lancashire cup second round.

## DERBY COUNTY 2 EVERTON 4 (Game 7)
*October 22, 1888. The Liverpool Mercury.*

Everton on Saturday journey by special saloon to Derby to take part in their League fixture. On arriving on the County ground they were received very courteously by the executive. The ground which is very open and nicely situated was in excellent condition. There was over 3,000 spectators present, who applauded during the course of the game the good points of both sides, and cheered accordingly, when deserved. Everton won the toss and at five minutes past three Higgins started the ball with a strong sun in his face. The first good point noticed was a splendid bit of combination by McKinnon and Watson but, Roulston went to the rescue, and starved off, enabling Bakewell to get to Joliffe's end, where he was wide in his finishing touch. From the goal kick, Everton broke away in grand style and forced a corner, which was nicely taken, and Costley put on the first point of the game. From midfield Derby showed up in a grand run by their left wing, and Catterton was conceded a corner by Ross, which, however, came to nothing. After Everton had made two incursions to the home quarters, Farmer shot in swiftly, and Costley again scored amid a round of applause by the spectators. By this early reverse the County seemed to renew their exertions and severely tested the visiting defence in which Holt and Weir were prominent, and at length from a pass by L.Plankett, Catterton headed a nice goal. Even play then followed until half time arrived with the score –Everton 2 goals Derby County 1. On changing over the County were the first to show up and H. Placett and Higgins had two attempts to beat Joliffe but, the Liverpool custodian stalled them off. Everton had now two free kicks to clear, and got away in a dashing run, Betswick conceding a corner and McKinnon shot a third point for the Evertonians. An appeal that the ball had been over the line was not sustained, and the goal was allowed. Again Everton

showing good tactics kept hovering round the home end, and
Chadwick with a smart shot again beat Betswick. Derby now
played up well, and at length Joliffe succumbed to Bakewell
who headed a second goal for his side from a pass by L.Plackett.
Encouraged by the spectators the Anfieldites were again busy
near the Everton end, but Farmer eventually checked, and play
was taken to the home quarters, but no further scoring took place,
Everton thus gaining their first League fixture away from home
by 4 goals to 2. The game all round was a pleasing one, and
both sides worked hard. The losers backs and half-backs played
a sterling game. While the forwards the brothers Plackett and
Higgins were the most conspicuous and found plenty of work
for the visitors. The winners, though not at their full strength,
showed determination in and combination, that selfishness of the
forwards so often see being entirely absent. Ross and Dobson
were in good form. Especially the latter, who was mainly
instrumental for his side winning. The half-backs were all that
could be desired while the forwards at times displayed great dash
and judgement. **Teams Derby County: - TH. Bestwick, goal,
Latham and LG. Wright, backs, Williamson, Hopewell, and
W. Roulston, half-backs Bakewell and Catterton right wing,
Higgins centre, H. Plackett, L. Plackett, left wing, Umpire
W. Shaw. Everton: - Joliffe, goal, Dobson and Ross (captain)
backs, Weir, Holt, and Farmer, half-backs, McKinnon and
Watson right wing, F. Sugg, Centre, Chadwick and Costley,
left wing, Umpire W. Briscoe Referee H.Jope**

**TRANMERE ROVERS 1 EVERTON RESERVES 0**
*October 22, 1888. The Liverpool Mercury.*

Reserves played in new jersey of Red and White stripes
Everton Reserves travelled over to Tranmere hill, on Saturday
but being short of four of the usual team and three of their being
forwards, the usually good combination of the Reserves was

all at sixes and sevens, Everton having the best of the play throughout-lost their first match this season by a goal to nothing. Dick assisted the Reserves thus being unwell, and not playing in his usual position but right wing forward; he was not the shining light he generally is. Some very good play was shown by Myer and Shepherd for Tranmere Rovers and they were admirably assisted by the centre half. The forwards play was disjointed-little of no combination being shown. McAfee at times was very brilliant with his fast runs on the left. Milward Chadwick, and Keys (who by the way was unfit to play on account of recent illness) all missed exceedingly easy chances for goal two were clear cut. A.Berry passing in front of goal and being missed by every one. An irregular incident accrued while going on the field. The Everton side turned up in new jerseys (Red and White strips), and a gentleman said, "They have deserted their old colours, and will be beaten," although defeated Stockton's boys were in no way disheartened and are looking forward to next Saturdays encounted with Bootle. **Teams: - Tranmere Rovers: - H. Sherdian, goal, T. Myers, and F. Shepherd, backs, J. Bradfield, J. Roberts, and G. Sherdian, half-backs W. Litter, J. Morgan, A. Taylor, C. McAfee and WH. Rouledge, forwards; Everton: - an other, goal, A. Chadwick and N. Ashcroft, backs, T. Fayer, H. Pollock (captain), and WH. Jones half-backs J. Keys, A. Dick, A. Milward, A. Berry and R. Fell, forwards.**

## EVERTON REVIEW
*October 22, 1888. The Liverpool Mercury.*

Everton went to Derby for the first time on Saturday to fulfil their League engagement with the County team and met with greatest courtesy yet shown them, the spectators and players evincing a refreshing impartiality to the visitors, which contrasted strongly with their neighbour, the Notts County in their behavior to the strangers. Leaving Smalley, Dick, and Waugh who are on the sick list, the Everton eleven were not the strongest, but all played a plucky game throughout, and succeeded in winning their first League match away from home thus getting higher in the League list. In the first half of the game, the Liverpoolians were fortunate in having the sun in their favour and were not long in play before they succeeded in putting on the initial point. The home left then showed up but failed to get through the opposing defence and Everton again scored from a well placed shot by Farmer, which was duly and properly notched by the 3,000 spectators present. Even play followed for a time, but Derby were striving hard and Catterton headed the first point for his side, half an hour from the beginning of hostilities. Nothing further in the scoring line was done up the half-time and Everton crossed over with the lead of a goal. Both clubs worked hard on resuming, the homesters being very near equalizing by a speedy shot from L.Packett but Joliffe saved splendidly and again the Derby colours were lowered this time by McKinnon. Holt now put in some neat work and helped his side to add another point, but just before the call of time, a foul goal was scored by Chadwick, a pleasant and enjoyable game ended in favour of Everton by 4 goals to 2. As Derby play their return match at Anfield-road on Saturday next no doubt the Everton spectators will receive the good treatment their club enjoyed when at Derby.

**DENTON 0 EVERTON 3**
*October 23, 1888. The Liverpool Courier.*

Everton journey to Denton yesterday to take part in a match for the benefit of E.Bromily, who unfortunately had his leg broken whilst playing at the end of last season. The following team faced each other. Everton: - Joliffe, goal, A. Chadwick and Ross (captain) backs, Weir, T. Fayer and Farmer, half-backs, Costley,

E. Chadwick, Sugg, McKinnon and A. Berry forwards, - Denton:
- Lowe, goal, Cooke and Seddon backs, Edwards moffatt, and
Clake half-backs, Walton Plant, Dowe Warnock and T. Seddon
forwards. 5,000 people were present, the home team was late
turning out, being half-an hour after the advertised time for kick
off. Everton won the toss, and elected to play with the sun at
their backs. The score at half time was Everton 2 Denton 0; final
result Everton 3 goals Denton 0.

**EVERTON 6 DERBY COUNTY 2 (Game 8)**
*October 29, 1888. The Liverpool Mercury.*

Nearly 8,000 Everton supporters put in an appearance at Anfield
on Saturday, to witness the above return fixture. The Derby
executive, not being satisfied with their clubs decisive defeat by
the Liverpoolians resolved at a meeting on Monday to send the
strongest team possible to reverse the previous result; but this
they were disappointed, as three of their first men failed to put
in an appearance at the last moment and the local team had to
supply them with a substitute in Harbour who proved worthy of
his place. On the other hand, Everton again played last week's
eleven, with one exception, Smalley being sufficiently recovered
to take on his accustomed place between the posts. Ross again
won the toss, and elected to play with a strong wind, at his back.
Higgins kicked off. The home left were the first to become
conspicuous and Williamson just cleared in the nick of time but
from a return Sugg hit the bar twice with well directed shots, and
then Derby left wing got away, and Needham beat Smalley with
a good shot. Ross now went centre forward and Sugg partnered
Dobson. This change worked well, and seemed to arouse the
homesters, who kept raining in shots to Marshall but some time
later before Ross was able to equalise with a scorcher. Again
Everton got up and Marshall had to give a corner to save his
charge, which was nicely taken by Farmer, and McKinnon who

was in waiting headed through a second goal for Everton. From the midfield kick off, L.Packett and Needham raced down, Dobson and Weir relieving and the leather was soon again in the Derby quarters by beautiful passing of the home right and centre, but Marshall was found on the alert, and L.Plackett called on Smalley, who threw away, Dobson enabled Everton to again invade Marshall's end, and McKinnon and Holt had the hardest of luck with their shots, the Derby custodian surpassing himself with his remarkable saves. Sugg having pulled up Higgins near in, Ross was soon at the other end and Marshall in saving conceding another corner. Which however, was worked clear, and the Derby left pair again got down but L.Packett was wide in the finish. Williamson saved Chadwick but Costley was lying handy, and all but beat the custodian with an oblique shot. Two corners were nicely cleared by Derby, but just before the whistle sounded for half-time, Marshall, in working a corner kick of Weir, put the leather to the foot of Watson who guided a third goal to the home team. Everton had the best of the play up to this stage, but had a fine goalkeeper against them, whose skill was duly noticed on taking up his position at the Oakfield-road end. Resuming the home forwards seemed to show up with greater dash against the wind, and soon assumed the command. Higgins and L.Plackett paid a flying visit to the visitors end to which, Holt and Dobson attended, and then commenced a mean attack on Marshall's charge, which at length succumbed to McKinnon who beat that custodian for the fourth time. Followed by Ross kicking a fifth point a minute later and breasting goal six shortly afterwards. Chatterton having collided with Holt was useless for the remainder of the game. Again Ross was conspicuous in working a pass from Watson, but Marshall shook him off. Three corners having been cleared by Derby. McKinnon was again soon in good work, taking the ball down in fine style and Marshall had to fist out two warm ones from him. L.Plackett at length was rewarded by screwing a second goal for his side

amidst applause. Ross having headed a corner kick over the bar.
L.Plackett again tried to augment the visitors score but Dobson
cleared, and Holt saved a return under the bar. From now to the
finish Everton completely hemmed in the visitors with splendid
passing but failed to add to their total, one of the hardest games,
so far as the homesters were concerned, again ending in favour
of Everton by 6 goals to 2. **Teams; Everton:- Smalley, goal,
Dobson and Sugg, backs, Weir, Holt, and Farmer half-backs,
McKinnon, Watson. Ross (captain) Chadwick and Costley
forwards. Umpire E. Berry: - Derby County: - Marshall
goal Williamson and Rowiston backs Harbour, Selvey, and
Hopewell, half-backs Chatterton, H. Plackett, Higgins,
Needham, and L. Plackett, forwards. Umpire Richardson,
Referee Mr. Fairhurst (Bolton).**

## BOOTLE RESERVES 2 EVERTON RESERVES 3
*October 29, 1888. The Liverpool Mercury.*

These teams met for the second time this season at Hawthorn
Road. About 1,500 people witnessed the match. Milward opened
play and Bootle were first to get near goal, but the attack was at
once eased Briscoe beating Woods, a corner being only gained
from Milwards kick. The game proceeded on even terms for a
time, and then Devlin, from the right nearly enabled Ferguson to
score, Barbour heading into goal a moment later. Bootle again
closed up in a threatening manner, and on the ball being well
played a warm tussle in the goalmouth gave the home team the
lead, Joliffe succumbing to the scrimmages. Everton now put
Howarth and Spencer on their mettle and, assisted mainly by
the activity of Ross the invaders were well taken in hand Keys
shooting over, and nothing coming of a corner. Replaying to
a movement of the Bootle forwards Falls and Berry got up to
goal on the left, and Keys making ample amends for a faulty
appreciation of a previous pass scored a good goal for the

visitors. Pollock headed clear from a free kick taken by Woods but Bootle at once returned though not permitted to become dangerous. Spencer sent well up the centre from which Everton raced on the left Fall's shot being handled whilst Briscoe went just outside in an excellent attempt. A corner however, was forced and this being turned to account, the score stood in favour of Everton by 2 goals to 1. The closing incident of the first half being a fair attempt by Briscoe who was a little wide of the post with ground shot. On resuming Everton gave hands, and had to fall back Morris's screw shot being taken out of its intended course by the wind, a further shot meeting with no better success. Milward was then seen tussling with Woods, and the latter getting the upper hand Bootle again made tracks for goal, Joliffe chucking out and in a moment Griffiths had to resort to a like maneuvers a return going over the bar. An aggressive action on Bootle's right caused anxiety relief coming from a corner placed by Morris and then Howarth cleverly beat Falls and stayed a rush. Morris following up and taking play inside the Everton quarters, from whence the visitors rushed down the centre, Griffiths failed to meet Milward's final kick and so gave Everton a further goal-a claim of offside not obtaining the approval of Mr Lamont. Moffatt kicking up, hands fell to Bootle in front of goal, But Everton were equal to the emergency, Keys in turn trying a long shot of merit from the right. A smart bit of forward play worked the ball hard in front of the visitors goal. Morris shooting in brilliantly, and from a free kick right in the goalmouth, Bootle cleverly beat Joliffe. Everton then had a turn, Griffiths kicking clear. Barbour and Morris headed a brisk run, and with great emergy infused in the game, both ends rapidly reached. As the end came, Bootle pitched repeated hot scrimmages in front of Joliffe, but the defence proved exceptionally strong and no opening being found for the rain of shots the home team had to accept a defeat in an even contest of 3 goals to 2. **Teams Bootle Reserves: - Griffiths goal, Spencer** and Howarth, backs, Dodd, Moffatt and F. Woods, half-backs T. Morris, Devlin, F. Ferguson, R. Anderson, and A. Barbour forwards. Everton Reserves: - C. Joliffe, goal, A. Chadwick, and H. Wharmby, backs, T. Fryer, H. Pollock (captain), and WH.Jones, half-backs, J. Keys, W. Briscoe, A. Milward, A. Berry, and R. Falls forwards.

## EVERTON REVIEW
*October 29 1888. The Liverpool Mercury.*

In their return engagement with Derby County, Everton had a very easy task set before them to repeat their first success over the Peakities and instead of a score of 4 goals to 2 the margin was enlarged to the breath of 6 to 2, and might have been much wider had the Anfieldites deemed it necessary to avail themselves of the ever recurring chances. This was Everton's eighth League contest and having now won five-Accrington, Notts County, Aston Villa and Derby County twice being their victims-they are fairly in the running for a high if not the highest position in the championship. Dick-who by the by, has got the advantage over Notts County officials in their complaint to the League of his conduct at Trent Bridge-had no place in the team for a second time Dobson again justifying his selection, and with Smalley in his old position between the posts instead of Joliffe the eleven was the same as did so well at Derby a week ago. On the converse of the shield, however, the visitors came with a quartet of different hands to these of the previous tussle with Everton. Marshall, Habour, Selvy, and Needham, Bestwick, Lathron, Wright, and Bakewell-at the chances excepting Marshall, who was irreproachable in goal, cannot be voted an undiluted success. With a sequence of bad fortune, the Derby officials are experimenting to ascertain the spring of their weakness, which on Saturday proved in forwards and halfs. Everton had the advantage of a strong wind on opening operations, and Marshall dropped in for a lot of warm work, but still Needham breaking loose easily beat Smalley and that was before the game was five minutes old. This aroused Ross to reform, he resorting to his usual tactic when matters are not running smoothly of himself taking charge of the centre Sugg then assisting Dobson in the back department. Ross soon drew up level with a shot of no indecision, McKinnon followed with a second goal and before half-time Marshall made Everton a great present of a third in attending to a corner. Though facing the wind, the home club continued to put goals on merrily they had reached half a dozen Ross laying claim to a couple, and McKinnon the remaining one. Whilst the last point of the match was accredited to L.Pickett, Dobson was the most useful, and finished back on the field Sugg doing satisfactorily in his new position as defence. Holt despite his injury at Derby, and which made it doubtful if he would be able to play takes premier honours at Half though Farmer and Weir ran him close. Ross was all right at centre, but McKinnon who has evinced a gratifying improvement of late, was the most accomplished of the home forwards. Of the visitors L Packett was far in front of his colleagues always excepting the goalkeepers.

# NOVEMBER 1888

## EVERTON 2 BOLTON WANDERERS 1 (Game 9)
*November 5, 1888. The Liverpool Mercury.*

In weather, the reverse of pleasant to spectators and players this return match was played at Anfield-road on Saturday in the presence of 6,000 spectators, which number would, no doubt have been doubled had the day been a good one for football. It will be remembered that at the last meeting of these clubs, at Bolton, Everton, were defeated by 6 goals to 2. Principally owing to the indisposition of four of their players and the bad state of the ground but, on Saturday the home club was at the full strength, and managed to wipe out the previous defeat by 2 goals to 1. The visitors brought a strong eleven including Gillan, who was to have kept goal for the home club this season, and Bethal Robinson. The ground considering the rain was as good as could be expected, but a strong breeze militated against an accurate game. Ross lost the toss, and started the half against the wind and hill. Chadwick and Brown were first to get conspicuous in a nice dribble up the left, and the former had hard luck with the finish, Gillan managing to clear at the expense of a corner which was fruitless, and then Robinson had to kick out to save from Brown a minute later. The Wanderers now got towards Smalley, Milne finishing with a sweet shot. From the free kick, Holt got possession and sent in a warm shot to Gillan, who had to concede another corner to save his charge, but the wind carried the ball over the line. Dick intercepted Brogan and Davenport in Everton quarters, and sent the ball to Brown, who gave Ross a chance, but the latter's shot went wide. Again the opposing right pair went down, but were erratic in their shooting. After Ross had tried to find an opening, Dobson successfully tackled Davenport in his bid for goal, and the ball rolled harmlessly out. A wide shot by Watson having been sent in, Smalley had a warm handful from Davie Weir, which he easily negotiated, and the ball was taken to the other and where Gillan was again tested by Chadwick, but only a corner was the outcome, which was also worked. Weir then gave Ross another chance, but his finishing touch was wide. With this let off the "Trotters" soon rushed to the home quarters and where Weir managed to stave off Barbour, and then Tyrer sent in a strong shot, which Smalley had no difficulty in getting away. Again Everton paid a flying visit to the Wanderers ground, and McKinnon slipped, as he was in the act of sending the leather home. Excitement now ran high, as Chadwick ran the length of the field from a throw in, but the chance was missed. Luck was against the home team, Gillan neutralizing himself in keeping his clean clear. A free kick falling to Everton well in, Farmer put the ball between the posts without any player touching it. Even play then set in, and when the half-backs whistle sounded neither side had scored. On changing over, with the wind in their favour, Everton soon bore down on Gillan, who had to dispatch two shots, from Watson and Farmer, but Failed to stop one from Brown, who gave his side the lead, amidst the greatest enthusiasm. From midfield Everton again pressed and soon Ross beat Gillan a second time; but the home umpire had previously claimed for a foul and, the point was accordingly disallowed and a free kick given, which Robinson got away. A foul was here given against Roberts for tripping McKinnon, which however, came to nothing, and Tyrer and Milne ran up, but Dobson eased, and McKinnon was unfortunate in his attempt to add to the score, the ball grazing the upright. The Everton left pair passed neatly up, but Chadwick was wide, in his kick, which let in the visitors, who had a free kick awarded them close in goal, from which the Wanderers equalised. Striving hard to get the lead, both teams were working well, and the various goalkeeping were kept busy. Dick and Dobson having stopped dangerous rushes, the home club at length got a throw in from the corner, and Ross registered a second goal to the delight of the home supporters. The Visitors from now to the end of the game had to act on the defensive, although Barbour was spoiled by Dobson in an ominous-looking run, and soon a hard and fast game ended in favour of Everton with the score- Everton 2 goals, Wanderers 1. **Teams Wanderers: - Gillan, goal, Robinson and Roberts, backs, Bullough Scrowcroft and D.Weir half-backs, Davenport, Brogan, Milne, and Tyrer, forwards. Umpire Harrison, Everton: - Smalley goal, Dick and Dobson, backs, J. Weir, Holt, and Farmer. Half-backs, McKinnon, Watson, Ross (captain), Chadwick, Brown, forwards, Umpire E. Berry, Referee J.Cooper.**

## CHESTER COLLEGE V EVERTON RESERVES
*November 5, 1888*

**Everton team: - C. Joliffe, goal, A. Chadwick and an other, backs, W, Harbour, H. Pollock (captain), and WH. Jones half-backs, J. Keys, W. Briscoe, A. Milward, A. Berry and R. Falls, forwards.**

## EVERTON REVIEW
*November 5, 1888. The Liverpool Mercury.*

Saturday's enjoyment was disturbed by thorough going and most cheerless of November weather, and dangerous and dullness were as Handy Andy would put it. "Like bad luck-everywhere". The ill-fortune, however, from an Evertonian appear only to the meteorological conditions for did they not average-not overwhelmingly, but effectuate-their previous reverse at the hands-or rather to be accurate, at the feet of their old notorious, and yet respected opponents Bolton Wanderers. On a slippery ground, and in the presence of a large company, which would have been greatly increased under favorable skies, the defeat of a month back was turned into victory, and the score reversed in the shape of 2 goals to 1. Instead of 2 goals to 6, Everton thus emerging from nine League tussle with six wins and three losses. They have now settled their account with four clubs having played home and away with Aston Villa, Notts County, Derby County, and Bolton Wanderers, the remaining contest, the first of the series having given Everton a success over Accrington, and the Anfieldites are now planted deeply in a forward position among "the twelve" The game on Saturday was of a highly-strung order, the pace being sustained almost throughout, despite the heavy state of the turf from the rain that fell for many hours previously, and continued till the interval. There was also a stiffest breeze sweeping from Anfield to the Oakfield-road goal, against which and the slope the home representative had to content at the outset and, yet they fully held their own during the first half, ends changing with both goals intact. On resuming Everton immediately went down to goal in business-like fashion, and were not long before they scored. Ross shooting through, only to be denied, owing to his own followed this. Umpire's prior claim for foul, and shortly after the Wanderers pulled up level from a free kick in front of Smalley. Some ten minutes later Ross took full scope of a chance and, with a shot there was no disgrace in allowing to get home, scored the winning point. Dick reappeared in the team, and shaped all the better for the leisure of the last three weeks, for he was always safe, in the first half especially so. Dobson also played a grand game, and it would be hard to say which was the more useful in their respective styles of defences. All the half-backs were efficient, Holt excelling in accurate kicking, and Weir in tackling. The Forwards were remarkable for hard work rather than combination, but this will be accounted for by the uncertain footing on the saturated ground. W.Brown at length resumed football after his suspension and made a favorable impression on the outside left, his passes being generally well timed, but he was poorly, backed up by Chadwick, Watson and McKinnon also were not at their best. Neither Mills, Roberts nor Harrison had charge of Bolton's goal, but Gillan-an associate of Everton in their practice games-and he and Smalley were both clever and about equally safe. All the visitors backs were smart, which Davenport and Brogan were the most dangerous of the Wanderers front line.

### BLACKBURN ROVERS 3 EVERTON 0 (Game 10)
*November 12, 1888. The Liverpool Mercury.*

The first meeting of these clubs this season took place on the historic ground at Leamington-street. The Rovers colours being similar to those of Everton, the home team courteously allowed the visitors the privilege of turning out in the famous blue and white they appearing in Red and Black jersey. Ross lost the toss, and Milward kicked off against a stiff breeze, and Chadwick securing possession, darted off but was checked by Forbes. Hands now fell to Everton in midfield, and Dobson shot through without touching anyone. Play became very exciting, but as yet no good play had been shown. Everton forwards were out of it, and the Rovers had not displayed any combination. The game went on in a ding-dong fashion, and a good run by Brown and Chadwick, and a final shot by the latter enlivened things a little. The Rovers backs and half-backs, did not allow the visitors forwards to remain long at their end of the field, and John Southworth was noticeable for good passing. Townley next showed what a fine turn of speed he has, by sprinting past Dobson, and then centering beautifully, but Ross cleared and immediately, Beresford secured a corner, which was unproductive. After some even play in midfield, Walton passed to Beresford, who put in a clinking shot, and Townley, who was lying under the bar headed through, but the point was not allowed owing to off-side. Farmer and Watson now showed a pretty bit of passing, and made some headway, but found the two-Internationals-Forest and Forbes-too good for them and again the Rovers forwards worked down the field, and a long shot by Almond was only partially cleared by Smalley, and unfortunately struck the crossbar and rebound through the goal. Everton now put more vigour into the game, and the play was improved. Both backs were deservedly cheered for fine defence and kicking, Forbes, not being tested in the same manner as Ross showing to great advantage. Playing up hard, Everton passed for a short time, and shots by Milward, Chadwick, and Farmer were with some difficulty cleared. Beresford and Southworth were then noticeable for missing two easy chances. The visitors again pressed and Brown had a shot, but being a disjoined effort, and not supported by the other forwards, was easily repulsed. Just on half-time Forbes missed his kick and Southworth kicked over the bar to save. On returning it was seen that the team, whose composition was not the best to start with, was again alternated Farmer going centre and Milward outside right. It was now thought that the visitors would assume the aggressive, having a good wind at their backs, but the Rovers played a surprising game, and from the kick off at once commenced an attack on Smalley, Fecitt and Townley making some fine runs, and bothering Dobson rather more than he relished. From the kick out, Watson, Farmer, and Chadwick made a considerable headway, but when coming near goal they seemed to lose their heads, and the shots were either weak or went wide. The Rovers were certainly now having the best of it, and Townley brought down the house for a rapid sprint and accurate centre which Nat.Walton promptly shot through. From now to the finish the Rovers played a winning game, and although Ross went forward and put Farmer half-back and Sugg full-back, no material difference was noticed for the Rovers forwards kept pegging away at the Everton goal, and after a shot of Southworth's had been repulsed in a weak style another goal was added from a scrimmage, and thus a very exciting game resulted Blackburn Rovers 3 goals; Everton nil. **Teams Rovers: - Arthur goal, Jim Southworth, and Forbes backs, Douglas, Almond and Forrest half-backs, Beresford, Walton John Southworth, Townley and Fecitt, forwards. Everton: - Smalley, goal, Dobson, and Ross (captain), backs Weir, Sugg, and Holt half-backs, Farmer, Watson, Milward, Chadwick, and Brown forwards.**

### EVERTON RESERVES 2 PADIHAM 0
*November 12, 1888. The Liverpool Mercury.*

The Lancashire Senior Cup Round Two
The Reserves team having disposed of Turton in the first round of the above cup competition, they were deputed to play the above match on Saturday, and although considerably weakened by the enforced absence of Falls, Keys, Milward, and Pollock, who have not the necessary qualification managed to win easily. At the last moment Fleming did not turn up and consequently the late injured player Cookson was prevailed to play. A large crowd of 3,000 assembled. The Everton team as follows: - Everton, Joliffe goal, Higgins, and Chadwick, backs Jones Fryer, and Parry half-backs, Harbour, Berry, Costley, Briscoe, and Cookson forwards. Upon commencing hostilities the Reserves at once assumed the aggressive and by superior play, bombarded the visitors' goal continually, and eventually were rewarded by a goal from the foot of Cookson. This reverse roused the Padiham team somewhat, and they played up with increased vigour, but up to half-time no further score was added. In the second half Padiham started off with a bit of dash, but failed to keep it up, and again Everton bore down upon the visitors goal, and but for wretched forward play and miserable shooting (a point not usually noticed in the second team) must have scored on several occasions. Still the visitors were not discouraged,

and kept pegging away, but found the defence much to good for them. Higgins, Chadwick, Fayer, Parry, and Jones, all being in splendid trim. At last Costley found an opening and increased the score to two. At which number the Reserves won their way in the third round of the Senior cup. Chadwick played with all his accustomed skill and coolness, and was the best back on the field. Fayer also played one of his old games. Parry, Jones and old Mike were very safe, but the less said about the forwards the better the play being but poor, and they are usually the strongest point of the Reserves team.

**BURNLEY 2 EVERTON 2 (Game 11)**
*November 19, 1888. The Liverpool Mercury.*

Everton visited Turf Moor on Saturday for the second time this season to decide the first of their two League matches with Burnley, but were not represented with their full strength, whilst the home club put a powerful team in the field. The team was the same, which beat West Bromwich Albion with the exception that McFetteridge played at centre instead of McKinnon. The attendance was large taking into account the uninviting character of the weather, and great enthusiasm was evinced throughout the contest. The couple of hundred excursions from Liverpool, especially making their presence known when their champions did anything brilliant. Everton had the disadvantage of contenting against a strong wind, which swept from goal to goal, and a rather prominent hill. On Costley, setting the ball in motion, and Burnley lost no time in driving players down the slope, as Sugg missed his aim. Ross checked a rush on the right, but it was Dobson who effectual cleared and enabled Chadwick and Brown to get well away. Friel relieved, and though Sugg intercepted, Everton lines were crossed, and on Friel again pitching play in front, Sugg was the more prominent in breaking the attack. Both wings tried a run, but could not pass

Berry and Lang and then Burnley closed up in strong formation. Brady failed to take Yates pass across the goal mouth, but was uncomfortably near to scoring a moment later. The home forwards could not be shifted, and out of smart maneuvering, Gallacher beat Smalley when the game was ten minutes old. Everton went up on the left as far as Berry would be permit and from a throw in at the half-way mark the Visitors were once more in trouble. Here Sugg relieved the invaders in check by grand heading, but on Farmer trying to also head, and being six inches lower than the ball, Brady and McKay put themselves in command, overpowered Ross, and Smalley venturing out of his lair and falling McKay shot through. Farmer next pulled up Brady, but Brown found near in, the kick by Abrams, however, being cleverly turned to use by the ex-Stanleyite. Chadwick followed up and a free kick falling to the lot of Everton near goal, Sugg in a good aim caused Cox to fist out, Watson banging the return through before the custodian had time to steady himself. A lusty cheer saluted Everton's success against the wind and hill, and from this time forward, the play was most determined. Burnley on resuming put the visitors defence on their mettle but disaster was gamely averted, more particularly by means of Sugg and Dobson's heading capabilities. Again Burnley attacked hard. Smalley stopped a volley grandly whilst Sugg gave a corner in converting a miskick by Ross, and Smalley further negotiated a most brilliant shy from the centre a moment later-indeed the attack was maintained right up to the interval, but the defenders were clever, and ends exchanged with the home club leading with only a one-goal margin. From McFettridge kick off, Costley at once showed how much easier it was to travel down the slope with a rear wind than when having these accidental advantage against him, but the backs easily cut up his progess so Fleming and Watson tried a wing movement with a better effort, the latter going just outside from Brown's pass. No relief came from the Burnley goal kick, for

Fleming centred to Costley, who toe to Chadwick, and the latter equalised in a spanking shot. The home team at once recovered from the shock, Brady and McKay trying vainly to get the better of Ross. Everton next had a chance on the right but Fleming was too gentle, and the Burnley right wing broke away, anxiety being increased when Dobson gave hands in stopping Yates. Ross cleared with the head, but a nice bit of forwards play again located operations at close quarters, in attending to which, Dobson got accidentally knocked on the knees. He however, though limping, played on gallantly to the end. The remaining portion of the game, despite a heavy showers, was carried on with great energy and brilliancy, both goalkeepers being several times upon to attend to ticklish shots, but neither side could demonstrate superiority, and a splendidly-contested and level match terminated in a draw-2 goals each. **Teams; Burnley: - Cox, goals, Berry and Lang, backs, Keenan, Friel, and Abrams half-backs, Brady, anf McKay right wing, McFetteridge, centre, Yates, and Gallacher, left wing, Everton: - Smalley goal, Dobson, and Ross (captain), backs, Holt, Sugg, and Farmer, half-backs Fleming, and Watson, right wing, Costley centre Chadwick and Brown left wing. Referee Mr AS.Ormerod (Accrington).**

### EVERTON RESERVES  2 SALTNEY 0
*November 19, 1888. The Liverpool Courier.*

The league contest at Burnley deprived the Anfield supporters of a first team fixture on Saturday. The contest being an encounter between Stockton's triumphant eleven and the Saltney team from Chester. The weather was very bad, and the heavy rain made the ground very sodden. They were about 2,000 spectators present when the teams faced each other. The Chester team came with two men short, but able substitutes were provided from the home reserves. **Teams follows Everton: - Joliffe, goal, A. Chadwick,** and M. Higgins, backs WH. Jones, T. Fayer and H. Pollock (captain) half-backs, Cookson, Harbour, Milward, W. Briscoe, and J. Keys forwards. Saltney: - Jones, goal, Blake, and Whittingham backs, Davies, Williams, and Sewell half-backs, Hallows, Scott, Parkinson, J. Merith, and Willams, forwards. This match was advertised to commence at 2-30 prompt, but it was 3-45 before the Saltney representative put in an appearance. Having won the toss Milward kicked off, for Everton with the wind, Milward twice giving Jones trouble, but the custodian was all there. After some good play Jones scored for Everton amidst applause. Score at half-time 1 goal to nil for Everton. On resuming again attacked but the ball was worked over the line. Some splendid play by Briscoe came to nothing after at length Jones success in beating his name sake, in semi-darkest and the whistle sounded Leaving Everton victories by 2 goals to nil.

**EVERTON REVIEW**
*November 19, 1888. The Liverpool Mercury.*

In the face of defection and absentee through indisposition, and the consequential "reconstruction" it was an open secret that Everton engaged in their first League match with Burnley, with pardonable misgivings. Moreover, unpromising as the teams seemed as chosen, it was doubtful right up to the appointed time of starting, whether it would not be still further weakened. Only six of the team reached Burnley by the train selected by Mr Barclay two others wandering too far from the platform at Preston whilst waiting for the saloon to be tacked on to the proper train, but these and others turned up with the excursionists, and a move was then made to the well-arranged enclosure at Turf Moor. Dobson was still missing, but just when he had been given up as lost, and Dick was preparing for the emergency, the ex-captain removed anxiety by putting in a welcome appearance, for Dick is at present hardly sufficiently convalescent for such a tough piece of business as was in prospective. When a hearty cheer of greeting had subsided, and players had taken up their positions, it was noticed that McMahon was displaced by McFettridge and Milward and Weir by Costley and Fleming as compared with the teams that fought respectively for the League Championship the week previously. Everton were at once on their mettle on Mr. S. Ormerod giving the signal for a commencement, for they had to attack if they could uphill and in the teeth of a half gale. Burnley of course, took all the advantage they could of the fortuitous assistance rendered them and pressed in quick succession, with the result that they led by two goals at the end of 20 minutes with hard and excellent play on either side. They had matters much their own way so far, but not for the hands near home, soon gave Everton the loophole they had been watchful for, Sugg shooting well, and Watson driving the return from Cox through-a surprising point against such a combination of odds. The second half was utilized by Everton in attacking more frequently, but they could only score once, and as this was the sum total of goals of the game-hard and brilliant and always interesting it ended as it should do in a draw of two goals each. Of the players, the home forwards were much the cleverest quintet and often went away in fine combination, particularly when storming the hill in the second half, Chadwick and Brown for Everton were all that could be desired on the left, except that the latter showed a temptation to resort to his old besetting sin of spring. Costley and Watson were fairly good but Fleming spoilt himself by availing rather than seeking tackling. Smalley, Dobson, Ross and Sugg were the salvation of Everton, Sugg being especially effective at centre half-back; while Friel and Lang were ever conspicuous among the Burnleyites. The result of a draw no doubt satisfied the most sanguine hope of the Everton committee, who of late have no sooner surmounted one difficulty, than another has arisen, and new desertion has supplemented illness is depriving them of material to select from, in connection with the League matches. The majority of the twelve clubs, have this week reached the turning point on the journey having got to the eleventh milestone and the order based on Mr McGregor theory of two points for a win and one for a draw.

### EVERTON 3 BURNLEY 2 (Game 12)
*November 26, 1888. The Liverpool Mercury.*

This return League fixture was played at Anfield-road on Saturday in the presence of 8,000 spectators. Burnley had the same team that did battle the previous week, and came in the full expectation of lowering the Everton Colours. The home club was greatly altered. Sugg taking Dobson's place at full back owing to an accident to the latter's leg, while a new centre and right wing donned the Everton colours for the first time, there by leaving Watson out. The weather was fine, but a strong wind prevented an accurate game being played Burnley had the misfortunate to lose the toss and McFettridge set the ball going against the wind. Ross pounced upon the leather, and sent in a long shot, Farmer slightly wide with his finish. Burnley from the goal kick, dribbled along on the right and were within when Ross intercepted, and Costley missed an easy chance owing to erratic shooting. Holt gave Costley another chance, and the Burnley custodian had great difficulty in negotiating. Coyne then broke away in good style, but the wind carried the ball away from his toe just as he was on the point of shooting. With this let off Burnley transferred play to midfield where Coyne again relieved, and, assisted by Davie and Fleming dribbled splendidly to the visitors quarter, where Lang had to concede a corner from which, however, nothing came. Fleming in a pretty shot, but Lang was playing well, and managed to stave off disaster, and sent to his left-wing pair, who trundled the ball along but Ross relieved with a shot which sent over Cox's head. Everton continued to hover around the Burnley end where Holt put in some nice shots, but failed to effect a downfall, Berry staving off danger by giving a corner. Yates and McFettridge carried play to the home end and the former tested Smalley with a clinking shot; but the Everton custodian fisted cleverly, and enabled Davie to do a grand dash up the field, Lang saving at the expense of another corner, which also was worked clear, as was one a minute later. In clearing, Yates collided with Holt, and play was suspended for some considerable time. On resuming Everton played with renewed vigour, and the Burnley goalkeeper and backs were taxed to the utmost. Yates and Gallacher managed to pass Sugg by tricky play, but Holt went to the rescue, and planted the ball up the field, where it was carried over the line. Abrams was penalised for a foul throw and Davie from the free kick, had the hardest of luck, Lang saving miraculously. At length Everton broke through the defence and from hands Chadwick beat Cox there by giving the home team the lead. With this reverse Burnley worked hard, and Brady and McKay put in some good work, but failed to pass the back division, and Fleming getting the ball from Ross, ran up and screwed across, but the chance was not availed of, and play was taken towards Smalley, where Sugg eased and Coyne shortly afterwards added a second goal for Everton. The homesters continued to have the best of the game, and Berry, in attempting to clear his lines, put one through his own post for Everton. From this to half-time the Anfieldites had many chances but failed to augment their total, and the whistle sounded for half-time with the score Everton 3 goals Burnley 0. On changing over against the wind, Davie worked right through, and sent across to the left pair, who, however, allowed the ball to roll out. Gallacher and Yates from the throw in got nicely along, and McFettridge was spoiled by Ross sending back, and Costley screwed to Davie who gave Cox a warm handful but that player fisted away, and

hands was given against Holt from the return. Brady having
sent over the bar, Friel spoilt the Everton forwards in a dashing
pass, which was followed by Coyne and Davie being cheered
for their neat short pass, but the wind assisted Cox to save their
finish in touch, Costley and Chadwick them went away in good
style, and the latter put in a splendid shot which, Cox just saved
in time, Everton again tried to improve matters and Lang had a
great deal to do to stave them off. At last Burnley took up the
reins, and continued for some time to keep Smalley busy, he
having to do yeoman service to keep the visitors at bay. From a
corner to Everton, Burnley got away, and McKay beat Smalley
for the first time. Continuing the pressure Brady owing to lying
off-side was unable to gain a second point. A minute later Sugg
gave a corner, from which Brady was enabled to add goal 2.
From now to the finish both goals were in jeopardy as each
club was working hard, but no other point was registered a hard
and evenly-contested game thus ending in a win for Everton
by 3 goals to 2. **Teams; Everton: - Smalley, goal, Sugg, and
Ross (captain), backs, Weir, Holt, and Farmer, half-backs,
Fleming, Coyne, Davie, Chadwick, and Costley, forwards,
Umpire E. Berry, Burnley: - Cox, goal, Berry and Lang
backs, Abrams, Friel and Keenan half-backs, Brady, Mckay
Mcfettridge, Gallacher, and Yates, forwards. Umpire J.
Kearsley, Referee WH. Jope.**

### STOKE SWIFTS 0 EVERTON RESERVES 0
*November 26, 1888. The Liverpool Mercury.*

These eleven's met for the first time at Stoke on Saturday, in fine
weather. **Teams; Everton: - C. Joliffe, goal, A. Chadwick, and
WH. Warmby, backs, C. Parry, T. Fayer, and WH. Jones
half-backs, J. Keys, W. Briscoe, A. Milward, J. Costley,
and W. Harbour, forwards; Stoke Swifts: - Hassle, goal,
Say, and Monter, backs, Tunstcliffe, Farmer, and Holdlen**

**half-backs Broadhurst, Forester, Milward, Slade, and Wainwright forwards.** Everton won the toss, and played with the wind, in the first half Stoke were the first to press, and gain the first corner with proved useless. A number of capital shots were put in by the home forwards but Joliffe was in fine form, and was heartily cheered for the save which he preserved his charge. Good passing by Everton forwards resulted in Briscoe making a deserving attempt to score, the ball hitting the post and rebounding outside. Milward was prominent for the same tricky play on behalf of the visitors, but was eventually pulled up when near goal. The same player shortly afterwards sent in a good shot, which was cleared by the goalkeeper. Both teams worked hard up to half-time, but when the whistle sounded, no goals had been scored. On changing over Everton showed much better form and as the result of a combined run, an oblique shot was sent in from the right wing. The Stoke goalkeepers certainly appeared to put the leather through his own goal, but for some reason or other the point was not allowed. After this piece of hard luck, the visiting team continued to have the best of the game and several times came near scoring. Stoke tried hard but, Joliffe kept goal splendidly, and repulsed shot after shot in grand style and the game was finished in semi-darkness, and despite the strenuous exertions of both teams, neither could gain the advantage, Result a draw, no goals having been scored.

**EVERTON REVIEW**
*November 26, 1888. The Liverpool Mercury.*

The commissioners deputed by the English Council to adjudicate in the matter of the allegations of misconduct against Dick (Everton), Hodgetts (Aston Villa), Russell (Preston North End), Sloan (Stoke) etc, have accomplished their task with completeness and expedition, if not with equity and leniency. The commission sat in Birmingham on Wednesday, and in

Nottingham on Thursday-an arrangement convenient for Aston Villa and Notts County, but not for Everton, who thus had to devote time to two sittings in two different towns-and the upshot, of it all is that Dick is suspended for two mouths and Hodgetts one month, whilst Russell and Sloan escape penalties. Football of course must be conducted in a respectable manner. The laws of play are readily understood, and should be respected, and above all proper behaving ought to be observed but the punishment now inflicted is more harsh than the exigencies of the offences seen to warrant. Hodgetts is not known as a rough player and Dick as he has generally been painted is not vindictive in his tactics, though he no doubt often raises the fire of even heavier opponents by the effective use of muscular thighs in tackling; and even admitting that both men had committed a grave error under provocation, a strong reprimand would have justly met the case. Birmingham people whilst ready to blame Dick are sensitive that great injustice has been doled out to Hodgett. If this be so, with what greater reason have Evertonians to complain of wrong for according to the commissioners finding Hodgett was declared to have actually delivered a blow whereas Dick could only be proved guilty of an attempt to strike ? However the fist of the commission has gone forth-the law in their eyes has been broken and vindicated, and the opportunity of lunging at the League perhaps gleefully embraced. Will the matter be allowed thus to rest? Violation of rules is not to be tolerated and fighting should be put down in a drastic manner, but the Association must be general and sweeping in their vigilance, and remember that roughness is not an exclusive peculiarity of League matches any more than cup ties, but is liable to bubble up at all and sundry contests. It so happens that the players put through their facing at this latest inquiry, all belonged to League clubs. Whilst other clubs-out-side the twelve-equally involved in misconduct, have been overlooked, and if the Council wish to displace a suspicious of antagonism to the League, they will make haste to apply their power indeterminately without fear of favour. The commission having disposed of some cases of infringement of professional rules, wound up their labours by issuing a homily for distribution among clubs, and especially applicable to referees, on a rigid observances of laws and penalities and the desirability of commission endeavouring to maintain a reasonable demeanmour on the part of spectators. Birmingham, Nottingham and other patrons will take note of this latter seasonable advice, it is to be hoped and then there will be small cause for confusions.

The return league engagement between Burnley and Everton proved quite as tough a struggle as that of the drawn game at Turf Moor the previous week. Burnley entrusted the reputation of their club to the same hands that made an even fight at the first meeting, but Everton were a very dissimilar eleven. Dobson is still suffering from the accidental kick he received from McKay and, with Dick ineligible Sugg was transferred from centre half-back to fullback, Weir stepping into the middle line, whilst the Forwards embraced the long talked of new blood in the persons of Coyne (Vale of Leven), and Davie (Renton) room being created for these strangers from over the border by dropping out Brown and Watson. Everton had the advantage of a strong breeze in the first half, which was so well utilised that they had the substantial lead of 3 to 0 at the time the interval was announced. Burnley replied with a couple of effective shots on an exchange of ends, giving the Anfieldites, with a score of 3 to 2, their seventh victory in connection with the league. Smalley played another grand game in goal, saving at times when it seemed impossible almost to cope with such a fierce attack. Sugg although at times doing some especial work, was a weaker defender than Ross. Burnley having covered this flaw, disposed their forces accordingly, and with Sugg once overcome a cross over was resorted to which tactics gave Burnley their two goals. Farmer, Holt and Weir each did so well at half-backs that it would be unfair to make a selection for superiority. The two new forwards both made a favorable impression. Davie showed be possessed judgement at centre, and, what is more to the point, was not slow in parting with the ball though it could be done with better advantage; and altogether he bids fair to be a great acquisition when a sufficient trial has allowed him to become familiar with his wing men. Coyne partnered Fleming, and treated the spectators to the neat short passing of Scotch brand, remaining one of McNee in the Dunmbartonshire and Lancashire match, and he often came in for an approving cheer. Fleming was hardly powerful enough for his colleagues whilst Chadwick greatly overshadowed Costley, was perhaps the best of the home front line.

# DECEMBER 1888

**WEST BROMWICH ABION 4 EVERTON 1 (Game 13)**
*December 3, 1888. The Liverpool Courier.*

This League match was played at West Bromwich. West
Bromwich kick off in the presence of about 7,000 spectators.
Just after the kick off, Dobson gave a corner from which nothing
resulted. After a throw-out, Sugg passed to Davies, who turned
to Coyne and that player shot outside. The home men then
pressed and Smalley had to save, and in the opening play Sugg,
Costley, and Dobson showed up well, Bayliss passed right
across to W.Perry, who neatly headed through and immediately
after, Smalley threw out grandly, Costley and Chadwick were
next prominent, when Sugg coming in sent in a slow shot, which
Roberts kicked away. From some pretty play in front of goal
Everton give a corner, the result of which was that after Smalley
had saved, Perry headed through. The following play settled in
midfield, but Davie had a shot, which Roberts handed off. From
good play on Bayliss, Davie received a pass and just kicked
over the bar. The home forwards by capital passing got down
the field, and Bassett with a long shot scored. Score at half-
time:- West Bromwich 3; Everton nil. Immediately following
the restart Sugg was hurt in the right foot and had to retire.
Smalley in saving gave a corner, but Weir headed away and
them Davies put in a splendid run down the right, Chadwick
eventually sending a shot which went outside Sugg on making
his appearance was cheered. A fine shot was then sent in, which
Smalley kept out, Everton raced down, and Coyne sent one in
which Roberts fisted grandly, Weir then kicking over. After Sugg
had again retired the play became faster, and Chadwick sent in
a beauty, Roberts just being able to repulse it. The home men
sustained a hot siege on Everton's goal and two good chances
were missed. At length the visitors got away, and Chadwick

propelled a grand shot from the left corner, which Roberts never attempted to stop. Everton were playing a little better now, and E. Chadwick made another grand attempt, Roberts fisting out timely and immediately Farmer had a try the ball just going outside. Costley was then disabled and had to go off the field. Davies then raced down finely but could not avail himself of a good chance. West Bromwich again pressed Dobson twice kicking away grandly. A corner was given however, from the scrimmage in front of goal another point was added to the home team's score. More exciting play followed in front of the upright, but the home men could not get through, Everton in semi-darkness playing fairly well with their 9 men. Final result-West Bromwich Albion 4 goals; Everton 1 goal; **Teams; Everton: - Smalley, goal, Dobson and A. Chadwick backs, Farmer, Weir and Sugg, half-backs, Costley, E. Chadwick, Davie, Coyne, and J. Davies , forwards. West Bromwich: - Roberts, goal, Walker, and J. Horton, backs, Bayliss. C. Perry, and Timmins half-backs Pearson Hendry, W. Perry, Wilson and Bassett, forwards.**

## EVERTON RESERVES 1 BURSLEM PORT VALE RESERVES 1
*December 3, 1888. The Liverpool Courier.*

The Everton first team having to play their league contest at Birmingham on Saturday, the Anfield enclosure was occupied by the reserve team, who had for their opponents a very promising eleven from the Midlands. The Lancashire County Association had the services of Ross and Holt in their engagement at Edinburgh, this necessitated the home executive drawing upon the Reserve to complete their first team, and in consequence of this the team that appeared on the field was very much weakened by the absence of A.Chadwick and Watson. A new man from Wrexham made his debut on the outside right in place of Keys. Teams; Everton: - Joliffe, goal, Pollock (Captain), and Wharmby backs J. Jones, T. Fayer and J. Parry, half-backs Briscoe, Cookson Brown, Keys, and Jones, forwards. Vale:- Broomhall, goal, Tadall, and Skimmer backs, Chadwick, Surees, and Farrington half-backs Sproston, Wood, Hood Stokes and Kirkham forwards. The Visitors having won the toss, W.Brown started the ball a few minutes before three. Burslem started with nine men. For a time the play continued in the centre. Good passing by the Visitors carried the ball into close proximity to the Everton goal, but it was kicked over the line. Everton then retaliated, and rushed down the field and for a time the play was in the neighborhood of the visitors's goal. A rush by the Burslem visitors caused Joliffe to save. A foul was given against Everton close to the home goal, but the ball was cleared. A long shot again caused Joliffe to use his hands and the leather was quickly transferred to the opposite goal, but Fryer kicked over. From a throw in the visitors forwards became dangerous, but Joliffe was all there, making a splendid save. From a goal kick Everton rushed down but failed in front of goal. Burslem now pressed but hands in front of goal removed play into the centre, Briscoe rushed down and passed to Brown, who was tripped and from the free kick, Everton were near scoring. Parry passed to Jones, who made a good shot for goal, and immediately afterwards Briscoe was again prominent with a good run and splendid shot, but Broomhall saved. A corner now fell to Everton but the ball was cleared and a long shot again caused Jolliffe to use his hands. Wharmby gives a corner and Briscoe again prominent for tricky play. From a free kick Everton near scoring, and in the scrimmage in front of goal, Fayer received a severe kick in the face and had to retire. Cookson was also down and also retired, Everton though playing with only nine men held their own. Keys proceeded in two brilliant runs. The visitors pressed but the good defence of Everton prevailed disaster. After the ball had again been in Burslam territory, good passing carried the ball into home territory and the Visitors scored. Immediately after this the whistle blew. Hood restarting the ball and for a time play continued in the centre. Good passing by the Everton centre forwards carried the ball into the neighborhood of the visitor's goal, but the backs cleared, Burslem carried the ball down the field, and looked dangerous, but kicked over. A free kick was given in front of Everton goal, but nothing resulted. A foul was given against the visitors for tripping Brown when close to the goal, but the ball was cleared. From a goal kick the Burslem forwards rushed down and caused Joliffe to save. A corner now fell to the visitors, but the ball was headed over. From a miss kick by Wharmby another corner fell to Burslem, and Joliffe saved grandly. From a throw in Kirkham rushed down the field, but Pollock checked and returned the ball. Good passing caused Joliffe to use his hands. Everton now played up strongly, but from a free kick Burslem again sent the ball down the field, Everton came again and obtained a corner, from which a goal was scored by Brown. After some even play in midfield hands against Everton allowed Burslem to get near the goal but the ball was kick over the line. A corner fell to Burslem and a hot tussle took place in front of the Everton goal, but the home defender stayed unbroken. A long shot again caused Joliffe to use his hands, saving at the expense of a corner, but the ball was kicked behind. From the kick out Everton rushed up the field, and obtained another corner but the dexterity of Joliffe kept the visitors from scoring. Although Everton falt the loss of the two men injured, yet they played up well, and after a well fought game the match remained a draw. Result Everton one goal Port Vale one goal.

## EVERTON 3 LONG EATON RANGERS 1
*December 10, 1888. The Liverpool Courier*

The English cup tie prevented South Shone fulfilling their engagement with the Everton on Saturday, and therefore's match was made with the Staffordshire organization who have a very excellent reputation. The home executives have been trying to improve their team, introducing a new play, Morris of Oswentry, going centre. Ross was unable to play his absence from the back division being keenly felt. Fully 7,000 spectators were present when the teams put in an appearance, J Holt the popular half-back receiving quite an ovation in recognition of his services for the county on Saturday last. Dobson having lost the toss, Orchard kick off Vesey and Locker raced up the left, their good intentions being foiled by Farmer and Dobson. From a throw in Chadwick and Costley dribbled down the left, and passing to Morris he put in a regular beauty which defeated Start five minutes from the commencement. A brilliant run by Hardy gave the defence some trouble, Dobson with a good punt removed the danger. Everton now pressed on the right, a shot from Weir just going outside. From the kick out, Holt passed to Coyne who again shot in, Start again proving equal to the condition. Everton renewing the attack brought the sphere well in front and after a great piece of passing again defeated the goalkeeper. (Chadwick). The Rangers began to play much better, their passing being much admired, after a good shot from Plackett Winfield called upon Smalley to clear; Weir was now cheered for some grand tackling, his play at this point being superb. A grand run by Davie enabled Morris to get in and he in turn passed to Chadwick, his final effort again proved successful. J.Start and Hardy with a beautiful run brought the play well into the Everton quarters. Erratic shooting and solid defence kept the goal intact. Half-time Everton 3 goals Long Eaton Rangers nil.

After the usual interval for rest, Orchard put the ball in motion. The visiting van took up the attack and a scrimmage was formed in the Everton goal mouth, Dobson and Sugg removing the danger with some fine kicking. Play was now confined to midfield for some time until Coyne broke away and passing to

Morris he missed a grand opportunity by shooting over. The Rangers right now put in a dangerous rush, Dobson having to concede a corner, the place kick going behind. A run by Davie placed Everton in position, a shot from Coyne striking the upright. The Rangers obtained another corner, the ball being well placed by Clifton, but Smalley and the backs were hard to beat, and again Davie and Coyne were on the job, a shot from the latter going outside. From the centre of the field the Rangers raced down, and passing the home halfs, Vessy got possession, and with a terrific shot he placed the ball to Smalley's hands, who appeared to throw over the bar. A plea for goal was raised, and to the astonishment of both players and spectators a goal was conceded. Chadwick removed the venue with a brilliant run, and passing to Morris he ought to have scored, but missed a grand opportunity by being too slow on the ball. Give and take play followed, each goal being visited in rapid succession until Holt passed to Davie, who forced a corner the ball going outside. Everton now pressed with great determination, but the fine back play of the visitors prevented any further scoring. A very pleasant game ended favour of Everton. Final result: Everton 3 goals; Rangers 1 goal. **Teams Everton: - Smalley goal Sugg and Dobson (Captain), backs, Weir, Holt and Farmer, half-backs, J. Davies, Coyne, Morris, Chadwick, and Costley forwards. Rangers: - F. Start, goal, Winfield, and Wiseman Backs Clifton, Plackett, and Newton half-backs, JS. Hart, Hardy, Orcard, Vessy and Locker forwards.**

### SKELMERSDALE 1 EVERTON RESERVES 4
*December 10, 1888. The Liverpool Courier.*

Played, at Skelmersdale on Saturday, Everton took a fair team. Pollock won the toss and played against the wind. Everton at once pressed, and after some brilliant individual play Briscoe scored, but, to the amazement of all the referee disallowed the point. Directly afterwards Taylor put in a good shot, which the full-back headed through. Skelmersdale got a foul off Milward in front of the Everton goal, just before half time, and they improved their chance and scored. Upon the re-start Everton played a good passing game and goals were scored by Milward (2), and Bob Watson. Watson, Keys, Milward and Briscoe, which finished up with Milward scoring, should give especial notice to a brilliant combined run. Everton won by 4 goals to 1.

## BURSLAM PORT VALE 2 EVERTON 2
*December 11, 1888. The Liverpool Courier.*

Played on the ground of the former in foggy weather, which prevents accurate play in the first half each side scored, but during the latter portion were decidedly unlucky, one of their players kicking through his own goal result a draw 2 goals each. Goals Ballam and Weir own goal for Port Vale, Morris and Chadwick for Everton, attendance 2,000 **Teams Port Vale: - Maudslett, goal, Bateman, and Skinner backs, Chadwick Shields, and Elson half-backs Povison, Balham, Randle Ditchfield and Reynolds, forwards. Everton: - Joliffe goal, A. Chadwick and Ross (captain) backs, Weir, Sugg and Watson, half-backs. Farmer, Angus, Morris, E. Chadwick and Costley, forwards.**

## STOKE 0 EVERTON 0 (Game 14)
*December 17, 1888. The Liverpool Courier.*

When the Everton team arrived in Stoke at noon on Saturday to play their fourteenth match in the League competition a dense fog overhung the town, but towards the time to kick off it lifted a little. As Stoke had defeated Blackburn Rovers, and were only beaten at Burnley by one point, in their last two matches, a grand even game was anticipated. There was only one alteration in the usual Stoke team, Ramsey being absent and Sayer taking half-back instead of forward. Everton had their full team. The following opposed one another: - Stoke: - Rowley, goal, Clare, and Underwood, backs, Sayer, Shutt, and Smith, half-backs Lawton, McSkimmer, Sloane Edge, and Milarvie, forwards. Everton: - Smalley, goal, Dobson, and Ross (Captain), backs, Weir, Holt, and Farmer half-backs, J. Davies, Watson, Morris, Chadwick, and Costley, forwards. Everton won the toss, and Sloan kicked off for Stoke. Smalley had at once to use his hands, and a foul took place right under the Everton posts. A goal kick gave temporary relief, and by means of long kicks the visitors forwards took the ball up, being well returned by Clare, Costley got off, but was well tackled by Clare, who kicked out, long kicking being the order of the day. Lawton fastened on and ran up, but Ross robbed him splendidly. Milarvie had a clear run, but spoilt by heading out. From the throw out Davies, and Watson took it up and the Stoke goal was placed in jeopardy, Morris trying a shot wide of the posts. From the kick off play was taken to the centre and Milarvie and Edge broke away, Dobson defending well. some nice passing between Morris and Costley took it up, Clare robbing them, and Edge and Sloane returning, the ball was kicked behind, Costley retired for a short time, being hurt, and Sloane's followed suit, but returned in a few minutes. Sloane broke away, and the Everton goal was in danger; a goal kick relieving when Davies got off and shot in effectual. Costley was here carried off the field, his knee giving away. Dobson next showed some rather tackling; Malarvie breaking away Rowley saved grandly at the expense of a corner. Davies and Watson taking it up again the former shot, Clare returning well. Even play followed, Chadwick screwing in from the corner forced Rowley to again fist out. Shutt was next conspicuous by some good tackling. The home left getting off passed Dobson, Smalley having to kick out, a corner being conceded was well placed, and a shot attacking the

crossbar, and after Ross had headed out. Half-time arrived with
a clean sheet. On resuming the Everton goal was visited with
out success and Stoke continued to press for some time, when
Chadwick got off, Clare returning and Smalley had to kick out
a corner immediately after being conceded. It was well placed,
but the Everton back play was too good. A free kick was taken
dangerously near the visitor's goal, but relief was obtained, a
grand piece of defensive play by Smalley and Dobson being
deservedly cleared. Twice shortly after was Rowley called upon
to save, which he did grandly. Edge raced up the left, Dobson
eventually robbing him and returning well, Rowley again
having to save. The home forwards then got off, but could not
pass Ross. Chadwick and Holt raced up the left, Rowley having
to kick out Chadwick's shot. Milarvie and Edge than had a turn,
passed Dobson and a final kick went across the goal mouth.
Some close play near the Everton goal followed Ross defending
well. Darkness coupled with the fog now made it extremely
difficulty to follow the ball. Final score Stoke nil Everton nil.

**EVERTON RESERVES 3 STOKE SWIFT 0**
*December 17, 1888. The Liverpool Courier.*

The Anfield executive provided an excellent bill of fares for their
supporters on Saturday, Bourne having won the toss, Milward
kicked off and immediately assumed the aggressive. A grand
pass by Angus enabled Keys to try a shot which Hassell cleared.
A good run by Wainwright brought the play to the other end
where Chadwick kicked clear. Hutchinson and Broadhurst raced
up the Stoke right where Higgins cleared after a rather persistent
attack. Good passing by Brown and Angus gave Milward an
opening, who shot through, but being off-side the referee refused
a goal. From the centre of the field the home forwards raced
down, Briscoe finished up a great movement by scoring a very
fine goal. Encouraged by this point Milward doubled down the

centre, and passing to Angus he shot in but Hassell removed the danger, but only for a minute, Angus meeting the ball again with a terrific shot again defeated the goalkeeper. The Champions commenced to passing on the right, and passing the home left Higgins was forced to concede, but nothing profitable resulted. Everton again came to the front and after a beautiful run Briscoe registered goal no 3. Half time arrived Everton winning by 3 goals to nil, after the usual interval A.Milward put the sphere in motion against the wind. Brown forced a corner, which Bourne headed clear for some time the play was confirmed to the Stoke quarters but the fine defence of Mountford and Hasell kept their goal intact. A splendid game ended in a 3-0 win for Everton. **Teams; Everton Reserves Joliffe, goal Higgins and A. Chadwick backs, WH. Jones, H. Pollock (captain), and T. Fryer, half-backs, W. Brown, Angus, W. Briscoe, J. Keys, and A. Milward forwards. Swifts: - Halsall, goal, Bourne (captain), and Mountford, backs, Harbour, Farmer, and Ryder, half-backs, Hutchinson, Broadhurst, Wainwright, W. Lunnicliffe, and Milward, forwards.**

### PRESTON NORTH END 3 EVERTON 0 (Game 15)
*December 23, 1888. The Liverpool Courier.*

The first of the League fixture between the above organisations took place at Deepdale on Saturday. Eight hundred spectators accompanied the team, Everton were short of Davies, Sugg, and Dick. Teams:-Preston North End:- Trainor, goal, Howarth and Holmes, backs. Robertson, Russell, and Graham, half-backs, Ross, Gordon Goodall, Dewhurst, and Drummond, forwards. Everton: - Smalley goal, Ross (captain), and Dobson, backs, Farmer, Weir, and Holt half-backs, Angus, Chadwick, Brown, Briscoe, and Watson, forwards. Ross lost the toss, and Goodall kicked with the advantage of a strong wind, and immediately Preston took up the attack. A grand shot from Dewhurst was well repulsed by Dobson. Everton now showed up on the right, Briscoe kicking over the bar. A grand combined run enabled Goodall to score five minutes from the start. From the kick-off Preston again pressed, Ross robbed Gordon in the nick of time. Goodall went away with a fine dribble, Holt foiling effort by good tackling. Dewhurst and Drummond now raced down the left and passing to Goodall to kick over. Everton now improved in the play. Angus and Chadwick put in some good passing, on the left. From the pass Brown shot in Trainer clearing, Ross forced the play to the right, but could not break the fine defence of Ross and Dobson. Brown broke, and passing to Angus he forced Howard to conceded a corner, but nothing tangible resulted. Everton now passed on the right. Trainor having to save in succession. The ball was now confined to the home left. Drewhurst missed a grand opportunity by kicking out. Everton now had a free kick against Russell. The Ball was well placed, but an erractic shot spoiled the advantage. Score at half-time: - Preston North End 1 goal, Everton nil. After the usual interval, Goodall put the ball in motion, and immediately North End rush away, Dobson intercepted a grand move, and Everton removed the venue to the other end, where Brown experienced very hard lines, a foul against Everton near the goal mouth, where some good heading was shown by Dewhurst and Drummond, a second goal being scored amidst the hearty cheers of the Prestonians. From the centre, Brown put in a beautiful run, Trainer having a grand shot from Angus. Ross now stopped a dangerous run on the part of his brother and Chadwick was again busy at the other end, Smalley was saved from some splendid defence. Weir now passed to Chadwick, who raced down, and another corner fell to Everton, the place being nicely taken. Angus just missing his mark with a splendid shot. Ross took a free kick well in front of the Preston posts, the ball passing between untouched. The visitors now caused some trouble Howarth and Holmes removing the danger with some fine kicking. Preston now infused more life into the game and after some fine passing Dewhurst scored a splendid goal owing to a misunderstanding on the part of the visiting backs. From now to the end of play was very even. Everton ought of scored but lack of combination in front of goal robbed them of a couple of goals. The Everton team played a spirited game. Result Preston 3 Everton nil.

**EVERTON RESERVESS 4 PRESTON NORTH END RESERVES 1**
December 24, 1888. The Liverpool Mercury.

The new stands on the Anfield-road enclosure have greatly improved the appearance of the ground, and though they were not so well filled as we expected there was a good number of spectators, when the following teams faced: - Preston North End Reserves: - Culshaw, goal, Hays, and Whittle, backs, Worthington, Dempsey, and Joy, half-backs Irvin Gilleade, Inglis, Dobson, and Gillespie forwards. Everton Reserves: - Joliffe, goal, Higgins, and A. Chadwick backs T. Parry, H. Pollock (captain) and T. Fayer half-backs, Falls WH. Jones, A. Milward, J. Keys, Morris, forwards.
Milward kicked off and Morris at once tried a long shot, which went wide. North End made an attack, which was checked by Higgins. Whittle returned, and Irvin passed to Gillespie who shot wide. Hands spoiled the home forwards when well within the enemy quarters.Irvin was cheered for good play on the right, Gillespie again shooting wide. Milward playing in good form troubled the visiting backs, and hands in a dangerous position was given again North End. Jones took his kick which went behind. Inglis robbed the home halfs and passed to Dobson, Higgins brought him up, but Gillespie shot wide. Everton had now to concede a corner. Inglis took the kick which went behind. Inglis initiated a bit of pretty passing. The defence being too good the visitors were unable to score. Thus did the Everton forwards make a good attack, and a splendid attempt to score

was made. Culshaw had to concede a corner and from the kick
Irwin made a splendid dribble nearly the whole length of the
field, and Joliffe was cheered for a grand save. Jones made a
good run up the left and passed to Falls, who made a poor shot.
The attack was kept up, and for pretty passing in front of goal
Milward beat Culshaw and scored Everton's first goal. A tussle
took place between Irvin and Morris, Morris getting the best of
it. Jones and Falls raced up the left, but Jones shot very wide.
Dobson and Irvin was cheered for a fine run, and Irvin cleverly
kept the ball in and made a good but futile shot. Milward put in
a good dribble in the centre, and passed both backs and Everton
had a chance, which they lost by bad following up. Higgins
made a grand save. Inglis returned to Joliffe, who fisted out.
The North End forwards now made a pretty combined dribble
and Higgins gave a corner. Inglis tried a high shot, which just
missed its mark. Joliffe again was cheered for a grand save,
keeping the globe out when it seemed impossible to do so.
The game was very exciting, North End sending in shot after
shot Joliffe still keeping his charge intact in champion form.
Inglis ran down the right, after even play, and just shot wide.
Everton took the ball up from the kick, and gained an abortive
corner. Inglis again made a grand single-handed dribble and had
hard lines. Half-time arrived with the score Everton Reserves
1 goal, Preston North End Reserves nil. In the second half,
Inglis kicked off and Jones raced down the left, and Whittle
caused laughter by neatly robbing Milward. The wind, which
was blowing from end to end was in Everton's favour, and
a different complexion was put on the game. Culshaw being
called upon to save by Milward. He just fisted out, and Milward,
playing in grand form, took the leather into the goal mouth, and
with a fast shot which struck the upright, defeated Culshaw, and
made the score two to nil. Jones was now loudly cheered by the
delighted crowd for a grand dribble down the left. Heys robbed
him and North End attacked. Chadwick making a huge kick

Keys raced up the right and Culshaw had to fist out a good shot. Keys robbed Jones cleverly and kicked to Fryer, who returned, and the home forwards salted down in line, and an exciting bit of play ended in Falls scoring the third. Bad shooting spoiled North End and Everton again were swarming in front, Milward doing the needful amidst loud cheering. Joliffe now made a mistake, which nearly gave a goal to North End, fisting the ball straight up, Dobson headed in and the leather just missed the goal. Everton gained a corner and kept up a stall on the North End goal without anything tangible being scored. North End with four goals against them were playing well, and tried hard to break the ice. Their Forwards dallied rather too long in front and lost the advantage gained. Everton playing a winning game gained a futile corner and "hands" in front of goal also helped them without result. Dobson and Gillespie raced up the left and Dobson amused the crowd by shooting nearly to the touch line. Irvin now went half-back and North End had the best of the argument for some time. Keys and Morris broke away, Milward spoiling their efforts by missing his kick. Not to be denied, Morris raced up the left, and sent in a grand shot which was well saved. North End now made a determined effort, which was successful. After passing nicely in front Gillespie got the leather, and sent in a good high shot, which Joliffe only partially stopped, and North End had secured their first goal. Final result:- Everton Reserves 4 goals, Preston North End Reserves 1.

**EVERTON 3 ULSTER 0**
*December 26, 1888. The Liverpool Courier.*

The series of matches arranged by the Anfield executive for the Christmas holidays took place yesterday morning in beautiful weather. The Ulster team are very popular with the Everton patrons, but their display was rather inferior, no doubt due to the fact that they arrived from the sister isle a few hours before they had to take the field. Fully 6,000 spectators were present when the teams put in an appearance at 10.45. Ross having lost the toss. Milward started hostilities against a very strong breeze. For a few minutes the play was confined to midfield until Angus with a screw shot, tested Pinkleton, who kicked clear. Davie forced his way up the centre until met by Pollock, who robbed at a dangerous moment, and again Everton were busy on the right, Watson missing a rather easy chance from a pass by Fall. Hands against the Irish captain gave Falls an opening, his shot being well cleared. Pinkleston was again called upon immediately after to stop a stinger from Weir. Miller and Martin looked dangerous on the right, but could not break through the fine defence of Ross and the veteran Mike, who gave the ball to Milward and after some fine passing on the left Milward scored the first goal. From a throw in by Leslie, Coyne and Davie dribbled up the left, Ross removing the danger with a strong punt. Milward receiving the pass forced a corner. Which Stevenson kicked over. Tierney now raced up the centre, his final effort going very wide. Weir brought the ball down the right Pinkleton saving shots from Watson and Keys, who strove hard to increase the lead. Two corners now fell to Everton, Leslie kicking clear a grand shot from Pollock, who experienced hard lines shortly after with a beautiful header. Watson accounted for a fine screw by Milward. After a short run by Coyne, Angus got the ball well in front from a corner kick, Phillips clearing in the goal mouth, and again Weir rushed in from half-backs and banged the ball through. From the kick off the Ulster van went away with a fine combined run, Coyne finishing with a wide shot. Angus now pressed on the left, and getting well down Milward again shot in, Pinkleton again clearing. Joliffe was now called upon to clear from Meyers. This brought half-time. Score Everton two goals Ulster nil. After the usual rest Martin re-started, the play being confined to the home right Watson having hard lines with a grand shot, which struck the uprights. Ross made an alteration

Falls going in goal, and Joliffe going left wing forward, the play of Joliffe causing great amusement for the spectators. Coyne and Meyers broke away, Higgins again proving a stumbling block, and again Everton assumed an aggressive attitude, Pinkleton repelling a strong shot from Angus. Martin with a rear turn of speed dribbled up the right, and passing Ross, Fall kicking clear. The home van pressed forward to the other goal, and from now to the close of the game the home team had pretty much their own way, the sphere rarely going over the centre line Just before the close Joliffe increased the score. From a pass by Falls. Final Result Everton three gaols Ulster nil. **Teams Everton:- Joliffe goal, Ross (captain), and Higgins, back, Weir, Pollock and Stevenson half-backs, Angus, Falls, Milward Watson, and Keys, forwards. Ulster: - Pinkleston, goal, Watson, and Downes backs Phillips, Tierney, and Leslie half-backs Miller, Martin, J. Millar, Davie, Coyne forwards.**

**EVERTON RESERVES 3 BLACKBURN PARK ROAD 2**
*December 26, 1888. The Liverpool Courier.*

Lancashire Cup Round Three
At the advertised time for commencing this important fixture, the weather was something wretched. A very heavy downpour and a regular gale of wind was the order of the day throughout the whole of the match. The ground was very slippery and the players experienced great difficulty in keeping their feet. At 2-30 the players made their presence on the field, the home team being rather weak owing to the numerous conditions that council the Lancashire senior cup. Dobson lost the toss, in front of around 4,000 spectators, and Brown put the ball in motion, and passing to Briscoe it was odds on Everton scoring. Frankland clearing with a hugh punt, from which Nackerath screwed across to Gargett, who with a long shot, beat Joliffe ten minutes from the start. Immediately after Dobson fouled, Eastham nicely placed the free kick. Holt

clearing in the goal mouth. Bricoe and Jones worked beautifully down the right, a shot from the latter taking effect to the delight of the spectators. A.Chadwick was next conspicuous with a grand bit of tackling and passing to Brown, he struck the Blackburn upright with a splendid shot. Whitaker and Mackereth pressed on the left, a grand pass from the latter being badly missed by Garner. Briscoe beat Jackson in a warm tussle, and Jones getting possession he gave Noble a rare fistful to clear. The Blackburn right again came down with a great dash the final effort of Mackereth going over. Dobson now took the kick out, and with a powerful lunge kicked the ball from his own goal within a few yards of the opposite end, the finest kick ever seen on the Everton enclosure. Two corners next fell to the home club, Noble stopping a rare header from Higgins. Farmer next stopped a rush by the Blackburn men, and passing to Harbour, missed a grand chance by kicking outside. Half time, one goal each. After a slight rest Lighbrown put the ball in motion, and immediately the visitors broke away. Dobson in working the ball clear had the misfortune to hands the ball, and from the free kick Joliffe stopped a regular beauty from the foot of Garner. The home right again raised the siege, and after some grand running Harbour obtained the lead by shooting through. Everton now had the best of the game, but the greasy state of the ball rendered accurate shooting impossible. After some exciting play in the Blackburn quarters Whitaker got away, but Farmer robbed him, and dribbling nicely down the centre sent a splendid shot, which took effect. Even play followed until Garner got passed Chadwick and with a low shot defeated Joliffe a second time. Shortly after the official whistle sounded. leaving Everton winners by three goals to two. **Teams Everton: - Joliffe goal, Dobson (captain), and A. Chadwick, backs Farmer, Holt, and T. Frier, half-backs, Harbour, Higgins, Brown, Briscoe, and Jones, forwards. Blackburn Park Road: - Noble goal, Frankland and Yates, backs, Jackson, Eastham, and Hartley, half-backs, Mackereth, Whitaker, Lightbrown, Gargett, Garner, forwards.**

## EVERTON 0 BOOTLE 0
*December 27 1888. The Liverpool Courier.*

This important and much talked of fixture between these two local rivals took place at Anfield-road yesterday, the unhappy difference which have lately prevented their meeting being amicably arranged. The clubs have met often in local Cup ties and in friendly competition during the past ten years, and Everton may fairly claim to have established superiority over their Bootle friends being the victors in nearly every encounter. Notwithstanding this fact, the Bootle club has always come up smiling, and it may be said coincident of turning the scale this time "new men and new methods" have been tried, and at the present juncture this is more noticeable than on any previous encounter, there being very few men now playing for either team who played in last year's cup tie. There is, however, to some extent a similarity of fortune in the position of the Evertonians club, who have always in these encounters been enable to place their full strength in the field. This year the hospital contingent is very strong and they are minus the services of Smalley, Dick, Waugh and Costley. From the Bootle team we miss the old Veteran Veitch their other changes being, however, an improvement upon last year's eleven. The weather was not too propitious, the ground being sloppy from the rains of the last few days, making accurate play impossible and causing evident amusement to the vast crowd, who thronged the new comfortable enclosure as the players endeavored sometimes in vain to keep their foothold on the treacherous turf. The kick off was advertised for two o'clock, but long before that hour the throng of partisans were crowding the approaches to the ground and when the teams put in an appearance there would be fully 16,000 spectators present. Ross having won the toss Galbraith kicked off for Bootle amidst much excitement. The Bootle left rushed down and a foul was given against Dobson but nothing tangible resulted. Bootle continued to press and Ross was compelled to kick out. Everton now rushed up, but Angus shot wide. From a foul Galbraith shot, but Joliffe fisted out. The game was very fast, and Everton rushed up Brown shooting well in compelling Jackson to concede a corner, which came to nothing. From a free kick off Davies got up, but the ball went out Everton having slightly the best of the game. Dobson relieved a rush by the Bootle left and the venue was quickly changed. Angus passed to the right, but Davies missed a good chance. MacFarlance playing grandly. The Everton left got up, and Chadwick shot but Jackson saved. The Everton forwards again got up but the ball was kicked out. Ross, Dobson and Weir relieved a good rush by the Bootle forwards. From a foul against Holt, Bootle got away, but the ball went out. Give-and-take play followed. The Everton left got well up, but Farmer dallied, and the ball was worked away. Even play followed, the game being very fast. Dobson tried a long shot, and Jackson fisted over. The corner, however, came to nothing. Dobson shooting wide immediately after Everton pressed, but the ball was forced out, Davies hugging the ball too much. The play continued in the Bootle half, and Jackson saved a low shot from Chadwick. The Bootle left got away, but Dobson relieved grandly. Davies was now prominent with a grand run, the ball, however, going out. A foul against Bootle was taken by Weir, and Chadwick just missed scoring, Briscoe heading wide a little later. Everton still pressed, and Chadwick again narrowly missing scoring, the same player immediately after striking the upright amidst great excitement, Davies shooting wide just after. A foul against Everton was kicked out by Campbell. Dobson compelled Jackson to handle. Bootle had a luck in, but Ross soon cleared. A foul was given against Campbell for tripping Weir, but nothing came of it. Half-time being called with a clean sheet. Brown kicked off after the usual interval. The Everton right worked down Briscoe and Brown clearing well. Bootle pressed and a corner resulted which was worked away. A foul against Bootle was taken by Weir, and Miller conceded a corner. The Bootle forwards got up, but Woods shot wide. Everton pressed, but McFarlane relieved. After a good rush by the Bootle forwards Jamieson, put the ball through but the point was disallowed for offside. Bootle continued to press, the excitement being intense Everton rushed off, and a foul was given against Bootle. The play ruled very fast and exciting, Everton having slightly the best of the play. The Bootle right got down, and a scrimmage ensued in which Ross was winded. Bootle pressed, and the ball went behind. Bootle now played grandly, the Everton defence bring severely tried. A foul was given against Campbell, and the Everton forwards got down, Miller relieving Everton having hard lines. Everton still pressed, but found the Bootle defence too good, Brown and Holt being noticeable for good play. Chadwick screwed across but Briscoe missed, a corner resulting which proved fruitless. Davies shot wide soon after. Hands was given against Jamieson, Chadwick shot in well but Jackson fisted grandily, Davies shooting badly just after. Dobson saved a good rush. Davies shot behind after good play by the Everton forwards, Everton pressed, Angus shooting behind. Even play followed. Everton now pressed, and sent a hot shot wide. Ross took a free kick for a foul against Bootle, Campbell being noticeable for dirty play, but the Bootle left worked up, Dobson relieving, Davies shot wide. A foul was given against Everton and one against Bootle immediately after offside against Everton and from the free kick Bootle got up, but Dobson relieved. Time was called with the result a draw. Result; Everton 0, Bootle 0.

**Teams; Bootle, Jackson goal, McFarlane, and Miller backs, A. Allsop, W. Hughes, and W. Campbell, half-backs, J. Woods, H. Galbraith, Jamieson Jones, and D. Galbraith, forwards; Everton: - Joliffe goal, Ross (captain), and Dobson backs, Farmer, Holt, and Weir, half-backs, Angus, Chadwick, Briscoe, Davies, and W. Brown, forwards.**

## ACCRINGTON 3 EVERTON 1 (Game 16)
*December 31, 1888. The Liverpool Courier.*

The Everton team left Liverpool on Saturday to meet the champion drawests in their League match at Accrington. The latter played their full strength whereas Everton were minus Holt (ill) and Farmer. A modest number of spectators was present. Teams Accrington: - Jk. Horne, goal, McLellan, and Stevenson, backs, Pemberton, Tattersall, and Howarth half-backs, Brand, Kirkham, Barbour, Bonar, and Lofthouse, forwards. Everton:- Joliffe, goal, Ross (captain), and Dobson, backs, Weir, Sugg, Parkinson, half-backs, Watson, Briscoe, Brown, Chadwick, and Angus forwards. Everton started with ten men only, one being a substitute. Everton won the toss, and Barbour kicked off with the sun in his eyes. At once the homesters pressed, Lofthouse sending one in over the bar. Chadwick then came on. Pemberton stopped Watson well. A free kick well played by Pemberton resulted in a goal kick. Chadwick took it up the centre, dodging splendidly passing to Parkinson, the latter to Watson, who rushed the first goal. After the kick-off Ross was cheered for fine tackling, and returning well forced a corner, Chadwick heading over at once taking it down. The home team took it down, Lofthouse being conspicuous forcing Joliffe to concede a corner. A pretty pass by Brown to Angus was neutralised by off-side play. Hands against Ross right in the goal mouth resulted in Brand scoring, Howarth playing grand. On restarting both Dodgson and Stevenson kicked well, Horne having to use his hands for a corner kick. Lofthouse raced down, a severe struggle taking place near the Everton goal, Brand kicking behind. Pretty passing by all the home forwards was neutralised by Brand's off side play. A grand shot by Chadwick was well repulsed by Horne. The visitors were then pressed, the ball eventually bounding over the bar. Brand showed magnificent dribbling, Weir clearing more than once. Howarth bringing Chadwick up. Ross kicked well, Brand racing down the left. A foul by Watson well placed was repulsed by Dobson. Chadwick passed to Brown the latter to Angus who was tackled by McLellan. From a grand centre by Lofthouse, Kirkham shot against the bar Joliffe throwing out, a grand run up by Watson and Briscoe giving Howarth and Stevenson plenty to do. At half-time the score 1 all. On resuming Stevenson was called upon to defend Barbour, eventually sending behind. Good kicking by Howarth, Parkinson and McLellan followed Stevenson conceding a corner. Watson was next conspicuous for some tricky play. Hands by Howarth in the mouth of the home goal, Pemberton relieving well, and Dobson kick over the posts. Harbour ran up, placing the visitors goal in jeopardy. A throw in gave little relief only to be returned by Stevenson. Dobson and Sugg showed good defensive play. Howarth shot in twice. Dobson kicking out. From a long shot, however, Howarth scored. After the kick off Howarth had another shot which hit the crossbar, the visitors goal being fairly besieged. A goal kick gave temporary relief, Ross showing brilliant form. A couple of free kicks fell to the homesters near goal, and from a scrimmage it was sent through. Accrington had by far the best of the game for some time, Weir tackling well, and Ross kicking splendidly. Once when the ball had passed Joliffe Ross kicked across. Everton then pressed a little, Dobson by a long kicking sending in over. After Horne had fisted out, a good run down by Watson was not utilized owing to his not being supported. A corner to Everton was well repulsed. A grand game resulting-Accrington 3 Everton 1 goal.

**EVERTON RESERVES 1 BOOTLE RESERVES 1**
*December 31, 1888. The Liverpool Courier.*

Everton first team being engaged in a league fixture at Accrington the rival Reserves had the run of the ground at Anfield-road on Saturday. As Everton have already been victorious over the Bootle second string twice this season the meeting was looked upon with interest and there were about 3,000 spectators present, when the teams put in an appearance. The Everton team was somewhat weak, the absence of Joliffe, Chadwick, Briscoe, and Brown being much felt. Teams: - Everton: - Lindsay goal, Ashcroth, and Higgins, backs, Fayer H. Pollock (captain), and Farmer, half-backs, Keys, Harbour, Milward Jones, and Kelly forwards, Bootle: - Griffiths, goal, Woods and Howarth backs, Hobley, Dodd and Moffatt, half-backs, Galbraith, Morris, McCowan, Barbour and Deane forwards. Pollock having won the toss, Milward kicked off down hill, and immediately Farmer had kicked out. From the throw in by Hobley, McCowan dribbled up the centre and from a fine pass by Morris, Galbraith shot in, Lindsay clearing. Everton now raced down and from a accurate pass by Milward, Kelly put in a magnificent screw which Griffiths fisted over the bar, nothing tangible resulting from the corner. A grand rush on the Everton right forced another corner, Pollock heading over the bar, Morris and Galbreaith removing the venue to the Everton uprights where Ashcroft cleared in the nick of time. Higgins now gave Milward a grand opening, and taking full advantage of the position, he forced his way until tripped by Woods, for which he was penalised, Farmer shooting over the bar from the free kick. Barber put in a nice dribble up the Bootle left until he was prettily relieved by Fayer who turned over to Keys, who gave to Milward. He again forced his way until tripped by Hobley, for which a free kick was conceded. Milward scoring with a low shot a quarter of an hour after the start. From the midfield Bootle pressed Everton having two men short for some time owing to injuries to Keys and Milward. From a corner kick Deane missed a grand opportunity by shooting outside, Milward resumed and from a pass by Kelly Milward put to a splendid run, the ball going outside. Barbour now shot in, Lindsay clearing. Higgins gave a corner the ball going over. Half-time Everton 1 goal Bootle nil. After the usual rest, McCowan put the sphere in motion and again Milward was busy, his shot at goal going over. Bootle got nicely into action, and from a pass by Morris, Galbrath had a shy at Lindsay, who threw out as Galbraith pressed. Ashcroft kicked clear, Morris renewed the attack, and from a good return Hobley defeated Lindsay with a low shot. Bootle still kept up the pressure a shot from Morris going over. The Everton vanguard fought hard to break away, and the absence of Keys as the right weakened their attack. Jones got in a good pass. Howarth heading clear a shot from Kelly. Morris and Galbraith, with very good passing caused the Everton backs some trouble, Fryer removing the danger with a long kick. Farmer worked the leather up the field, Milward just missed scoring. Everton obtained two corners, nothing resulted. Hands against Pollock gave Bootle an opening, Higgins heading clear in the goalmouth. Milward and Kelly brought relief in the home left Howarth kicking clear. Galbrath gave Morris an opening, he shot striking the upright. Milward was again prominent with a superb run Howarth robbing him, when meeting in position. Good passing brought both well into the Everton quarters, Lindsay saving a good shot from Barbour who was subsequently given offside. Fayer threw in to Harbour who forced his way up the field, Woods kicking out to save. A very pleasant game ended in a draw. Everton Reserves 1 Bootle Reserves 1.

# JANUARY 1889

## EVERTON 2 THIRD LANARK 2
*January 2, 1889. The Liverpool Courier.*

Continuing their holiday tour the 3rd Lanark travelled out from
Manchester, and opposed Everton at Anfield enclosure yesterday.
Recent frost had rendered a hard and extremely dangerous
ground. It was nearly half-an-hour past the advertised time
when Milward on behalf of the homesters placed his foot to the
ball, and within a couple of minutes from the start Marshall had
scored for the visiting team. The restart was followed by another
attack, but although danger threatened the home quarters were
cleared, and Farmer and Watson, took in the ball from midfield,
and gave Brown a splendid chance on the left of goal which to the
disappointment of the home supporters ended in failure, the ball
being shot barely a couple of feet outside the post. Undismayed
by this abortive attempt the Evertonians ranged themselves
in front of the Lanark citadel, and during a hot melee Davies
headed in only to find Downie not-out consummate skill. For
some time afterwards Everton continued to have the best of the
play, Milward at this time being one of the most conspicuous of
the players. At length the siege was raised, and on a return to the
lower ground Jas Oswald sorely tested the defensive powers of
Joliffe who, however kicked away and averted a second disaster.
With the ball again in midfield, Farmer took a free kick for hands
and in close following Milward and Watson were conspicuous
in good play. The visiting centre and right relieved admirably
where upon Chadwick and Brown inaugurated a reversal of
positions, and Dobson having beaten Marshall, Chadwick and
Milward rushed up. Downie momentarily repelled the attack,
which however was renewed, and a moment later Milward
equalised amidst the enthusiastic plaudits of the crowd there
being at this time about 6,000 persons present. Desultory play

ensued, during which the players were partially obscured by the fog. Watson made a temporary raid, which being repelled the Volunteers were again skirmishing vigorously on the lower ground. At length Ross missed his kick, and taking full advantage of the centre setups Oswald rushed up and beat Joliffe for the second time. Closely following the re-start Chadwick sent in a neat shot, which Rae repelled. Again the sphere was brought up, only however, to be shot outside. The Scottish right-Marshall and John Oswald-now contributed neat passing play, the result of which was that the home lines were again beleagued. With relief at hand the ball was again travelled upfield, when Brown essayed a shot which was headed safely away. Soon afterwards Ross was favoured with a free kick, and from a resulting corner Everton were within an ace of scoring. From now to half-time the play was of a fairly even character, and when the official whistle was blown for the change of ends, the score stood, 3rd Lanark 2 goals, Everton 1 goal. James Oswald having resumed, the ball for a time was dangerous near the visitor's posts. At last the sphere came bounding through the fog to midfield, false cries of "goal" having previously been raised. Again nothing could be seen of the players until from a free kick the play was momentarily located in the centre of the field. Everton were now having much the best of the game, the Visitors indeed not having crossed the dividing line since the change of ends. A dark mass was now seen surging through the fog, which at this time was so dense that neither goal could be seen; but although a footing in the home half was gained, the raid was quickly repulsed and a moment later a tremendous shout revealed the fact that Everton had scored a second goal and equalised the score. Now that the teams were on equal terms the play became more vigorous even than before. Suddenly the misty canopy was raised and the 3rd Lanark were occupying the higher ground. Joliffe having kicked out in front of goal, Holt made a thoroughly artistic run, and, aided by Davies and Watson on the right the visitors quarters again became the venue of play. Brown centred to Davies who headed in grandly where upon Downie fisted out in admirable style, and for a time more even play prevailed. For a moment the sphere was at the Everton corner, and danger being cleared, Holt contributed an additional fine piece of play. Still the men of the Lanark pressed on, and after a grand dribble James Oswald shot across the goalmouth, and thus a grand advantage was lost. Johnson however, returned with the ball, but fell on the frozen ground. Just when success seemed to be within reach. The Evertonians, and especially Joliffe, were having an anxious time of it until the tension was eased by means of a kick from the front of goal. Davies now made a clinking run down the right, which was responded to by a most brilliant run by Johnson on the right which culminated in a free kick for Lanark in front of goal. Nothing occured, however, but although a moment later Downie was sorely tried, his charge remained intact. A grand passing movement on the part of James Oswald, Johnson, and Hannah towards the close of the game jeopardized the home goal, which however, was promptly relieved and as the whistle was shortly afterwards blown, a well contested and most amicable game was brought to a close, the result being a draw of two goals each. **Teams; Everton:- Joliffe goals Ross (captain) and Dobson, backs, Weir, Holt, and Farmer. Hal-backs Watson Davies Milward Chadwick, and Brown forwards. 3rd Lanark: - Downie, goal, Fairweather, and Rae, backs, McFarlane, Ferguson, and Thompson, half-backs, T. Oswald, John Oswald, Hannan, Marshall, and Johnson, forwards.**

## EVERTON 2 CAMBUSLANG 1
*January 3, 1889. The Liverpool Courier.*

The third match of the latter's English holiday tour was played on the Anfield enclosure yesterday. The weather was again very foggy, and of course greatly militated against accuracy of play. The visitors were strongly represented, whilst the homesters also had a full eleven for the occasion of the two previous matches of the tour, the scotchmen had won one (Preston North End), and lost one (Bolton Wanderers) whilst on New Year's day, Everton played drawn game with the 3rd Lanark R.V. thus the fixture proved to be an interesting one, and when the teams faced, there would be about 2,500 persons present. Milward kicked off on behalf of Everton, whose forwards were pulled up by Downes, and the Scotch van dashed down to the Everton goal. A throw-in accrued to the visitors near the corner and the home citadel was seriously menaced till relief came through the ball being shot over the line by H.Gourlay. Neat passing by Chadwick and Angus was spoiled by Russell, and Camburslang again assumed an aggressive attitude, but again failure attended the shot at goal. A free kick to Everton in the centre was taken by Ross, Davies and Watson were prominent on the right but were promptly robbed by Russell, who dribbled down the centre. Ross was passed, and the Everton goal looked like being captured. The Latter, however, rushed back, and after some brilliant tackling secured the ball, and the home forwards were again swarming round the Scotch goal, Milward here compelled Downs to handle. The Cambuslang custodian threw sharply out, but Angus secured the ball and shot outside the posts. From the kick out of goal, the "Scots" claimed a free kick in the Everton half and this being granted them, hot play ensued round the home posts. The fog here became very dense and it was with difficulty that the movements of the players could be followed. Cambuslang, however, forced a couple of corner, the first of which went outside whilst the second was headed away by Sugg. Angus dribbled well on the Everton left but kicked too far ahead and Fryers got the ball away. Joliffe was forced to handle at the other end. The venue of play, however, was quickly removed to the upper ground, and Angus shot in capital style, the ball just passing outside the posts. Everton were having by far the best of the game and except for an occasional breakaway by the visitors forwards were pinned within their own quarters. After several unsuccessful attacks on the Scotch goal. Chadwick shot the sphere past Downs this feat being greeted with encouraging cheers by the home partners. Ross foiled several attempts to score by the Cambuslang right wing, who now became troublesome, and after a run down by the home forwards the Sum was equalised. From the centre kick, Chadwick, Angus and Farmer showed good points for Everton but they were met by the sterling defence of the Scotch backs, who kicked and tackled capitally. A combined run by the Everton left brought danger to the visitors goal, but the latter put the leather over the line. Everton still pressed, but a long kick by Gourlay took hostilities to the home citadel, where a corner kick was conceded the visitors this proved futile, as did a quick shot by Buchanan. A run down the field by the Everton forwards, met with no better success, but a few minutes later loud cheers proclaimed the fact that Milward had placed the homesters ahead- doing the trick from a pass by Watson. Cambuslang next showed dangerous tackles, Sugg kicking out of goal. The Visitors, however, returned, but half-time was called with the score:- Everton two goals, Camsbuslang 1 goal. Caldon re-started the ball on behalf of Cambuslang, but Davies securing possession of the sphere, rushed down the field. Unfortunately, however, he kicked two far ahead, and the ball rolled harmlessly over the line. A free kick accurued to the Scotchmen from "hands" off Holt, and the ball being well placed, hot play ensued in the home half, Joliffe having to hit away a shot from the foot of Prendeleith. Dobson further removed the danger, and the Everton forwards crossed the half-way line. They were driven back however, and play again raged in the Everton quarters. Holt attempted to clear, but was prevented by Hendry holding him round the back. Farmer, however, was successful in clearing, and the forward rank of

Everton menaced the Cambuslang goal. A corner resulted, from which Everton had extremely hard lines in not scoring, Downes clearing in the nick of time. Play was suspended owing to a slight accident to Davis, who however, resumed a few minutes later. Play was still down at the Cambuslang goal, but no impression could be made on the Scotch defence. Low and Prendeleith ran nicely along the Cambuslang left wing the latter sending in a swift shot which Ross repelled in capital style. Angus replied on behalf of Everton, but nothing accrued. An attack by the homesters was cleared by means of a free kick. Dobson replied by a huge punt, but the visitors were not to be stalled off, and the left wing again broke away. This was followed by extremely neat passing by the Cambuslang forwards, Ross meeting them in grand style. Low returned but shot yards wide of the posts. Undaunted by this the Scots returned, and looked like equaslising, being prevented however, by the defence of Ross Joliffe, and Dobson. The latter took a free kick for the home team, who attacked the Cambuslang goal strongly, the ball being shot over the line. Milward was next seen dashing down the centre with the ball at his toes. Downs robbing him in the nick of time. Everton, however, kept up the pressure, and a free kick was awarded them in the Cambuslang half. Ross took the kick and sent the ball through the visitors posts. The homesters claimed for a goal, but as the ball had not touched any of the players, during its flight the point were disallowed. Cambuslang next assumed an aggressive attitude and siege was laid to the home goal. In their attempt to score they were fouled by Ross and Joliffe and the home van were next attacking in hot style. Gourlay relieved, but Dobson returned the ball with a nicely judged kick. A free kick to Everton right in front of the Cambuslang "sticks" was taken by Dobson, this being followed by a couple of corners, both of which were got safely away. Holt tried a long shot from the centre right off the touch line Downs relieving in good style. The whistle now blew for a cessation of hostilities Everton having won by two goals to one. **Teams; Cambuslang: - Dunn, goal, Downs, and Foyets, backs, Hendry, J. Gourlay, and Russell, half-backs, Low, Prendeleith Caldow, H. Gourlay, and Buchanan forwards. Everton:- Joliffe goals, Dobson, and Ross (captain), Holt, Sugg, and Farmer half-backs, Watson, Milward, Angus, Davis, and Chadwick, forwards**

**EVERTON REVIEW**
*January 5, 1889. The Liverpool Courier*

Everton were most unfortunate in meeting Accrington in the League fixture minus Farmer and Holt, the former of whom oddly missed his train so that the team had to make the journey with only ten men. A useful recruit, however, was picked up on the way in the person of Parkinson, of Bell's Temperance, a promising Youth, who played a capital game, and was partly the means of Everton's scoring the only goal. Turning to the game, the play during the first half was of a grand character, Chadwick, Ross, Parkinson, Brown, and Watson for Everton and Brand (who dribbled magnificently) Howarth and Lofthouse for the "Reds" all deserving credit for their heroics efforts. Watson scored for Everton and from hands of Ross, Accrington equalised the score, at the interval standing one goal each. The second half, was also well contested, the Accringtonians, in particular, playing grandly, Dobson and Ross put in some fine back play for the Evertonians. Notwithstanding which Accrington scored twice Howarth successfully with a long shot. Everton failed to get on even terms, and were defeated by three goals to one. The match between the Reserves of Everton and Bootle did not produce an edifying display, but was on the contrary voted one of the worst games ever played at the Anfield enclosure. Certainly Everton were inadequately represented, and although the Bootle second string is not so strong as it was a season ago, a fair chance was presented of lowering the colours of the rival club after a lot of scrambling play each side scored a goal, and as in the last of the games between the senior teams the match remained drawn.

## EVERTON 1 BLACKBURN ROVERS 0
*January 7 1889. The Liverpool Courier.*

The return League contest between the above clubs took on the Anfield ground on Saturday. An Attendance of fully 6,000 spectators testified to the immense popularity of the engagement. A good deal of curiosity was evinced as to the composition of the Rovers teams owing to them having to play off their Lancashire Cup tie but when the players put in an appearance it was noticed that the Rovers were fully represented. The recent frost had made the ground somewhat dangerous for the players. At the time of starting the ground was enveloped in very thick fog. At 2-20 Southworth having been successful in the spin of the coin, Milward kicked off and immediately the Rovers became aggressive. Joliffe having to clear from Townsley. A long punt by Ross gave Everton relief. Angus and Chadwick forced the play on the left the ball going outside. From the kick out J.Southworth ran up the centre "Hands" against Holt gave the Rovers a chance, Dobson heading clear. Brown and Watson with a grand passing run caused Forbes to concede a corner. The ball was nicely cleared by Almond after it had struck the upright, Milward was noticeable with a fine shot, which McCowan fisted out. A grand run by Whitaker put the Rovers on the aggressive Weir kicking clear. The Rovers left still pressed, until Farmer passed to the left, and from a pass by Angus, Brown kicked outside. From the kick-out the home forwards got well in the Rovers quarters, where Milward shot in, McCowan clearing. The ball was met by Watson, who scored 15 minutes from the start. The spectators greeted this success with tremendous applause. The Rovers left forced play, Dobson heading clear. From a throw in by Douglas the Rovers took a foul in the goalmouth. Ross working the ball clear with some fine tackling. Whittaker and Townley ran up the left, J.Southworth missing a grand chance by kicking outside. A throw by Farmer enabled Chadwick to break away, Forbes robbing him at a dangerous moment. Half-time Everton 1; Rovers 0. After the usual interval Southworth put the sphere in motion, the fog being heavier than before. Townley immediately put in a screw shot which Joliffe cleared. The Rovers took a couple of corners that were well cleared by the Everton defence. A good bit of passing by the Everton forwards removed the venue to the other end, where Southworth kicked clear. Watson now forced his way up the right, Farmer relieving him and passing to Watson, who put in a stinging shot, which McCowan again cleared. Everton kept up a persistent attack, McCowan stopping shots from Angus and Milward. By good passing the Rovers again paid Joliffe a visit, a good shot from Douglas going over the bar. From midfield Milward had a magnificent forward movement Watson finishing with a grand shot. Which was well charged by Southworth in a marvellous manner. The Rovers attack on the left, Ross and Weir clearing their lines with some fine kicking. Chadwick got possession in the Rovers quarters and passing to Angus he again shot in, Southworth clearing. The Rovers getting into line again Everton were pressed, Ross kicking clear. Chadwick sprinted up the left and passing across the goalmouth, Forbes kicked out. Turner renewed the attack the ball going over the bar. The Rovers rights broke away but could not break through the Everton defence. The home team brought the ball into midfield, when the official whistle sounded. Result Everton 1; Rovers 0. Previous to the engagement of the match it was decided that owing to the condition of the ground and fog that whatever the result might be, the match would be to deferred to a draw and count accordingly. **Teams; Blackburn Rovers: - McCowan,** goal Southworth, and Forbes backs, Douglas, Almond, and Forrest half-backs, Douglas, Watson J.Southworth (captain), Whittaker, and Townley, forwards. Everton: - Joliffe, goal, Ross (captain) and Dobson backs, Farmer, Holt and Weir, half-backs, Angus, Chadwick, Milward, Watson, and Brown, forwards.

## SOUTHPORT OLD BOYS 2 EVERTON RESERVES 1
*January 7, 1889. The Liverpool Courier.*

Played at Southport on Saturday before a good attendance of spectators. A dense fog extended the field, so that it was with the utmost difficulty that either the players or the ball could be distinguished. In addition to this, owing to the recent frost, the ground was rendered very hard and slippery making it dangerous and uncomfortable for the players and preventing them from giving as good an exhibition as they otherwise would have done. A start was effected about 3-30 by the home team kicking off. Everton having the slight wind at once assumed the aggressive and experienced hard lines on several occasions. About ten minutes from the commencement Smith scored for the Old Boys with a splendid screw shot and his effect was greeted with a loud shout of approval from the Old Boys supporters. This reverse seemed to awaken the Evertonians somewhat and they went to work with renewed vigour but the defensive tactics of the Old Boys back division nullified their efforts, and several corners fell to the visitors, but nothing resulted there from, and half-time arrived with the score:- Old Boys 1 goal, Everton nil. In the second half the visitors assumed the offensive, and a smart dribble on the part of their forwards ended in a goal being scored after the kick off. The game was contested on the most even terms until with three minutes of time when Dutton the centre-forward for the Old Boys shot another goal. The Evertonians on the plea of off-side disputed this, but the referee allowed the point. Everton then left the field. Final result Old Boys 2 goals, Everton 1 Reserves 1 goal.

**EVERTON 2 STOKE 1 (Game 17)**
*January 14, 1889. The Liverpool Courier.*

The return League contest took place at Everton on Saturday, fully 7,000 spectators present. At 2-40 the teams took up their position on the field. Stoke started with 10 men, Ross having won the toss, Wilson kicked off against the wind. From a long return by Farmer the Everton forwards forced Rowley to clear. Again the Everton right worked the leather into the Stoke quarters, Rowley having to fist out a hot shot from Chadwick. By neat passing Lawton and McSkimmer removed the play to midfield. Holt returned, and again Rowley saved from Watson. At this point the Stoke eleventh man joined his team. A grand run by Chadwick and Angus forced the Stoke captain to concede a corner, the place kick was nicely put, Underwood cleared. The visiting right forced their way, Ross stopping the rush with some fine tackling. From a throw in by Farmer, Chadwick struck the upright the ball going outside. Hands against Stoke gave the home team a grand opportunity, from a pass by Holt, Ross shot through; a claim off offside against Milward was sustained and no goal conceded. A combined run by the Stoke forwards caused the Everton defence some trouble, Ross heading clear. The home right wing put in a splendid run, Davies compelling Rowley to concede another corner, and from a pass by Watson, Milward scored a well-earned goal. From midfield Watson dribbed up the centre, Farmer intercepting the pass and again Milward and Chadwick called upon Rowley to save. The Stoke left removed the danger Joliffe having to clear from Lawton. Weir was now prominent with some fine half-backs play, and passing to Milward he in turn put in a regular daisy cutter, which Rowley kicked clear. Davies was now cheered for a magnificent run down the right Clare robbing him at a dangerous moment. Edge and Milarvie in a fine run up the left , Ross kicking out to clear. Half time Everton 1; Stoke nil.

After the usual interval Milward kicked off, Rowley received a magnificent reception from the spectators on taking his place in the goal-mouth. His display in goal is undoubtedly the finest that has been seen at Anfield enclosure this season. Weir was immediately called upon to stop McSkimmer, who had worked his way down the left. A couple of fouls now fell to Everton Ross having hard lines with a stinging shot. Lawton and McSkimmer put in a most determined rush. Ross kicked out and Angus took up the attack, and passing to Davies he headed through. From the centre of the field Wilson forced the play down Ross receiving a nasty kick, which accusitated his working for a little time. From a throw in Chadwick received from Holt, and again Rowley fisted clear. The home van would not be denied. Rowley saving shots from Chadwick and Milward. From a goal kick Lawton removed the venue with a strong run. Farmer removed the danger with a timely kick. Weir now left the field having received an injury. The Stoke forwards played much better, but could not break through the fine defence of the home backs. Edge gave Dobson some trouble, Joliffe clearing from Milarvie. After a splendid run by Ross Angus passed to Milward who kicked over the bar. Another visit was paid to the Everton citadel, where Angus gave a foul for "Hands" After a warm tussle in the goal mouth McSkimmer secured the first point for Stoke. Joliffe in saving from Ramsley conceded a corner, Milward kicking clear. Watson broke away, Chadwick missing a fine opportunity by kicking outside. From the throw in Watson put in a splendid run, Milward missing a good chance by dallying in the goal mouth. Again Everton pressed, but could not score. Even play followed Chadwick put in a fine screw, which Rowley saved, and a well fought game ended in favour of Everton by 2 goals to 1.

**Teams Stoke: - W. Rowley, goal, T. Clare (captain) and A. Underwood, backs, R. Ramsley, G. Shutt, and E. Smith, half-backs G. Lawton, R. McSkimmer, A. Hogg, R. Milarvie,**

and J. Wilson, forwards. Umpire Lockett. Everton: - C. Joliffe, Ross (captain), and Dobson backs, Farmer, Holt and Weir half-backs Angus, Chadwick, Watson, Davies, and Milward, forwards. Umpire Mr Berry referee Mr Fitzroy Norris (Bolton).

## EVERTON 0 PRESTON NORTH END 2  (Game 18)
*January 21, 1889. The Liverpool Courier.*

In glorious football weather this important return fixture took place on the Everton enclosure. For a long time previous to the start the roads leading to the ground were lined with ardent supporters of the home side. At the time of commencing hostilities there would be fully 15,000 spectators present. The champion League team were strongly represented the only absentee being Fred Dewhurst the Preston captain. The home organisation was minus Weir and Smalley their places being filled by Joliffe of the Reserves and Kelso of Newcastle West End. At 2-45 the teams put in an appearance the visitors receiving a very cordial reception. Ross having won the toss Goodall kicked off down the hill, and immediately Thompson raced down, Farmer relieved and passing to Angus, he passed to Watson who shot in Trainor saved in a marvellous manner two minutes from the start, Everton having hard lines in not scoring. Ross and Drummond broke away down to left, Dobson heading clear. From a throw in by Kelso, Milward raced down the centre. Howarth kicked clear. Hands against Dobson gave North End a chance Joliffe fisting out a warm one from Gordon. Preston now took a corner, Graham heading over the bar. The home right removed the play to the other end, Angus missing a good chance in the goal mouth. The Everton right forced Holmes to kick out. Kelso threw in, Trainor again saving a good shot from Davies. From midfield the Preston van raced down, Farmer relieving Gordon of a dangerous moment. From a corner kick the Preston men showed some neat passing in front of the home upright, Russell kicking over. Again Preston came dangerously near, a shot from Thompson going outside. The game was stopped for a few minutes owing to an injury to Farmer. From the goal kick the visiting forwards caused the Everton backs some trouble. Ross clearing with a long punt. A grand run by Davies forced Holmes to concede a corner, Trainor fisting out in grand style. Jimmy Ross was now conspicuous with a splendid run, Dobson robbing him on the touchline. Kelso now placed his wing in position, Davies put in a superb run, Russell taking clear. The Preston left removed the venue, Ross striking the Everton crossbar with a terrific shot. Gordon ran down the right Farmer robbing him, and passing to Chadwick he shot in, Trainor giving a corner which proved abortive. Russell took a free kick for a foul against Holt. Half-time Everton 0, Preston North End 0.

After the usual rest Milward put the ball in motion, and after even play in midfield Gordon ran up, and passing to Drummond he shot behind. Again Preston came to the front, Kelso saving in the nick of time. The Everton patrons were now treated to a fine bit of passing by Kelso, Watson, and Davies, which caused Graham to concede another corner, which proved abortive. Again the Preston forwards with good passing brought the ball up the field and from a pass by Goodall, immediately Jimmy Ross scored with a low shot. The Everton forwards broke away in line, and looked like scoring until Russell tripped Milward for which he was penalised, from the free kick , Trainor stopped two shots from Kelso and Chadwick. Goodall removed the danger with a fine run, and, passing to Drummond, he had a grand opening Joliffe kicking clear. Holmes with a long kick put Gordon in possession, who shot behind. Angus and Chadwick came away with a fine passing run, Howarth with an excellent bit of kicking removed the danger. Goodall again rushed up the centre and after passing his opponents he lowered the home citadel a second time. Dobson being at fault from the restart, Milward pressed, Russell proving a stumbling block. The Everton left were now prominent, a shot from Chadwick going outside. Holt was now cheered for a fine defence, his pass to Davies going over the line. Kelso threw in, and again Gordon was first. Ross kicking over, Robertson threw in Farmer again holding the Preston right in check. Hands against Preston looked dangerous, Kelso again cleared, Milward made off, Howarth kicking clear. Again Chadwick broke away, and passing to Davies he lost a good opportunity by being too slow on the ball, Robertson kicking clear. Short passing put the Preston forwards on the aggressive Ross finishing a spendid movement with a fine shot which the home custodian cleared. The offical whistle sounded leaving the North End victors by 2 goals to nil. **Teams Preston North End: - Trainor, goal, Holmes, and Howarth backs, Robinson, Russell, and Graham, half-backs, Gordon, Drummond, Goodall, Jimmy Ross, and Thompson, forwards. Everton: - Joliffe goal, Dobson and Ross (captain), Kelso, Holt, and Farmer half-backs, Davies Watson, Milward, Chadwick, and Angus, forwards.**

**PRESTON NORTH END RESERVES 4 EVERTON RESERVES 0**
*January 21, 1889. The Liverpool Courier.*

No details

**WOLVERHAMPTON WANDERERS 5 EVERTON 0 (Game 19)**
*January 28, 1889. The Liverpool Courier.*

The Everton team journeyed to Wolverhampton on Saturday to play the first League fixture with the Wanderers. Smalley was in the team for the first time for some weeks. There was a good attendance between 2,000 and 3,000. Milward kicked off, and Farmer, which gave the Wanderers a chance, called upon

Ross to clear a foul but Holt headed the ball away, and White kicked behind the posts. Baugh was cheered for a fine return and a warm scrimmage took place in front of the Everton goal, and the Wanderers rushed the leather past Smalley. White and Hunter raced past Ross, but Holt was in the way and pulled them up finely. The Everton forwards had not yet found their feet, and the home team were having the best of it. Lowder kicked outside, when Angus had a chance, and from the throw in Baugh give the leather to the forwards, and Wood shot the leather past Smalley for the second time. Baugh, a grand back, was in good form, and gave his forwards lots of work which they did in first class style. Angus and Chadwick broke away but could not get passed the home backs, the peculiar formation of the ground telling against them. Milward initiated a fine passing movement taken up by Chadwick, and Angus. The strong wind told against their efforts and the "Wolves" was in the visitors half, an off-side goal being scored. The Everton forwards broke away in line, and Davies tested Rose for the first time and found him all there. The referee gave an unfair decision against Everton, and spoiled what shaped to be a dangerous move. Brodie made a fine dribble down the centre, and tried a daisy cutter, but Smalley cleared in grand style, only to see Knight return with a high shot out of his reach. Again the home forwards, aided by the hill, were too good, and after Smalley had quickly thrown out several times, Wood shot it pass him for the fourth time. Ross now gave the first corner, which was futile and half-time arrived with the score- Wanderers 4 goals Everton nil.

In the second half, the Wanderers kicked off, and Everton now having the wind and hill showed very different play to the last half, and Ross was quickly called upon to save. Stevenson over ran the leather but soon recovered possession and Everton gained their first corner which was abortive. The Wanderers retaliated, and Smalley had to fist out. Milward tried a long shot, and Rose just kept it out, but keeping up the pressure, Everton gained a corner, but the sphere was kicked behind. The Wolves changed the venue, and after a scrimmage Brodie scored the fifth goal. Everton forwards took up the attack and after pretty passing Watson tried a long shot, which went wide. Brodie initiated a pretty movement, and the Wolves had hard lines, the ball just going outside. The crowd were evidently delighted with the show of the Wolves. The visitors tried hard to retrieve the fortunes of the day without success. Hunter raced up the right, and tried a shot which just missed its mark. Again the home right wing were running up in grand style, But George Dobson who throughout had played a grand game robbed them. Brodie ran and passed in splendid form. Ross proved a stumbling block, and Holt gave the leather to Davies, who was spoiled by Lowder. Again the Wolves were swarming in front, but shot behind. The game continued to be in favour of the home team, the visitors forwards being weak. Lowder and Allen being too many for them. Dobson was tried at half, Holt going back, but the charge did not make very much difference final score Wolvers 5 goals; Everton nil.

**Teams Wolverhampton Wanderers:- Rose, goals, Baugh, and Flectcher, backs, Allen, Lowder, and Hunter, half-backs, White, Brodie, Wood, Knight, and Wykes forwards. Everton: - Smalley goal G. Dobson, and Ross (captain) backs, G. Stevenson, Holt, and Farmer, half-backs, J. Davies, Watson, A. Milward, E. Chadwick, and Angus, forwards.**

## EVERTON RESERVES 6 NORTHWICH VICTORIA 0
*January 28, 1889. The Liverpool Courier.*

Fully 3,000 spectators welcomed the Reserve  forces of Northwich and Everton, who tried conclusion on the Anfield enclosure on Saturday. The home reserves were well represented, Bobby Jones receiving a very cordial reception on coming on the field. At 3-15 the teams faced each other, and Pollock being successful in the spin of the coin, Beaman kicked off against the wind. The opening incidents were in favour of the Cheshire men, until Chadwick cleared his lines with a good punt. The brothers Brown broke away and forced a corner, which was well placed, by Weir, the ball dropping nicely between the posts. Briscoe headed through five minutes from the start. This early reverse roused the visiting team, who broke down the left, and from a pass by Upton, Joliffe was called upon to save from Bowyer. From a throw in by Fayer, Keys dribbled up the right and passing to Taylor he in turn gave to Brown who headed through. A claim of off-side was raised but the referee decided in favour of the home club. Todd passing on the Northwich left brought the play into the Everton quarters, where a couple of corners were taken, nothing tangible resulting. From midfield Taylor put in a splendid run and again W. Brown got possession of the sphere, and from the touch line he put in a capital screw across the goal mouth, Briscoe increasing the lead with another fine header. Rowbottom and Hubbard raced down the right, Pollock kicking clear, and again the Home left was busy. Winstanley gave a foul for "hands" the free kick passing between untouched. Everton still pressed, and after some fine passing in the Northwich goal mouth, Harper was again defeated by Briscoe but a claim for offside was sustained. Another good run by Rowbottom caused Pollock some trouble, the ball going outside. Williams threw in to Beaman who tried a shot that went wide. Weir brought relief, and again Harper was called upon to clear. Sands give his wing men a grand opening, which was spoilt by erractic shooting on the part of Hubbard. Chadwick robbed the Cheshire left, and passing to Taylor he ran up and scored with a rattling shot, the ball passing over Harper's hands. Score at half-time Everton Reserves 4 goals Northwich Victoria nil.

After the usual rest the teams changed ends. Taylor put the ball in motion. After a brief visit to the lower goal the visitors left rushed down, Chadwick and Pollock clearing in grand style.

Everton raised the siege, and after a grand struggle another goal was scored out of a scrimmage. From the centre Northwich assumed the aggressive. Joliffe conceded another, which was kicked behind. Bob Brown removed the venue with a splendid run. Everton obtained a free kick for "hands" Harper saving a good shot from Taylor. Play was now confined to the home quarters, a shot from Rowbottom going outside. Taylor and Brown removed the play to the other end, where another corner was taken Brown's final effort just missing the mark. A faulty kick by Fayer, let in Beaman who forced Joliffe to clear. Keys and Briscoe pressed on the right and from a pass by Taylor, Brown shot through a plea for off side was again sustained. The Everton forwards again came to the front from Keys going over, a good passing run by the Northwich van looked like scoring Chadwick kicked clear. The Everton forwards came again in line, Briscoe spoiling a good opening by rather selfish play. Bowyer and Upton got the better of Pollock a low shot from Hubbard going outside. Williams took a free kick, Upton missing a splendid opening by kicking over. Sands threw in Fayer kicking clear at a dangerous moment. From the kick out R.Brown dribbled down the centre Harper saving from Briscoe. Everton would not be denied, Harper fisting out from Brown and Taylor. A long kick Fayer enabled Keys to pass to R.Brown, who scored a very fine goal. The Northwich men made a good attempt at the other end and but could not break through the fine defense of Chadwick and Joliffe. Final Result, Everton 6 goals Northwich Victoria nil. **Teams Northwich Victoria swifts: - Harper goal, Molyneus, and Dugs backs, Wilhams, Winstansley and Sands, half-backs, Rowbottom, Hubbard, Bowyer, Upton, and Beaman forwards. Everton Reserves: - Joilffe goal, Pollock (captain), and Chadwick (a) backs, C. Weir, R. Jones, and Fayer, half-backs, W. Brown, R. Brown, W. Briscoe, J. Keys, and A. Taylor, forwards.**

# FEBRUARY 1889

## EVERTON 3 BATTLEFIELD 2
*February 4, 1889. The Liverpool Courier.*

The above teams met on the Anfield enclosure on Saturday
under very unfavorable circumstance. During the morning
Liverpool was visited with a very heavy storm, and at the time
for starting a very strong, bitter wind was blowing, which
made it very uncomfortable for the spectators, who numbered
about 5,000. The visitors were the first to put in an appearance
the home partisans receiving them very cordially. After two
months, suspension Dick took his place in the Everton rank, his
return being received with that recognition, which his ability
deserves. Ross having been successful in the spin of the coin,
Somerville started the game down hill, the ground being very
sloppy. The Battlefield men were the first to press. A shot by
Elliott was nicely cleared by Dick. The home right, with a good
passing run, removed the play to the end Milward forcing an
abortive corner. Ross sent forward, and immediately the visitors
recognised their advantage, and went away in splendid combined
run, Somerville finishing up the movement with a good shot,
which Smalley appeared to fist over the bar. A claim for goal
was sustained to the astonishment of the spectators. From the
restart the home left pressed forward, Ross being unfortunate
with a regular daisy cutter. Again Sommerville broke away,
Holt checking him and passing to Dobson, who shot in the ball
just going outside. Hector and Hendry paid Smalley a visit from
which the latter cleared at the expense of a corner, which Dick
headed clear. A throw in by Dobson gave Watson and Davies a
good opportunity, which Gow frustrated by conceding another
corner that was worked clear, by the fine defence of Hall and
Cook. Elliott brought relief with a fine run. Farmer worked the
sphere clear, and passing to Ross, the latter gave to Milward who

equalised, to the delight of the spectators. Encouraged by this success this home van renewed the attack, Davies causing Neill to clear. A pretty bit of work on the part of Ross and Chadwick enabled Brown to shoot through, but a claim for offside was sustained. Everton again broke away, Brown scoring a grand goal from a pass by Davies. Immediately afterwards Chadwick and Brown, passing brought the ball up the field to Ross, he scored for Everton with a low shot. Score at half-time:- Everton 3 Battlefield 1. After the changing ends Milward kicked off against the wind. The opening incident of the play was rather in favour of the home club. One of the visting backs displayed a sting of unnecessary dealing in defending his goal. Good passing by the visitors removed the play to the Everton quarters, where Holt was cheered for some fine tackling. From a long kick by Farmer, Davies, missed a good chance. Walker robbed Watson, who passed to Hendry, who put the Everton citadel in danger owing to Dobson missing his kick. Ross removed the danger with a long punt. Milward dribbled down the centre Gow again removing the danger, and passing to J.Cunninghan, put in a fine sprint Dick clearing on the touchline. Chadwick was now conspicuous with an excellent dribble. T.C.Hendry robbing him when further downfall of the Scotch goal seemed certain. Hector forced his way up the right, passing Farmer and Ross he brought the ball in front, Elliott increased the score with a fine goal. The play became very exciting. Watson and Davies forced the play with a strong run, Hall kicking out to save. Dobson was now called upon to check a fierce raid of the part of the Scotch left, and passing to Brown he allowed the ball to run out. From the throw in by Hendry, Hendry initiated another aggressive movement which Ross repulsed. Milward and Chadwick both had shots, which Neill cleared. The game ended in a heavy downpour the home team winning a very hard game by 3 goals to 2. **Battlefield: - Neill goal, Hall and Cook, backs, TC. Hendry, Walker and Gow half-backs, Hector,**

WT. Hendry, J. Cunningham, Elliott, and Somerville, forwards. Everton: - Smalley, goal, A. Dick, and NJ. Ross, (captain), backs, G. Dobson, J. Holt, and G. Farmer, half-backs, J. Davies, R. Watson, A. Milward, E. Chadwick, and W. Brown, forwards.

**EVERTON 1 WOLVERHAMPTON WANDERERS 2 (Game 20)**
*February 11, 1889. The Liverpool Courier.*

The return league contest was played on the Everton enclosure on Saturday in fine but rather windy weather. The recent frost had made the turf very hard and somewhat dangerous's for the players. It will be remembered that in the first contest a fortnight ago the "Wolves" defeated the Everton representative by five goals to nil. Although this is the greatest reverse the home team have received in the League matches, it was fully expected that the game would be of a more even character. The County match at Stoke deprived Everton of the services of Ross and that, which automatically weakened the back division. The Wolverhampton captain was also absent, his place in the centre having being taken by Wykes. At 3-30 the teams took up their position on the field there being about 10,000 spectators. The Wolves having won the toss. Milward kicked off against a strong wind, and immediately Dobson was called upon to stop Hunter and Cooper who made an excellent run up the right, Elgar Chadwick relieved his goal with a fine run Lowder kicking over the stand to clear. Farmer threw in to Milward and Brown came dangerously near scoring, the ball going outside. Albert Chadwick passed to his brother who forced Baugh to concede a corner which proved futile, although nicely placed by Farmer. Wykes now indulged in a splendid run up the centre, Dick checking him in midfield and again Watson and Davies forced their way down the right Mason clearing with a hugh kick. Play was now combined to the right, and Farmer having all their work to check the persistent attack of Hunter and Cooper. From a long pass by Dick, Milward rushed up to the other end, where Baugh saved under the bar from a grand shot from the foot of Davies. An excellent dribble by Knight gave Everton some trouble. Smalley having to fist out from Woods. Farmer brought the ball out of the goal mouth and passing to Brown he compelled Rose to clear. Everton still kept up the attack and obtained a free kick for "hands" and after a fine bit of passing Chadwick scored. Against great cheering on the part of the home patrons. From midfield Allen passed to Cooper, who raced away until met by Dick who transferred the sphere to Davies, and again Rose saved three capitals shots in rapid succession. Still the pressure was kept up by the home van until Milward kicked over the bar. Another grand run by the visitors enabled Allen to test Smalley, who cleared splendidly. Dick worked the ball clear, and passed to Davies, and again Rose kicked clear. Dobson, Dick and Smalley preventing any downfall of their goal, made a most determined rush by some grand defensive play. The visitors again pressed, until Dick saved in the goalmouth. Farmer gave a corner which Cooper headed over. The home left brought the play to midfield. Half-time Everton 1 goal, Wanderers nil. After the usual interval, Wykes re-started the game downhill. The play for a little time was confined to the Everton quarters, Chadwick heading clear a good shot from Cooper that looked like taking effect. Milward initiated an aggressive movement, which was well sustained by the home halves. Roberts improving considerably in his play. The defence of the visitors being very good, no opening could be effected. The home team, increasing the speed again pressed, Rose stopping a splendid shot from Watson. Mason passed to his forwards, who paid another visit to the Everton goal, Smalley saving when a goal seemed certain. Brown and Chadwick got possession, and passing to the right Davies put in a fine screw. Rose again proving equal to the emergency. Chadwick had hard lines with a long shot. Smalley was next called upon to save a good shot from Wykes. Good passing by Davies and Watson gave Everton another opportunity Davies shooting well. Dick negotiated a good shot, Allan and again Brown and Milward brought the ball to midfield. Where Fletcher returned to Wood, who dribbled down the right until relieved by Farmer, the ball passing over the line. A nice passing run by the visitors looked ominous, Smalley again removing the danger when surrounded by four of his opponents. From the kick out, Davies raced away Mason fastened on the ball and passing to Knight he shot through. A claim for off-side was abstained. Hunter and Cooper renewed the attack and after a warm scrimmages Wood equalised. Both teams tried hard score and each goal was visited in turn, Mason repelling a good shot from Brown. Fletcher with a long shot kick got the ball well in front. Dobson kicking clear. The home van again pressed, Mason removing the danger. The Visting forwards rushed away. Knight shot through the referee conceding a goal the player being distinctly off-side. Immediately the whistle blew. Result- Wanderers 2; Everton 1. **Teams Everton: - Smalley goal, Dick, and Dobson (captain), backs, Farmer, Roberts, and A. Chadwick, half-backs, W. Brown, E. Chadwick, Watson, Davies, and Milward, forwards. Wanderers: - Rose goal, Baugh, and Mason backs, Fletcher, Allen, and Lowder half-backs Hunter, Cooper, Wood, knight, and Wykes forwards.**

### SOCK AND BUSKIN V EVERTON
*February 13, 1889. The Liverpool Daily Post.*

A novel and most successful charitable movement was yesterday brought off on the Everton football ground, in the form of a pantomime football match between members of the theatrical profession now engaged in the different pantomimes going on in the City and members of the Everton Football Club. The entertainment was in aid of the funds of the Royal Infirmary and

Stanley Hospital, and no doubt these institutions will greatly benefit thereby. The idea however of coupling the names of pantomime artistes with football is not exactly new, as some years ago a similar thing occurred in Sheffield, when these engaged in producing the Pantomimes than being performed in that town played a "character" game with a local team of footballers with such success that the charity on whose behalf the performance was being enacted greatly profited. That a similar thing could be successfully brought to issue in Liverpool suggested itself to several master minds in the city; and amongst them were Mr. Albert Smith and Mr. Alfred Hemming, this one, as it well known, connected with one of the principal theatres of Liverpool, and the other as equally celebrated in sporting and football life in the old town. To this pair was left the task of "bossing the show" under the role of the joint secretary. They first of all obtained the co-operation of a host of talent from the different theatres of the city, who heartily entered into "the fun of the things" quite as much indeed as if they had been "invited" to perform at one of their own benefits. They then secured the patronage of his worship the Mayor and other gentleman, and decided that the "entertainment" should he given on behalf of the Royal Infirmary and Stanley Hospital, two very deserving charities connected with Liverpool. To secure a ground and opposing side were the next tasks, and there were found to be very small matters in the preliminary business, as the Everton Football Club executive, who possess an enclosure second to none in the kingdom for convenience of the (if we except press accommodation) heartily responded to the desire that the "match" should be played on the ground in Oakfield road, and they suggested that they should choose the one team, which was composed of Everton players. The town for weeks past had been liberally placed, and the public generously responded to the appeal made on behalf of the two insitutions by a large purchase of tickets. Unfortunately, the weather for several days past had not been very propitious for outdoor sports, and doubts were entertained as to whether or not the "performance" would take place. That it did do, so thanks are due to the energetic management, who set themselves the formidable task of clearing away the accumulations, of the "Downpour on Sunday". The job was successfully accomplished to the comfort of all, the only winter surrounding being small heaps of snow along the "touch line" and the adjacent house-tops on the latter of which were perched, clinging to the chimney stacks, several darling spirits probably with more nerve in their breeze than "coppers" or generosity in their pockets. Overhead the afternoon was fine and bright, with a brilliant sun's shining and as early as half-past one o'clock the "show" commenced by people wending their way Everton wards. At two the ground was well lined with spectators who aroused themselves by snowballing each other. A few minutes later the "itinerant" part of the business was begun by vendors of packets of "sweetmeats" and the winners of the football match for a penny. Others, fully equipped for the occasion were playing on barrel organs accompanied by a bevy of fair ladies from the respective theatres all eagerly "begging" on behalf of the charities. A splendid orchestra was divided by the Alexanders Prince of Wales, and Shakespeare staffs, who discgorged a fine sound of music to wile away the time while waiting for the more important performers who, at three o'clock promptly, came tumbling for the many thousands of spectators now assembled, truly, it was the greatest football match, ever witnessed on the Everton ground. The Mayor and his party now made their appearance, and were received with much cheering. The "Sock and Buskin" company, who in all numbered about twenty-six, kicked off, and immediately there was a scrambling in front of the Theatricals goal. The scene was indescribable, much noise and hullabaloo were perfect players as much as spectators became as if by magic connived with side splitting laughter; spirited devils, dwarfs, giants stages, villains

Highlanders, clerical, police, brigands, clowns, harlequins, fat boys, and pick witches character all became a mixed up mass with the Everton players. It made no difference which way the ball was kicked so long as the pantomimiste could have their little "go"and produce a laugh. More often the ball was missed than kicked, or else picked up and run off with. The two theatrical goalkeepers were in force with"drop curtains" which took up form of lawn tennis nets sewn together, so that when their charge became endangered the pulleys were immediately set to work. By a clever mixture of Rugby Association, and pantomimic tricks several "corners" fell to the Theatricals. Afterward Joliffe gave a "foul" by "fisting" the wrong side of the centre line, and here the pantomime business was great. On the cry of foul, Mr. Wheetley, one of the Artist produced from some mysterious corner a dead "fowl" and presented it to Ross, the Everton captain. This fine joke was of course successfully in "bringing down the house". At length by means of inducing Jolliffe to forsake his goal. McCarthy, one of the half-backs, picked up the ball and run straight up to the post, and flung it through, for which of course a goal was claimed and after Davies had been "taken into custody" for running too fast, half time was called, and refreshments in the shape of inflated balloons were handed round. This also afforded no end of amusement for the spectators and players. The score at this period was Theatricals 1 goal Everton nil. Then on changing ends, and hence great anxiety was shown by the whole team for their charge. They accordingly flocked round it, cutting capers, shouting, protesting in such a manner that they forgot all about goalkeeping, and Ross headed the ball through and equalised. From the start some capital and amusing "passing" was shown by the clowns who rushed everything before them, including the whole of their opponents, and put them and the ball through a second time. Messrs. Graham and many were compelled to do some clever tumbling feats to clear their goal, but the climax was reached when

"Pickwick" got "winded" There was such a stir, and commotion amongst the talent, and calls for "doctors" and "water" as discussed gave anxiety's for the life of Mr.Pickwick, but the "plant" was soon observed, and the neighborhood of Everton once more re-echoed to the sound of merriment. After enjoying a plentiful supply of cold water, brought forth in sturdy cans and buckets, Pickwick came round. Play was resumed, and Everton men being surprised, a third goal was scored for the combination by a very clever impersonator of a Liverpool "step girl" Another raid on the Theatricals goal caused an amusing stampede, and as Ross sent in his shot there were about two and twenty goalkeepers all fisting out. After the Everton goal had once more become "endangered" the whistle sounded time, the result being a win for the Theatricals by 3 goals to 1. It is needless to say that the game was immensely enjoyed by about 8,000 or 9,000 people. Amongst those on the stand were the Mayor (H. Cookson.) Mr John Houlding (chairman of the Stanley Hospital), Mr I.E.Bennett (secretary of Stanley Hospital), the Rev. Dr. Hyde, Dr.Costine, Mr E.Berry, and Mr E.H.Bryson. Miss Maude Branscombe and other ladies were very successful collectors of silver and copper coins on behalf of the fund. Photos of the professional players had from Brown, Barnes, and Bell, from Lord Street, the proceeds from the sale of which will go to aid the fund.

**EVERTON REVIEW**
*February 16, 1889. The Liverpool Courier.*

The League contests are fast drawing to a close, and the Evertonians do not as was confidently anticipated, improve their position. On the contrary, there has been a gradual falling to the rear, and as the remaining fixture are of the strongest possible character, the outlook is by no means a cheerful one. Still "a long pull and a strong pull" may effect wonders, and it is certain that every effort will be made to keep within the qualifying bounds for next season's competition. When it is remembered, however that the Evertonians have been competing against the very best teams in the country, the record is not bad. Rome was not build in a day nor was North End so formidable when first organised as now, and Everton must therefore take heart and "play up" as becomes a team surprising to championship honours. Their opponents last Saturday were the Wolverhampton Wanderers who on their first issue won easily by five goals to nil; but notwithstanding the severity of the beating hopes were entertained despite the absence of Ross and Holt, that if the result was not absolutely reversed the balance in favour of the "Wolves" would be much smaller than before. The Latter assumption proved correct, for the game was excellently contest, and should (in the opinion of many) have remained a drawn as "time" was up or alleged to have been, when the Wanderers scored their second and winning point. Play during the first half was very fast, Knight conspicuous for the Wanderers, whose forwards passed almost to perfection. Baugh and Mason also did well as back, and notwithstanding the constant attacks of the Everton van, they were kept out of goal, Rose was several times compelled to handle the ball, but wonderfully well. After half an hour's play Chadwick scored. Amidst tremendous cheering, for Everton after some fine passing by the forwards ranks. The "Wolves" played determinedly, Dobson Dick, and Smalley having all their work cut out to prevent the downfall of the home goal. This, however was prevented, and half-time arrived with Everton leading by one goal to nil. On resuming, the play rolled in favour of the Wanderers for whom Cooper almost scored. Roberts was playing half-back for Everton in place of Holt, and was a failure until towards the close of the game, when he improved considerably. The Wanderers showed a splendid defence, and the home forwards try, as they would could not increase their lead. Rose saved finely, shots from

Watson, Milward, and Davies, and Chadwick also had hard lines a fast shot just passing over the bar. After Smalley had saved grandly Knight defeated the Everton custodian but the point was disallowed. Wood then scored a legitimate point, and with the score equal play became faster than ever. Knight notched a second goal, offside not being sustained. This was the last point, and the Wanderers won by two goals to one-luckily it must be confessed.

Ever foremost in works of charity the Evertonians on Monday returned to antagonise a team of panomine players, 17 in number made conditions by which they could not possibly win, but as the public appreciated the entertainment, this mattered little. Two custodians, with a net in front of goal, presented an almost insurmountable barrier, and it is therefore by no means surprising that on a single occasion only were the Evertonians able to successfully shoot though goal. The antics of the pantomimic troupe were lubricious in the extreme especially the fatal scene between Wheatley, Joliffe and Ross. Disregarding off –side and other restrictive clauses of the rules of the game, "sock and buskin" elements were every where hands and feet being used in a style never before witnessed on the football field; and thus privileged, they won by three to one and completely "brought down the house."

## EVERTON 5 DUNDEE STRATHMORE 1
*February 18, 1889. The Liverpool Courier.*

This important engagement took place on the Anfield enclosure on Saturday in very boisterous weather. The heavy downpour during the early part of the field had rendered the turf very heavy. This, together with the strong wind, considerably militated against anything like a good exhibition of football. At four o'clock the teams took up their positions in the field there being fully 9,000 spectators present. It was a matter of regret that the trial match at Glasgow prevented W.Dickson accompanying his team his place being taken by his brother. Dundee having been successful in the spin of the coin Ross kicked off down hill and against the wind. The opening feature of the game favoured the home club a free kick by Farmer going outside. McGregor and C.Dickson removed the danger with a fine run up the right. Weir kicking clear in the goal mouth. Watson retaliated from the home side, Mason saving a good shot from the foot of Chadwick. The kick out gave the Scotch forwards another opening, and taking full advantage of the opportunity Dick was called upon, the Everton back being loudly cheered for a fine defence. Ross now led a very fine movement, Simpson relieving the Everton captain, when a goal seemed certain. McGregor was again well to the fore with another grand dribble, his pass being well repulsed by Dobson. Strathmore still kept up the pressure Dick conceding a corner, which proved fruitless. From a throw in by Steven the ball was taken into the Everton quarters. A grand shot by Dickson was well cleared by Dick, who conceded another corner, which was well placed by Laburn and after a warm scrimmage in front the ball was kicked through. The spectators duly recognised this early success of the visitors. From the kick-off Chadwick and Brown dribbled down the left. McFarlane transferred the play, Farmer kicking over the stands to clear his lines. In response in the demand of the spectators the home van came down the field, with an excellent passing run. Ross finishing up with a shot that took effect. Douglas made a good attempt to save. The visitors started from the centre, Smalley again fisting out a good shot from Murray. From midfield the home left ran down and passing in Ross increased the home total with a grand goal. Everton kept up the attack and obtained three corners in rapid succession, William Brown having hard lines-with a good header. Laburn threw in to McGregor who raced up the right. Dobson kicked clear, and passing to Ross, he and the left worked the ball down the left, Brown allowed the ball to go over the line. Good play by the visiting half-backs enabled their forwards to press, a shot from McLaren going over. Score at half-time- Everton 2 goals Dundee one.

After the usual respite Murray put the ball in motion. The Scotch right worked down, Holt came to the rescue, and put Brown in possession, Ross missing what appeared to be an easy chance from a pass by Chadwick. Hands against Watson gave Mason a free kick, Ross intercepted, and passing to Davies the latter scored but a claim for offside was sustained. A nice dribble by Murray gave Duncan an opening. Weir proving a stumbling block, and Everton became aggressive Chadwick scoring third goal after some beautiful passing by the home van. Both sides had the advantage of a free kick from the latter of which Brown almost scored. Farmer who passed to Chadwick nicely repulsed a dangerous rush by the Strathmore right. The ball was again hovering round the Scotch posts, Mason saving a good shot from Davies. A foul against Everton brought relief, but the visiting forwards could not break through they excellent defence of Weir, Holt, and Farmer, who fed their forwards judiciously, a long shot from Chadwick going over the bar. Weir robbed McLaren and Duncan, and dribbling up the wing Chadwick shot in, Douglas proved equal to the occasion. The game assumed a one-sided character, the visitors scarcely ever getting over the centre line. Good passing by the home forwards gave Holt a chance, his shot going over. A good run by Dickson caused Dick to kick over the line. From the throw in Murray kicked over. A mistake by Farmer let In McLaren, who made headway down the left. Dick with a strong punt, spoiled his intentions, and passing to Watson he shot in, Douglas saving. Ross met the sphere, and gave to Watson who scored a rather soft goal. Another rush forced Douglas to fist out from Ross, good passing by the home left enabled Watson to increase the score. From now to the close Everton had the best of the game. The Scotch continued to defend admirably. Dick took a free kick and landed the leather well in front, Mason kicking clear. Final score- Everton five goals, Strathmore one goal. **Teams Everton: - Smalley goal, Dobson, and Dick, backs, Farmer, Holt and Weir half-backs, W. Brown, A. Chadwick, Ross (captain), Watson, and J. Davies, forwards. Dundee Strathmore: - Douglas goal, Mason, and Simpson backs Laburn, McFarlane and Stiren half-backs, McGregor, C. Dickson, Murray, McLaren and Duncan forwards.**

**TRANMERE RESERVES 1 EVERTON RESERVES 5**
*February 18, 1889, The Liverpool Courier.*

On Saturday Tranmere played off their return fixture with Everton Reserves, and as this was the team that first broke the Everton record, of course great interest was taken in the match by the Tranmere's supporters. Teams Everton: - C. Joliffe, goal, A. Chadwick and J. Connor, backs. T. Fayer, H. Pollock (captain), and C. Weir, half-backs, J. Keys, W. Briscoe, A. Milward R. Brown, and D. Waugh, forwards Tranmere Rovers: - H. Sherdian, goal, T. Myers, and F. Shepherd, backs G. Sherdian, C. Roberts, and H. Fish, half-backs, W. Littler, J. Morgan, A. Taylor, J. Stevenson, and R. Edwards forwards. Everton turned out late, and a start was not made until 3-45. Everton won the toss, and Tranmere kicked off against the wind. Immediately Everton worked the ball down and forced it over. Hands against Tranmere looked dangerous and after a neat pass Milward scored the first goal for Everton. Again the visitors took it down, and again kicked behind. Tranmere now took the ball up the field but soon it was down again, and play was even for some time. From a throw in Everton came near to scoring for the second time, the ball striking the upright. Milward now put in some nice work but could not succeed in scoring. Waugh was now noticed making a grand run and centering to Milward the latter play overran the ball and Tranmere worked it up the field. Again Waugh raced down and passing to Brown another was scored for Everton. Littler here made a run up the right for Tranmere but he could not break through the Everton backs. Tranmere began to play up a little after this but could not do much against the wind and shortly after Everton had hard lines, the ball hitting the bar and rebounding back into play, but none of the Everton being there the ball was worked back. The home team were completely penned in, and the visitors gained a corner but the ball was kicked behind. Another corner soon followed, and Everton tried to rush the goalkeeper through, it passed over the bar. Play was continually on the left, and Waugh put in a splendid shot, which Sheridan failed to stop but he was ruled off-side, and the point scored was not counted. A foul right in the goal mouth looked dangerous for Tranmere, but now a dispute occurred, and play was stopped for some time. From the scrimmage in front of goal Everton again put through. Tranmere now took the ball, past the half-way flag for the first time amid great cheers, but not for long, Everton soon taking it back Brown scored another goal. Everton were again in front of goal, when the whistle blew half-time Everton 4 goals Tranmere Rovers nil. Final Result Everton Reserves 5 goals, Tranmere Rovers Reserves 1.

**EVERTON  0  WEST BROMWICH ALBION  1  (Game 21)**
*February 25, 1889. The Liverpool Courier.*

In rather dull weather this important League contest took place on Saturday, the ground being in very good condition. The English Cup Holders received a very good reception, regret being expressed at the absence of Bassett their popular forward who is away playing in the International Match against Wales (score 4-1 to England) at Stoke. After an absence of four months Waugh took his place in the Everton ranks, his presence being heartily welcomed. At 3-50 the teams faced each other there being an attendance of fully 10,000 spectators. Ross won the toss, Bayliss kicked off, against the wind. The opening points of the game were rather in favour of the home side. A long kick by Waugh landed the sphere in front of Roberts who conceded the first corner the ball going outside. "Hands" against Dobson gave the Albion an opening, the free kick going over the bar. The kick out was taken up by Ross, who forced his way down the centre Horton kicking clear. A tremendous rush by the Albion left was beautifully checked by Weir who passed to Davies, and again Everton became dangerous, Perry with a timely kick removing the danger. This was followed by a splendid run by Wilson who travelled to the other goal Dick cleared his lines with a huge punt. A good combined run by the home forwards earned another corner; Farmer placed the ball well in front, Roberts fisted out Waugh returned, the ball going over the bar. Play was confined to midfield. Holt was loudly offered for fine defensive play. Ross again fastened on the ball, and, passing to Davies he missed an excellent chance of scoring. Everton kept up the pressure, Chadwick kicking behind from a grand pass by Davies. A free kick near the Albion goal was taken by Dick, who kicked-over. This was repeated a minute later by Chadwick. A grand dribbled by Perry was nicely checked by Dick, who worked the ball clear, Dobson having to clear a minute later from Bayliss. The Albion improved considerably in their forwards play, Weir heading clear a grand shot from Crabtree. Pearson putting a pretty run, and passing to Wilson he almost brought about the downfall of the Everton Citadel. Dick kicking out repelled a good passing run by the visiting right, the throw in by E.Horton giving his side a rattling chance. Farmer came to the rescue, and passing to Chadwick he put in a low shot, which Roberts cleared. This brought half-time, Everton 0; Albion 0. Recommencing Ross put the ball in motion, and passing to Watson to break away, Timmins returned to Bayliss who scored three minutes from the kick off. Ross initiated a grand aggressive movement, Davies allowing the ball to pass over the lines. The Everton left was now conspicuous, Ross having hard lines in the goal mouth. Crabtree and Perry became almost irresistible with a spirited attack, Dobson again saving in grand style. Waugh and Chadwick brought relief with a grand run. Horton and Perry returned, the ball going behind. A throw in by Farmer was not utillised by his forwards, and again Perry troubled the home defence. Dobson with a strong punt cleared his lines. Ross handling when a goal seemed imminent spoiled another splendid run by the Everton left. Hands against Holt in the Everton quarters enabled Pearson to test Smalley. Whom played equal to the demand made upon him. A good pass by Waugh gave Davies a chance, which was not taken. Holt robbed Bayliss and passing to Ross, he again experienced hard luck in not equalising W.Perry indulged in a little gallery play, his effect being spoil by Holt, who passed to Ross, who rushed down the centre Green transferring the play to Bayliss, who raced down. Smalley fisted out from Pearson. Give-and–take play followed until Chadwick gave Watson mark. Everton continued to press, but could not break through the fine defence of the visitors. Ross struck the cross-bar a few minutes off time. Final result:- West Bromwich Albion  1 goal Everton nil. The following were the teams which faced: Everton: - R. Smalley, goal, A. Dick, and G. Dobson, backs, J. Weir, J. Holt, and G. Farmer, half-backs, J. Davies, R. Watson, JN. Ross (captain), E. Chadwick, and D. Waugh, forward. West Bromwich Albion: - Roberts goal, J. Horton and H. Green, backs, E. Horton, G. Parry, Timmins half-backs, W. Crabtree, W. Perry, Baliss, Pearson and Wilson forwards, Referee Mr Cooper.

**SOUTHPORT CENTRE 1 EVERTON 2**

*February 28, 1889. The Liverpool Courier.*

A large number of persons assembled yesterday at Southport to witness this match. A splendid match was witnessed, and at half time the game stood Everton two goals Southport nil (2 from Davies). Shortly after renewal of play the Central after their goal (Mullen) had been severely attacked, made a fine run and scored. Some most excellent play ensued, the game ending Everton, 2 goals Central 1 goal.

**EVERTON FOOTBALL CLUB AND THE MANAGEMENT**
*February 28, 1889. The Liverpool Courier.*

To the editor of the Liverpool courier
Sir-during the progess of and since the match West Bromwich Albion v Everton, of Saturday last, I have heard many hard things said of N.J.Ross, the captain of the Everton first team, his play in the above game. I myself did not consider he was doing as well as expected but under the circumstances which I have been assured of, and coming from a source I have no reason to doubt. I take this matter before the public, the chief supporter of the last mentioned club. The fact are as follows:- the visting team at once objected to the globe placed on the field for hostilities, on the ground that it was not true; therefore appealed to the captain of the home team for a new ball, and he in turn, as was his duty, appealed to one of the leading spirits of the management committee in the person of one of the management for his aforesaid article, and was immediately snubbed in the following terms:- mind your own business and go to your place, and play your game that is all you have to do. Now I maintain that such a speech was quite uncalled for before an audience of football members. Such treatment of a first class player is sufficient to cause him to be most careful in giving him content to play for the Everton club.

# MARCH 1889

### BURSLAM PORT VALE ROVERS 2 EVERTON RESERVES 4
*March 4, 1889. The Liverpool Courier.*

The match between these clubs was played at Burslam on Saturday in beautiful football weather. Teams: - Everton: - Joliffe, goal, A. Chadwick and H. Pollock (captain), backs, Fayer, C. Weir, and J. Weir, half-backs, J. Keys, W. Briscoe, A. Milward, Brown and J. Angus, forwards. Rovers: - Meakin, goal, Martin, and Udall backs Chadwick, Hond and Farrington half-backs, Sporston, Wood, Keeling Kirkham, and Randles, forwards. Milward kicked off against the wind, and after a bit of preliminary skirmishing the Rovers forwards got off very beautifully down the left and Randles scored after Joliffle had knocked out once. A minute later, however, Milward equalized from a scrimmage. After this the Rovers had another look in, and forced Joliffe to concede a corner. Which he by good defense prevented from being improved upon. Everton now showed much better form and pressed hard, Brown and Angus being prominent. A fine shot by Milward almost scored and Brown also almost brought about the desired result. The siege was raised, and the Rovers got a corner from which Hood scored. From now until the finish of the first half the Rovers had the best of the game. Joliffe played finely in goal half-time Rovers 2 goals Everton Reserves 1. Final Result Rovers 2 goals Everton Reserves 4.

### SUNDERLAND 4 EVERTON 2
*March 6, 1889. The Liverpool Courier.*

These teams met at Sunderland yesterday. The weather was fine, and the attendance large. During the first half Everton faced the sun. The game was hotly contested, each side stirring its atmost to avert defeat. During the first half Sunderland by good play scored three goals and their opponents one. On the resumption of play Sunderland played a hard scientific game which resulted in their favour by four to two. Snow fell during the game. Dick was hurt. Scorers Sunderland, Davidson, McLarhlan (2), Breckoupridge, Everton Davies and Chadwick. **Teams; Sunderland: - Kirkley, goal, Oliver and Simpson, backs, Mckenchine, Raylaton, and Gibson halfbacks, Davidson, Smith, Breckoupridge and McLachan, forwards. Everton: - Joliffe, goal, Dick and Ross (captain), backs, A. Chadwick, J. Weir, and Angus half-backs, Watson J. Davies, Milward, Brown, and E. Chadwick, forwards.**

## BOOTLE 3 EVERTON 3
*March 11 1889, The Liverpool Mercury.*

This important match took place on Saturday on the Hawthorne-road enclosure. An hour before the time announced, for the kick off people were to be-seen making their way to the ground, and at half-past three all the points of vantage had been secured. The ground, considering the heavy fall of snow which took place on Friday, appeared to be in very good condition, and these parts which had been most affected were covered with sawdust. The crowd was in good humor and it was apparent that many were present with their intentions of making it a hard day having "armed" themselves with watchmen's rattles, horns, etc. The match is the second which has taken place between the teams this season the encounter on boxing day not having decided who should hold the title of Champion, owing to it having resulted in a draw. As to who should win there was a great divergence of opinion, the supporters of both clubs being confident of the success of their boys, whilst others thought that no better result would be arrived at. Both teams had a hearty reception on their appearance on the field. Ross especially is having a very warm welcome. There were between six and seven thousand spectators when the following teams faced - Everton: - R. Smalley, G. Dobson and JN. Ross (captain) backs J. Weir, J. Holt, and G. Farmer, half-backs, J. Davies, R. Watson, A. Milward, A. Chadwick and W. Brown forwards. Bootle: - Jackson, goal, R. McFarlane, and FR. Woods, backs, A. Allsop, W. Hughes, and W. Campbell half-backs, J. Woods, Hughie Galbraith, right wing, T. Morris, centre, R. Jamieson, and W. Hasting left wing. Bootle won the toss, and played with a slight wind at their backs. Milward kicked off Bootle at once making a raid into the Everton quarters, Ross relieved the pressure. Wood nicely headed but Holt returned, and play was in the home half. A foul helped Bootle and Dobson gave the first corner. Nothing resulted. A foul was given against McFarlane, Ross took the kick. The ball going behind spoiled the advantage, and play was in the visitors quarters Campbell was cheered for several fine throws. Bootle continued to press Hasting at length sending in a poor shot. The game was at this point rather disagreeable, fouls being given, against both teams for unfair play. Bootle had hard times, a good shot just topping the bar. Ross kicked out F.Wood returned and Milward made a fine dribble down the centre. Hughes checked him. Watson and Davies taking up the attack. Jackson had to throw out. Bootle made a splendid attack initiated by J.Woods, Ross having to concede a corner, which was futile. Bootle were certainly having the best of it, Campbell was cheered for robbing Ross and sending in a grand shot which Dobson cleared. Everton had a turn Chadwick putting in a grand shot, Gailbrith disappointed his supporters by kicking over the bar, when he seemed to have the goal at his mercy. Smalley was cheered for a grand save, fisting out when surrounded by opponents, McFarlane robbed the Everton forwards when they become dangerous. Bootle at length had their reward, Morris amidst the cheers of the Bootleties from a goal by Woods, shooting the first goal. Milward initiated a pretty movement, but nothing came of it, and Bootle were quickly in the visitors quarters again. Ross playing in his inimitable style spoiled the home forwards time after time but could not prevent Bootle from scoring their second goal. Which was scored from a foul close to the goal mouth. Everton had a chance  but shot behind. Davies sent in a good shot from the touchline which just went behind. Everton soon had their revenge. Jackson muffed a shot, and Chadwick quickly took the advantaged and put it through. The Evertonians playing in better form attacked fiercely, but without result. The Everton combination was vastly improved consequently with the aid of Ross whose kicking was grand as they were having considerably the best of the game at this point. Twice was the Bootle goal  placed in jeopardy by passes from Watson and Davies. Half-time arrived with the score:- Bootle  2 goals  Everton  1goal. Morris kicked off and as at the commencement, Bootle were at once pressing. Everton soon relieved, and for some time Bootle had rather a warm time of it. Milward made pretty dribble which was taken up by the visiting forwards. Who spoiled themselves by kicking behind. Chadwick tried a long shot which was well saved by Jackson, Chadwick, and Brown ran and passed, Chadwick finished with a shot which went wide. A Red hot scrimmage took place in front of the Bootle upright, nothing tangible resulted, and fouls became the order of the day. Bootle had a turn after pretty play Galbraith passed Farmer and Holt turning the leather over to Jamieson, who was enabled to beat Smalley for the third time. Play became very exciting, Everton putting all in to wipe out the deficit. Bootle not to be denied met the onslaught plucky, and Ross had to concede a corner, which, being well placed, Smalley had to fist out a good shot. Hasting made a grand single handed dribble down the left Dobson spoiled him, and Davies who had gone centre raced up the centre in fine style. McFarlane proved the stumbling-block Bootle had for some time the best of the argument the leather rarely going over the centre. At length the pressure was removed but not for long, Bootle pressing again without result. Dobson removed the venue and Everton had the bad luck to have a goal disallowed for offside. They quickly had their revenge for Ross kicking to Davies that player neatly headed Everton's second goal. Bootle at once from the kick off attacked Everton's goal, Smalley having to save several good shots. The leather being kicked over the bar. Everton in turn were shooting, Watson disappointing the Evertonians by kicking high over the bar. The kick out brought no relief McFarlane having to concede an abortive corner. Another corner quickly fell to Everton with the same result as the last. Everton were now having all the game. Holt tried a long shot, which was easily cleared by Jackson. At length the game was made even; Milward racing up the centre turned over to Brown, who promptly shot in, past Jackson making the score three all.

## EVERTON RESERVES 3 AINTREE CHURCH 0
*March 11, 1889. The Liverpool Courier.*

This fixture came off on Saturday on the former's ground. At four o'clock the teams faced each other as follows: - Everton Reserves: - C. Joliffe, goal, A. Chadwick, and J. Connor backs, C. Weir, H. Pollock (captain), and T. Fayer, half-backs, J. Angus, R. Brown, D. Waugh, W. Briscow, and J. Keys, forwards. Aintree Church: - Morris goal, E. Jones and Taylor, backs, Ray, Jones, and Nidd, half-backs, Maskin, Shaw, Gorncok, Roberts and J. Jones, forwards. The home team were successful in the spin, and Aintree started at 4-30 with the sun facing them. Nidd stopped a dangerous rush by Briscoe and Rays, Roberts, and Jones taking the leather into the Everton custodian, Chadwick cleared. Again obtaining possession Ray pulling him up. Everton then became aggressive Waugh exhibiting good play, and caused the Church custodian to save, which he did smartly. The home forwards gave Nidd and Taylor plenty to do. The Everton forwards again troubled Morris who was successful in repelling a shot from Pollock. Jones then conceded a corner which Angus kicked to high. At length the forwards had a splendid chance and from a pass by Waugh, Keys scored the first goal with a terrific shot. The Custodian had not a look in. At half-time Everton were 1 goal to nil.

On resuming play Roberts rushed the leather into the Reserves quarters but was soon returned Waugh obtained possession and caused Taylor to concede a corner. For a short period the Reserves fairly penned the Churchites, Jones and Roberts eventually breaking away and called upon Joliffe to clear a shot from Curnock. The slouchy state of the ground plainly told on the visitors, who were continually rolling in their mud. Everton now put in a determined rush, and from the corner rushed their second point through. Shortly afterwards the Reserves were dangerous near Morris, and forced him to concede a corner to clear his charge which proved futile. The Churh played very hard managing to press the Reserves defence, and obtained a corner, which was worked away by Chadwick. Waugh was next conspicuous, and passing to Briscoe he added another goal to their credit. Final Result; Everton Reserves 3 goals, Aintree nil.

## EVERTON 2 HALLIWELL 0
*March 181889. The Liverpool Courier.*

Gloomy football weather favor this important contest on the Anfield enclosure on Saturday. The Halliwell team, although not one of the most powerful Lancashire teams have a good representative eleven, and have fought excellent fights with a number of the league club's. This is the second time this season that they have met this seaport combination. In the first match played in September last Mr. Goulding's eleven were beaten by the narrow majority of two goals to one. The team that represented Everton consisted principally of those who are ineligible to compete in the Lancashire cup tie. The forward division was fairly strong, but the defence was not equal to the standard of an Everton first team, the absence of Dick, the popular full-back, being keenly felt, especially when the Halliwell man got in close quarters. It will be a matter of congratulation to those who take an interest in the Everton club to know that although the accident Dick received at Sunderland was of a rather serious nature, he is now able to walk about, and it is expected will take his place in the team in a few weeks. At 3-45 the Everton team put in an appearance, Ross receiving a very cordial reception. The Bolton team, were rather late. There would be about 6,000 spectators present. Ross having won the toss, McGuinnes kicked off at 4-05 against a very strong breeze, and facing a drizzling rain. The visitors started with ten men. After good exchange in midfield Crombie put in a fine run his shot going over. A couple of fine throws by Weir, close in the Halliwell goal looked dangerous, the ball going outside from a long kick by Robb. "Hands" against Wilson enabled Halliwell to clear their lines, but Powell returned the ball. Wilson was now conspicuous in robbing McGuiness and passing to Waugh, the Everton forward broke away in combined run. The visiting backs relieved the pressure. Hewitson and Russell ran down the left, but a claim for off-side put an end to the invasion. Nidd, McDougall returning the ball initiated another spirited attack. The visiting van forced the pace on the left, Ross heading clear on the goal line. Everton again came to the fore. Fairclough rushed out of his goal, and evidently came off second best in a tussle with Davies. Everton were now favoured with a corner, which was taken by Davies, but the wind carried the ball over the bar. From the kick off Halliwell worked the sphere to midfield, the Everton halves returning, the ball going over-from a shot by Milward. Good passing by the Everton forwards again troubled the Halliwell defence, until Durham ran down the wing, Ross kicking out to save. Another fine run by Davis, and a pass to Milward caused Fairclough to handle. This was repeated a minute later from a capital shot by Angus. Ross returned into the Helliwell goalmouth, Watson missing a splendid chance by shooting over the bar. McDougall put in a fine shot at the other end. Joliffe saving grandly. Halliwell kept up the pressure, until Angus and Waugh with a spirited run changed the venue. Fairclough now saved two splendid shots from Wilson and Waugh, from the latter he was forced to concede a corner, which was taken by Davis, Milward, heading through amidst applause. From the kick off Milward ran up the centre and finished up with a fine shot just skimmed the bar. The visiting forwards improved considerably, McDougall heading out. From the throw in Davies forced his way-up the right, Fairclough saving a fine screw from Watson, Russell and Hewitson rushed down the left, Joliffe saving at the expense of a corner which proved abortive. Waugh passed by Angus, who ran up the left, Durham kicking out to save. From the throw in by Weir, Milward experienced hard lines in the goalmouth. A miskick by Wilson let in McGuinness, who ran down the centre, Nidd recovering the lost ground by a timely kick. Good passing by the visitors caused Joliffe to handle. This was followed by a capital sprint by Milward, he passed to Watson being intercepting by Robb, who kicked clear. Everton had now the advantage of a couple of corners, from the latter of which the ball almost passed through. One of the Halliwell backs was penalised for foul play, the free kick going over the line. Ross experienced some difficulty in stopping the Halliwell right, but Weir came to the rescue and passed to Watson, who called upon Fairclough to save. Milward showed up prominently, a shot from Weir just missing the mark. From the kick-out McGuinness put in a fine run, and finished up with a warm shot that struck the upright. Good heading by Waugh  and Watson gave Davis an opening but he allowed the ball to go outside. Another corner to Everton followed, which was worked clear, Ross returned, and Milward was again unfortunate. The ball still kept in the Halliwell quarters, Faircloorh saving when surrounded by several of his opponents. Wilson beautifully stopped a fine dribble by Russell. Durham returned, and Ross conceded a corner. This was followed by a free kick for "hands" against Wilson. Milward with a strong kick removing the danger. Ross took a free kick, and again Davies had a fine chance, the ball going outside. A warm scrimmage was formed in the Halliwell goal, Waugh missed a fine chance by kicking over the bar. Half-time Everton 1 Halliwell nil.

After the usual respite Milward restarted the game, Fairclough receiving a good reception at the other end. The Halliwell forward got well up, the ball eventually going out. Halliwell were again to the fore, Hewitson shooting wide. Ross relieved, and the Everton forwards raced down the field Waugh kicking rather wide. Bobby Watson elicited the plaudits of the crowd for a splendid run down the right. Fairclough conceded another corner, which was nicely placed by Nidd, Durham removed the play to midfield, where Wilson passed to Davis who scored a second goal for the home club. The Halliwell left wing pair showed up prettily. Russell shot clean into Joliffe's hands. A long kick by Ross enabled Milward to break away, McDougall robbing him when matters looked ominous for the visitor. Russell and Hewitson removed the venue to Joliffe's charge. Russell shot over, when he had the goal at his mercy. Another raid was made upon the Everton fortress, but errac shooting spoiled several excellent chances of scoring "Hands" against the stripes was well taken up by Waugh, the sphere going over from the foot of Angus. The Visiting forwards became very aggressive, shot after shot was sent only to find the home defence equal to the demand made upon them. Waugh got the better of Durham and passing to Davis he in turn sent a beautiful shot which took Fairclough all his time to save Wilson renewed the attack Fairclough being charged over the line by Milward. The

subsequent corner proved fruitless. Ross was again called upon
to clear, Joliffe being compelled to concede a corner, which was
got away by Waugh and Milward with a fine run. Ross now
stopped a further raid, Crombie allowed a splendid opportunity
to pass. Milward put in the finest run of the day down the left,
Watson just missing the goal. A foul for Everton in front of goal
was taken by Weir and worked clear by the visiting backs. Nidd
threw in to Ross but the ball rebounding McGuinness rushed up
the field. Powell relieving on the goal line. Halliwell pressed,
but could not break through the fine defence of the Everton
backs. The official whistle sounded, leaving Everton winners
by 2 goals to none.

**Everton: C. Joliffe, goal, J. Powell , and JN. Ross (captain)
backs, W. Wilson, Weir, and F. Nidd, half-backs, J. Davies,
R. Watson, A. Milward, D. Waugh, and JW.Angus forwards.
Halliwell: - Fairclough goal Lucas, and Robb backs,
Derham, Scowcroft, and McDougall, half-backs, Crombie,
Hay, Russell, Hewitson and McGuinness forwards.**

## HIGHER WALTON  3  EVERTON X1   1
*March 18, 1889. The Liverpool Courier.*

Lancashire cup semi-final
This match was played on the ground of the Rovers at Blackburn
in dull weather. The ground was soft in consequence of a slight
fall of rain. About 1,500 spectators assembled to witness the
match. The Everton club had previously relied on almost entirely
Reserve strength to pull it through but on Saturday there were
several of the first team men included. This was advisable, as
Higher Walton only a few weeks ago defeated the Blackburn
Rovers by 4 goals to 3. When at halt-time the Rovers were 3
to 1. A start was made at half-past three, and the Walton boys
diligently went to their work, giving the opposing backs no
little trouble. These were, however, equal to the task, and by

their aid play was retained mostly in mid-field, from whence Everton made occasion attacks which were not particularly dangerous. At length Chadwick and Costley had a chance, and by nicely dodging their opponents an opening was found, but Chadwick assayed a shot which the goal-keeper cleared before Costley could get up in time to complete the effort. Everton were still having the best of matters, and kept the play close to the Walton goal, Fair having a shot which went over. Rain now again descended, Higher Walton then became pressing in their attention, and a not remarkably fast shot was sent in, Smalley did not succeed in his endeavour to pick the ball up, and consequently gave it a kick, which Mather spoiled and headed the leather through, a fest which gave pleasure to the majority of the spectators, judging by the uproar. The ensuing play was of a derisory and uninteresting nature, Chadwick now and then betraying a too great regard for retaining the globe. By good forward work, and especially so on the left wing, Costley had an apparently good slight at shooting, but he failed to take advantage of it. Then came some exciting play at the opposite end after Higher Walton had gained a corner. J.Mather struck the crossbar, and then a good shot from the left wing went over the bar. A few minutes later the centre-forward shot a fine goal. Half-time Higher Walton 2 goals Everton nil.

Upon the resumption of the play the Waltonians assumed the aggressive and W.Mather mulled a grand opportunity. Fleming afterwards sprinted down the right, the ball however, going over the line, and Briscoe was at this point hurt and obliged to retire. The Evertonians were now playing with more spirit, and several good attempts were made to place the game on an equal footing. The Walton custodian being tried was not found wanting. Briscoe returned to the scene, and then Costley, was placed here for combat for a few moments. A capital front rank movement on Everton's part a little later Edgar Chadwick scoring with a rattling shot. Costley now being incapable of further exertion was obliged to leave the field, from a free kick which fell to the Waltonians the ball was shot in front of goal, and J.Mather scored a splendid goal. Later on Chadwick shot, almost scored. Final result Higher Walton 3 goals Everton 1 goal. **Teams: - Smalley, goal, Dobson (captain), and A. Chadwick backs, Fayer, Holt, and Farmer, half-backs, Fleming Briscoe, W. Brown, E. Chadwick and Costley forwards. Higher Walton: - Chatman, goal, Ose, and Daly backs, T. Taylor, Spencer and Baldwin half-backs, T. Mather, Oddon, W. Mather, E. Naylor, and T. Naylor, forwards.**

### EVERTON 3 SOUTH SHORE 0
*March 25, 1889. The Liverpool Courier.*

The champion team of the Blackpool district made their first appearance this season on the Anfield enclosure on Saturday. The previous encounter between the home club, and the visitors have generally been of a very even character when played at Everton, but like most of the leading organisations of the country, when the Liverpool representative have visited the Blackpool ground they have had to retire defeated. In fair, two years Everton with a good team were beaten by seven goals to two by the South Shore men. The visitors are a fine body of men, and although their game cannot be classed as scientific, they play with considerable dash and speed. The teams were 35 minutes behind time in taking up their positions in the field this being due to the late arrival of the visitors. Both teams were well received, Ross and Wilson being the recipients of a very cordial greeting from the crowd which numbered about 4,000. Ross having lost the toss, W.Wilson, who took the place of Milward in the centre, kicked off down the hill and against the wind. The home forwards immediately became aggressive, Langley saving a capital shot from Watson a minute from the start. R.Elston put in a fine dribble up the left. Holt cleared, Parkinson renewed

the attack. Smalley just caught a fine screw shot from Cookson. "Hands" against Holt looked dangerous and Dobson cleared with a fine punt. A good combined run by the home team was brought into play at the other end, where Chadwick caused Langley to use his hand. Hacking initiated another dangerous rush. Holt transferred the sphere to Watson, who shot wide. Everton had the advantage of another free kick taken by Ross, which was nicely placed, but was worked over the line by the right wing. A similar fate attended a corner kick a few minutes afterwards. The visiting right broke away, Ross misjudged his kick, and a corner was conceded which proved abortive. From a kick-off a grand forward movement was shown by Farmer, Chadwick and Waugh, which resulted in a further corner kick being taken by Farmer, who landed the ball well in front of Wilson who defeated Langley with a high shot. The visiting team appeared too smart under the reverse, and infused a lot of dash, a grand run by Hacking being beautifully nipped in the bud by a timely kick by Dobson. Holt robbed the visitors centre, and passing to Davies, he put in one of his terrific runs and finished up with a splendid shot which just missed scoring. Waugh and Chadwick put Everton on the attack Gosling relieving his lines by kicking over. The subsequent corner proved effective. The visitors had the best of the play for some time. Ross displaying marvelous defensive tactics in keeping his goal intact. Wilson came to the relief of his backs, and dribbled down the centre and passing to Davies the ought to have made a better attempt than he did of the opportunity offered. Encouragement by the cheers of their supporters, the Everton left forced a passage down the field, a shot from Chadwick being well-cleared by Langley, who a minute latter saved from Waugh. Elston retaliated with splendid sprint. Dobson cleared with a grand header. Edgar Chadwick ran the length of the field, Langley saving his shot with a grand punt. Half-time Everton 1; South Shore 0.
After the usual respite Cookson, put the ball in motion, and

passing to Parkinson a warm tussle ensued in front of the home upright, Ross and Dobson removing the danger with some fine kicking. Davies responded with a grand run up the home right. Watson shot over the bar. Play was confirmed to midfield until Watson relieved the monotony by passing his opponents. Wilson by judicious passing brought the play into the Shore goalmouth. Chadwick took another corner, the ball dropping amongst the Everton forwards, Watson scoring a second goal out of the scrimmage. Ross now negotiated a fine bit of passing by the visiting left, and passing to Watson he ought to have eased the score, but shot high over the bar. Dobson now came in for some well merited applause for the superb tackling, and putting his forwards in position, Wilson forced another corner from which Moore put the ball through his own goal. Chadwick with an overhead kick, gave Waugh another chance, his final effort going outside. Everton now held the upper hand but erractic shooting spoiled more than one chance of scoring. The visiting backs, in defending their goal, made a frequent use of their hands, and several free kicks were awarded, from the latter of which a goal was claimed but not conceded. Towards the end Chadwick became prominent a shot from the foot being headed clear by Gosling. This brought full time. Final; result Everton 3 South Shore 0,

**Everton: - Smalley, goal, Dobson, and Ross (captain), backs, weir, Holt, and Farmer, half-backs, Davies, Watson, Chadwick, Waugh, and W. Wilson, forwards. South Shore: - Langley, goal, Gosling, and E. Moore, backs, J. Watson, E. Sharples, and Wash (r), half-backs, A. Hacking, Richards Elston Roberts Elston, A. Parkinson, and H. Cookson, forwards.**

## CHESTER COLLEGE 1 EVERTON RESERVES 2
*March 26, 1889. The Liverpool Courier.*

This return fixture should have taken place on the Anfield road enclosure, but as the first team had induced the South Shore down, Stockton's boys journeyed to Chester and after a fairly even game won by 2 goals to 1. At the close they were very hospitably entertained by the Collegians and finished up a very pleasant day out with a musical evening, Messier WP Baylee and W Kearton being with the visitors, rendered several musical pieces all highly enjoyed. The Reserves seem to be great favourites at Chester.

## EVERTON 4 SOUTHPORT CENTRAL 1
*March 28, 1889. The Liverpool Courier.*

The return fixture between these teams was decided at Anfield yesterday, evening, there being only a small attendance of spectators. Everton kicked off against a slight wind. The Central forwards took up the attack, Duncan shooting wide of the posts. From the kick-out the Everton left dashed down, the field, and from a screw shot by Chadwick, Watson scored the first goal for the home team. Shortly afterwards Chadwick missed when right in front, and Shaw cleared the danger. The Visiting forwards now put in a neat run to the Everton goal, Graham shooting across without effect. Play now became even, the Central showing very good form, Horton especially furnishing a fine display at half-back. Davies and Watson dribbled down the Everton right Les giving a "corner" which however, was futile. A hot attack of the home forwards was well met by Hodgkinson, who transferred play to the centre. The home goal was next the scene of hostilities. Weir punted the misfield, but Shaw returned, and several shot were aimed at the Everton goal, none of which took effect. Ross cleared the danger with a long kick, and from a shot by Watson, Shaw gave a "corner". From the kick out of goal, Fecitt dribbled down the centre, and the Central left gave Dobson a serious amount of trouble. Ross however, relieved, but Graham and Duncan returned with the result that the scores were equalised. Harrison had a rare chance of scoring but failed. Milward dribbled finely, Gee clearing just as the whistle was blown for half time the score standing one goal each. Facitt having restarted on behalf of the Central rush was at once made for the Southport goal, Farmer sending in a neat shot, which Gee cleared. Following a dash on the part of the Central left the home forwards took play in front of their opponents goal. Milward sent in a stinging shot, which Gee cleverly saved. Watson, however, rushed up and scored a second goal for the home side. The Evertonians still kept up a hot attack on the Southport citadel, but although Milward and Chadwick were busy the shots were cleverly dealt with by Gee. At length Chadwick sent in a shot almost from the centre, which the Central custodian allowed to roll through his legs. Everton still kept an incessant and harassing attack, their forwards crowding in front of the Central goal. From a scrimmage Sugg shot the ball, striking the bar. The same player, however, headed through, notching the fourth point for the homesters. A run down by the Central forwards was spoiled by "hands". Play again verged in front of the visitors "sticks" Gee knocking out a shot from the feet of Chadwick. J.Weir then made a grand attempt to score, the ball dropping right in front of the Central goal. The danger was cleared, and the Southport forwards spurted to the other end of the field, and Joliffe, in attempting to clear, gave a "corner" from a long shot by Sugg, Gee fisted out only just in time. Everton were now having all the best of the play. Ross standing in goal with his coat on. The Central gained a corner kick, but no further point was scored, and the central were beaten by four goals to one. **The following are the teams: - Southport Central: - Gee, goal, Hodgkinson,**

and J. Shaw, backs, J. Horton, C. Weir, and Les, half-backs,
Harrison, Mullen, Facitt, Graham, and Duncan forwards.
Everton: - Joliffe, goal, Dobson, and Ross (captain), backs,
Farmer, Sugg, and J. Weir, half-backs, Waugh, Chadwick,
Milward, Watson, and J. Davies, forwards.

# *APRIL 1889*

## EVERTON 3 BLACKBURN ROVERS 1 (Game 22)
*April 3,1889. The Liverpool Courier.*

For some time past the Liverpool football community has
manifested a considerable amount of interest in this important
match. The teams have already tried play twice this season in
the League contest. The first match was played at Blackburn
last November, when the Everton boys were defeated by 3 goals
to nil, and the return match arranged to be played at Anfield in
January last, but when the teams came on the field it was found
that the frost had made the ground very dangerous and it was
decided to play a game, but whatever the result might be the
match was to be declared a draw. The game ended in Everton
victorious by 1 goal to nil, subsequently the league committee
refused to uphold the decision and ordered the match to be
replayed. It was a matter of extreme regret that Everton were
deprived of the services of Ross, who was unable to play owing
to an indiposition his absent been keenly felt. There was about
6,000 spectators present. When Everton kicked the ball off at
3-35. The ground was at very odd conditions, but soon after the
game commenced the rain stopped falling. Everton pressed at the
opening and shot gaining a corner, which could not be improved.
The homesters continued to have the best of matters and Milward
nearly shot over, and the same player retaining capital form put
the ball through, a claim for off-side being disallowed. Then the
Rovers became somewhat more conspicous, and a number of
shots were but along none of them, however, being close enough
to cause an excitement. A few minutes later though the visitors
had a free kick close to goal, and from this they equalised the
score. Holt was damaged, and went way for a few minutes,
being able to return to his place. Chadwick showed some good
play, and making one or two long kicks, Waugh attempted a shot

some distances from the goal, but just failed in his endeavor. An exciting dash was made towards the Rovers goal just before half-time, Milward and Brown appearing as if they would pop the ball through, but Davies spoiled the affair, and half-time arrived with the score Everton 1; Blackburn Rovers 1.

Shortly after the restart Holt made a beautiful shot, the ball just being headed out by Southworth, but the sooner had it been done, then, Waugh neatly kicked through. Everton were playing in good style, and were decidedly having the best of the tussle. Forbes was penalised for tripping Brown when close to the Rovers goal, from the free kick Davies added to the score. Things began to get very warm about the Rovers goal, Chadwick made an opening through, and travelled well up the field Townley was putting in some splendid runs down the left, whilst Wilson for Everton, was defending very finely. Haresnape made the Evertonians then charged Smalley, Townley just previously kicked over. Brown and Davis played up well, in a splendid run along the right and Forbes got back to the former and struck to his. Brown being away and shot through, the referee had however blown his whistle, and a good piece of play was devoid of result. Barton later on charged Waugh when the ball was elsewhere. Waugh fixed the Rovers half-back altogether, and there was further suffering and pleasant banter and shelf. Brown, Davies, and Waugh had spanking shots at the Rovers custodian, Arthur fisting away, Jim Southworth a Rovers back, had gone away, and Douglas filled his place. Final score Everton 3 Blackburn Rovers one. **Teams, Everton:- Smalley goal, Wilson, and Dobson (captain), backs, Farmer, Holt, and Weir half-backs Waugh, Chadwick, Milward, Brown, Davies forwards. Blackburn Rovers: - Arthur goal, Jim Southworth, and Forbes, backs, Barton, Douglas, and Forrest, half-backs, Beresford, Jack Southworth (Captain), Haresnape, Whittaker, and Townley forwards.**

## EVERTON 8 EARLESTOWN 2
*April 4, 1889. The Liverpool Courier.*

These teams met at the Anfield enclosure last evening. Wretched weather prevailed and only 500 persons witnessed the match. Earsletown were minus Sims and Fazackerley whilst Everton lacked the services of Ross, Holt, Watson, and Smalley, Everton kicked off, but the visitors were the first to attack, Nidd clearing the danger with a timely kick. Waugh and Chadwick made a nice run along the Everton left, and after some neat passing Farmer scored the first point for the homesters. From the centre-kick the visitors attacked, where upon Wilson put in some fine play, and they were repulsed. Waugh was again prominent, and sent in a hot shot, which Champion put through his goal thus recording the second point for Everton. The homesters were thus early having the best of the play, until a run by the Earlestown left placed the home goal in danger, J.Shaw sent in a grand shot which Farmer put over the line. Waugh cleared the ball from the corner kick, and the Everton forwards raced down the field, with the result that Davies topped the bar. A few minutes later the same player defeated Champion with a spendid screw shot right off' "touch" The Earlestown van were next prominent, a corner kick accuring to them. This proved futile, and at the other end Champion saved on his knees whist Weir sent in a spanker, which pressed outside the upright. Chadwick then notched a fourth point, which aroused the visitors who rushed down, W.Shaw scoring. Brown retaliated for Everton and at half-time the home players led by five goals to two. At the "half" only lasted thirty minutes, the scoring progressed at the taste of a goal in a trivia over four minutes play. Earlestown restarted, and Milward raced down the centre until Green robbed him. The home forwards, however, returned and Farmer took a "corner" which proved futile. Everton had much the best of play, which was mainly located round the Earlestown goal. As many as a dozen shots were sent in, but the ball went anywhere but between the posts. Following a raid by the Earsletown, forwards, Davies shot a sixth goal for the home side. Waugh next gave Champion a "handful" which he had the utmost difficulty in clearing in time. Wilson played a splendid back game for the home side, and repeatedly mopped dangerous rushes of the Ealerstown forwards. Chadwick shot a seventh goal for the Evertonians, who were playing in grand form. Weir again shot through the Earlestown goal, but the point was disallowed. Brown then rushed down the Everton right, and centering grandly, Waugh notched the eighth goal. Everton pressed during the remainder of the game, but failed to score any further points. Earlestown thus retiring beaten by 8 goals to 2. **Teams; Everton:- Joliffe goal, Dobson (captain), and Wilson, backs. Farmer, Weir, and Nidd, half-backs, Davies, Waugh, Chadwick, Milward, and Brown, forwards. Earlestown: - Champion, goal, Green and Jones, backs, Johnson, Howell, and Allison halfbacks, J. Shaw, W. Shaw, Conray, and Siddeley forwards.**

## EVERTON 4 WITTON 1
*April 8, 1889. The Liverpool Mercury.*

Everton encountered Witton for the first time this season at Anfield and quite 7,000 enthusiasts were present. Ross again absent, but his place was successfully filled by W.Wilson partnering Dobson. A new man was tried in the person of A.Parry (Chest St Oswald's), who seemed to satisfy the followers of the home club with his consistent and accurate passing to his right partner. Witton, who kept the crowd waiting 40 minutes came with their full strength. Dobson won the toss, and taking advantage of the slight-wind, kicked towards Stanley end. Grimshaw set the ball going, and soon Parry caused Sharples to throw out, a well judged shot. Coming again. Holt had the misfortune to handle, and the visitors getting down from the free kick, Rushton missed his mark. From the goal the home left, and centre did a grand rush towards Sharples, and Milward, unfortunately was ruled offside. Nothing daunting, Everton again were aggressive and after Wilson pluckily staved off Rushton, Sharples had to negotiable attempt from Davies and Chadwick. The visitors, who still kept pegging on, got towards Smalley, and Wilson put in a timely save from Smith, and placing the ball well up the field, Milward got possession and scored the first goal for the homesters. After this Witton strove hard to get on level terms, but failed to break through the defence of Dobson and Wilson, who enabled their side to hold the upper hand, and Farmer narrowly escaped notching another point. After the visiting custodian had attended to Parry, Isherwood sent in a scorcher to Smalley, who saved in a business-like style, a performance which Sharples initiated four times just on half-time. On charging ends, the spectators showed their admiration of the clever tactics of the visiting custodian by a hearty round of applause, which was the least that, could have been meted out to him. Milward restarted, and the Everton right were not long in getting down, but Davies failed to find another opening. The visitors mometarily held the reins, but Wilson proved himself equal to Turner and Horsefield by neatly robbing them when ominous looking and then Sharples was called upon by Waugh, responding in good style by throwing out the shot in clearing, which Smith handled the leather close in the goal mouth and from the free kick Farmer very cleverly added a second goal. Play still continued fast, considering the soft state of the ground, and Davies hit the crossbar, followed by Sharples escaping to the corner in steering a good aim by Milward. Rushton was again conspcouous and nicely eluding Wilson, had the goal at his mercy, but was yards off the mark. Amends however were made, Horsefield beating Smalley for the first time with a very easy shot. Everton, who seemed to be anxious to obtain as many goals as that scored against Witton the previous week infused more life into the game, and Farmer added a third point whilst Milward attended the goalkeeper, a feat performed by Parry but without success a minute later. As a final attempt, the strangers well fed by Iserwood, strove hard to increase, but found the home defence impregnable and just on the call of time Parry added the fourth goal for Everton, greatly to the delight of the spectators, who seemed to be proud of the capabilities of the last acquision to the team. Result Everton 4 goals Witton 1 goal. **Teams; Everton: - Smalley, goal, Dobson (captain), and Wilson, backs, Farmer, Holt, and Weir, half-backs, Davies, A. Parry, Milward, Chadwick, and Waugh, forwards. Witton: - Sharples, goal, J. Smith, and Shorrock, backs, Alston, Isherwood, Pickering, half-backs, Ruston, H. Smith, Grimshaw, Horsefield, and Turner, forwards.**

## AIGBURTH VALE 3 EVERTON RESERVES 4
*April 8, 1889. The Liverpool Courier.*

This interesting fixture fought out at Fulwood Park in gloomy weather and attended by only a few spectators. Everton kicked off at five minutes past four, and the home backs were soon busy, Jackson having to fist out two or three shots. Aigburth pressed and from a corner warm work followed, Joliffe setting out twice but being beaten at the third attempt by Tibbott, the goal giving great satisfaction to the spectators. From the kick off Angus had a chance, but he shot wide. Tibbott then headed a second notch from a scrimmage and the game got very lively. A corner to Everton was well centered by Nidd, an offside goal resulting. Hendry making a fine sharp shot at the other end, which however, just went outside, succeeded a wide shot by Weir. Another corner to Aigburth gave the same player a second chances, which the afore mentioned accepted in fine style, heading the ball through and adding goal No.3. Weir afterwards sent in a beauty, which Jackson failed to negotiate thus making the game one to three. Several corners to the visitors ended in Everton centering nicely and Weir heading another point for his side. After some minutes close work in the home goal against the homesters nearly proved an equaliser, but Jackson just got the ball away. At this point Everton had the best of the game, and Angus made the game 3 all with a fine oblique kick very low down. Score at half-time Everton reserves 3 goals Aigburth Vale 3 goals.

Resuming Everton pressed, and showed much the better combination a few minutes from the restart, and after a sustained improvement of the home goal, Robinson helped the ball through the upridge putting the visitors a goal to the good. Aigburth broke away once or twice, but the vistoring backs held their opponents well in check. Roberts played a fine game for his side, and was very prominent all through. The home team weakened and could scarely get on level terms with the visitors. Tibbott put in good work, but nothing came of it, the ball being chiefly in Aigburth quarters. Everton took a corner and Aigburth cleared. Nidd and Weir put in some good long kicking and Peers did similar work. Briscoe put in a warm handful, which Jackson got away, but the game was continued near the Aigburth goal. Final result Everton 4 goals Aigburth Vale 3 goals.

**EVERTON REVIEW**
*April 8, 1889. The Liverpool Mercury.*

Everton have apparently struck the right chord at last, and the the improving tendency of the forwards week by week bids fair to see the attack as uniformly strong as the defence has all along been. This week they have added two more victories of an unequivocal kind to their record- that of Earlestown by 8 goals to 2 on Wednesday, and again over Witton on Saturday by 4 goals to 1. It so happened that Bootle have recently met those two particular clubs, and on the eve of a certain interesting event it is impossible to refrain from indulging has it long since been proclaimed, "ardoruous" Bootle made a draw with Witton, and were only 5 goals to 3 better than Earlestown in the cup tie. These figures speak in favour of Everton. Of Everton's latest success, however, it was not a good game-not nearly so entertaining as the Earlestown match, when Everton's forwards were seen as they have not been seen of late-but this defect is to be attributed to the slippery state of the ground, which indeed, was flooded in places. The home team are stronger in physique than the visitors, and on the heavy "turf" the weight told effectively the Wittonians who were fast on the dry ground at Bootle, being now too slow for their heavier Anfield opponents. Play thus despite the clever all-round tactics of Witton went all in favour of Everton, and had the shooting been as accurate as the forwards were powerful in their raids, the score would have been a record one. Sharples delighted everyone with his prowess between the posts; he was relieved in a great measure by Smith, though Shorrock was almost as safe a back. Each set of halves were about equally effective Isherwood being about a match for Holt who played one of his best games though lame. Dobson and Wilson did their work well, and there is a great confidence in the department as when in other charge. Smalley had few opportunities of displaying his form. The Everton forwards were on the whole highly satisfactory, the left wing proving very strong. Davies had a new partner in Parry of Chester St Oswald's but on such a ground he had hardly a fair opportunity of showing his full worth. The wing was certainly not so effective as the one in charge of Chadwick and Waugh. Parry was very free in passing to Davies; a little more attention to Milward would have made his efforts telling.

**SOUTH SHORE 4 EVERTON 1**
*April 8, 1889*
No details.

# EVERTON X1 7 NORTHWICH VICTORIA 1
*April 11, 1889. The Liverpool Mercury.*

These teams met at Anfield last evening, before about 1,000 spectators. The home club depended almost entirely upon reserves men apparently saving their senior players for the Bootle match. The ground was in a muddy condition, but play was carried on briskly right from the start. Northwich were the first to become dangerous, but were stalled off easily, and Everton attacked strongly on both wings Angus scoring after a few minutes play. Fallows was nearly beaten two or three times in quick succession and after a flying visit to Joliffe, Parry and Milward went down in grand style the latter running close up and shooting the second goal. Everton returned to goal, repeatedly, Cross intercepting smartly when Parry and Brown had assumed a menacing attitude. There was no keeping the home forwards backs and a moment later Parry shot through, whilst Milward charged Fallows. The next goal came from Briscoe, who put through from a corner forced by Milward and placed by Angus. Two other goals followed within a few minutes Angus and Parry being the pilots, and at half-time Everton were leading by 6 goals to nil. The visitors backs proving no sort of barrier to the strong and well combined forwards runs of the home team. On Milward restarting, Victoria right wing broke away with the wind at their backs, but were pulled up by Chadwick and Pollock, and Fallows soon had to chuck clear from the right wing. Chadwick attended another breakaway to, and then Fallows was in two minds, though he cleared. A strong run by Northwich's right wing and down the centre took play in close proximity to Joliffe who was defeated by leather, an appeal for off-side not being entertained. The visitors brightened up just now and made the game more even, travelling once or twice quite powerfully at the home team. Everton, however, towards the close again assumed control and Angus running hard and centering Milward just managed a goal near the post, after an exciting scrimmage. Parry trying a shot of some merit in the renewed attack. In the waning light the home team moved often to goal in nice combination, but in the last moments or so the visitors gave trouble. No flaw was to be found in the Everton defence however, the result being:- Everton 7 goals Northwich Victoria 1 goal. **Teams. Northwich Victoria:- Fallows goal Maddock, and Cross, backs, Hankey Whitlow, and Dalton, half-backs, Rowbottom, Leather, Golden, Upton. And Pickering forwards. Everton: - Joliffe, goal, Chadwick (a), H. Pollock (Captain), backs, F. Nidd, W. Wilson, and R. Jones, half-backs, W. Brown, Parry, Milward, W. Briscow, and Angus forwards. Referee H.McIntyre.**

## EVERTON 1 BOOTLE 2
*April 15, 1889. The Liverpool Mercury.*

The third meeting of Everton and Bootle, which took place at Anfield on Saturday aroused all the interest of the two previous contests, and despite the increased tariff, there was the same dense crowd of about 10,000 spectators. The weather though threatening fortunately proved fine, and the ground, it was still muddy in places, was in a greatly improved condition to that of the previous Wednesday. Punctually at four o'clock Ross led his men on the field, followed immediately by Jamieson and his colleagues, both teams being popularly received. Bootle had two alterations compared with the eleven that played in the last match. Jardine displaced Jackson in goal, and Jones partnered Hasting. Morris playing centre half in place of Hughes. The changes in the Everton team were, Waugh, Wilson, and Parry also Brown, Holt and Watson, respectively. Mr Fitzroy Norris having addressed the players everything was in order for a start. Jamieson prompt to time kicked off, and Bootle at once moved uphill in spite of the wind against them. Wilson held Wood in check when going well, but the visitors were not yet stalled off, as Hasting returned on the left, and compelled Dobson to kick out. Keeping at close quarters, a free kick fell to Bootle, which was placed by MacFarlane, from which Wood centered nicely to Jamieson who beat Smalley and placed Bootle in the lead three minutes from the start. Before the ovation subsided Parry, Milward and Davies were away in strong combination and severely defeated MacFarlane and Woods, the shots by Chadwick and Parry being in one case wide, and in the other too high. Again the home team grew threatening. MacFarlane adroitly intercepting a splendid centre by Chadwick and then Jamieson led a rush which brought forth a clever defensive feat on the part of Ross, Davies at once replied in a dashing run, finishing with such a good pass to Parry that McFarlane deemed it essential to step across to kick out. Everton proclaim a series of exciting scrimmages in goal, Jardine fisted out coolly. Allsopp headed another critical movement, and all the visitors stood up manfully until relief came on the left. Hasting put over the bar, and with this let off Everton soon took up the bombardment in earnest Davies going behind from a corner, and Milward being just off the post in a shot taken at an easy position. A good run by Hasting and Jones shifted the venue, and a passing run, in which each of the five forwards had touched the ball improved the outlook for Bootle but Ross was on the alert to prevent mischief, as he did when MacFarlane placed accurately from Chadwick's foul of Allsopp near goal. Waugh came to the rescue in a neat dribble to Milward, who beat Allsopp but found himself foiled by Campbell, the latter driving on to the roof of the long stand. Farmer broke through from the throw in, and gave Chadwick an opening but the Blackburn man banged wildly over the bar, and on Farmer again dodging up Campbell was just to smart enough to divert Waugh's shot. Davies a moment later overrunning himself from a Wilson pass. Chadwick also received from Wilson, and tried a low shot which MacFarlane was keen enough to see would pass harmlessly out if left alone. Ross next risked a corner in attending to Wood, a corner falling to Everton soon afterwards. Play just now ran on even lines, culminating in Jardine carrying the ball out of his prescribed boundary. An exciting tussle arose from the free kick, Hasting eventually clearing. Further scrimmages were pitched in front of goal, and after Jardine had scooped away when on his knees, a sterling bit of play by Parry, Davies and Waugh was too clever to be combated. Parry equalising with a spirited return shot. There was jubilation once more in the home camp, and hopes ran higher as Parry, upon Farmer nipping a fine run by Jamieson and Galbraith in the bud, experienced rather hard luck in shooting behind. Bootle soon rallied, and went up two or three times in splendid formation, and just when Hasting was sailing along strongly, Wilson disputed his progess. Half-time was announced with the score Everton 1 goal Bootle 1 goal. On taking up positions for the second stage, Jardine was welcomed to the Anfield-road goal with a good cheer in recognition of his skill during a trying time, and was also congratulated by the referee. Campbell was the first to forge ahead when Milward restarted, with Jones in support, Weir checking them by kicking out. Hasting however, took up the theme, and though Ross slashed across to repel the attack, Smalley had to check out. Everton now ascended the slope by the aid of a hugh kick, Wilson's shot being clamly fisted clear by Jardine, whilst Milward went ridiculously wide from a long range. Allsopp was too tricky for Waugh at the half-line, but Everton closed up to goal in a determined manner, play setting in Bootle quarters for about 10 minutes. Ross came well up the field, and kept his forwards supplied, but only one good attempt was made to score, and them McFarlane met Parry's accurate shot very smartly. Jones and Weir had a tussle, the former getting free, only to find Ross breaking ever in front of Dobson, and kicking up the wing to Davies and Parry. Bootle were at once back to goal, the ball having been impelled by means of neat heading by Jamieson, Hasting and Galbraith. Dobson cleared by conceding a corner, and from a ticklish scrimmage that ensued Galbraith had a fine chance, but faltered, apparently fastened in the mud, and so gave Smalley time to pick up and chuck away. Waugh was near scoring a few moments later, lifting just over the bar, from a pass by Parry, after Chadwick had run well. Ross then found it safest to give a further corner, on Wood and Gaibraith running prettily, the latter placing behind, and this was followed by Jones shooting through, Subsequently to the whistle sounding for off-side. Both goals were repeatedly visited during some energetic play; but nothing remarkable occurred until Davies, Chadwick and Waugh each shot hard in succession, and Jardine coolly saved two of their shies and Woods the other. Milward soon had another favorable opportunity but again made a wretched attempt. Woods went well from a free kick, and though checked at the corner, he followed by giving Smalley a handful. Waugh and Chadwick, going nicely up the left, raised the hopes of the Evertonians once more, but the attackers were easily held in check. Wilson also had a good opening from a corner, but was too high, and then Bootle attacked very strongly time after time about the nearest shot being an overhead one by Jamieson. Ross, as he had done all through played a masterly and safe game staving many an ugly rush, and just when all had made up their minds that there was going to be another drawn battle, a run by Hasting, Galbriath and Jamieson took the ball within range, the captain tipped to Wood, who availed himself to the full of a good position, and thoroughly beat Smalley. The Bootletes at the slice of good fortune raised a great shout for there were but three minutes left, for play, and the match was practically won. However, Everton darted off up the right, and on Parry becoming dangerous, Campbell kicked over, but before the corner could be placed the signal was given for a cessation of hostilities, Bootle emerging out of three hard contest as Liverpool champions, by a bare margin of victory on the score of Bootle 2 goals Everton 1 goal. **Teams, Bootle: - Jardine, goal, Woods and MacFarlane, backs, Allsopp, Morris, and Campbell,** halfbacks Wood, Galbraith, Jamieson (captain), Jones, and Hasting forwards. Everton:- Smalley, goal, Dobson, and Ross (captain), backs, Weir, Wilson, and Farmer, half-backs, Davies Parry, Milward, Chadwick, and Waugh, forwards. Referee Mr. Fitzroy Norris. Umpires, Messr McMurray and Berry.

## CHURCHTOWN 0 EVERTON RESERVES 0
*April 15, 1889 The Liverpool Courier.*

These teams met at Churchtown, before a fairly large attendance. The game during the initial stages was of the keenest nature, and when half-time was announced although both goals were frequently visited, no major point were registered a result, no goals being scored.

## EVERTON 3 NEWTON HEATH 1
*April 16, 1889. The Liverpool Mercury.*

These two well known teams appeared at Anfield last evening it being the first appearance of Newton Heath on the ground. The visitors brought a good team with them and Everton were presented by two or three of their second team. About 3,500 spectators assembled. Williams kicked off, and Everton at once pressed. Farmer and Ross punted into goal-Briscoe sent over to Watson and he parted judiciously to Angus, who scored with a spendid oblique shot, four minutes from the start. Good play by Farmer kept Powell busy, but at length Dobson was beaten by Gotheridge. Ross cleared but Brown put the ball though when he had a good opportunity to pass. The play was kept on the Everton right, which was not to the best advantage. From a foul the ball was taken over the Everton lines for the first time. Parry passing by the whole of the home forwards took the ball down, and Angus obtained a foul, which Farmer put over the bar. Williams and Jarrett rushed away, but Smalley cleared. Watson was fouled when clear away, but the referee gave no foul. Excellent play by Holt gave Watson and Briscoe possession, they passing to Milward he shot into Hay's hands, who only partially cleared and Briscoe shot through. Good combined play on the part of the home forwards kept the sphere in the opponents goal, Milward at last give Hays a handful, which he had no difficulty in clearing. A good shot by Owen was diverted by Williams who headed out. Everton then secured a foul near goal, and Watson shot through, but as the ball was wrongly placed it was brought back. Williams started, and Tait and Williams ran down. Williams shot to Smalley's hands, and from some inexplicable cause he allowed the ball to fall and scored for the visitors. Back play by Dobson gave Jarratt a possible chance, but Ross came to the rescue. Hays next had a busy time, as he had to fist out five consecutive shots. Doughty and Gotheridge worked their way down, but found Ross good enough for them, and Angus gave to Brown, who raced away, but nothing came of it. This was directly afterwards followed by a foul in goal and Ross scored the third point for Everton. The home team still maintained the pressure but breaks away by Tait and Gotheridge relieved the monotony. Ross gave a foul in goal, but Holt sent up the field, and Watson forced the pace considerably, and the home forwards again became the aggressive. **Score Everton 3 goals; Newton Heath 1 goal, Teams Newton Heath: - T. Hays, goal, Mitchell and Powell, backs Burke, Owen, and Jones, half-backs, Tait, Jarrett, Williams, Doughty, and Gotheridge, forwards. Everton: - Smalley, goal, Dobson, and Ross (captain), Weir, Holt, and Farmer, half-backs, Briscoe, Watson, Milward, Angus, and Brown, forwards.**

## EVERTON 0 LONDON CALEDONIANS 1
*April 20, 1889. The Liverpool mercury.*

This was the first visit of the visitors to the Anfield enclosure and to show the interest it aroused they were greeted with a hearty welcome from close upon 14,000 spectators. The day was rather dull, but fine, and the ground in capital conditions for a good display of scientific football. Everton first appeared in the white jerseys they unfortunately played in last Saturday but as the "Scottish" were in the same costume the Everton team had to retire, and their re-appearance in the old blue and white colours was the signal for an outburst of hearty cheering. Ross won the toss, and played uphill, with a good breeze at his back. Barbour kicked off but Milward intervened and gave to the left, where the immense audience appreciated good play by Nidd. Angus passed well to Davis but the latter unfortunately "fouled" the ball, and Burns, on the visitors right, got clean away, but shot badly. Holt helped the kick off to Angus and obtained a foul near goal, but nothing tangible accrued. Everton were now decidedly the better team, and kept up a continued pressure. The home forwards made up an excellent combined run, but Farmer unfortunately headed wide. Stirling, the London Scotch goalkeeper, showed remarkable form, and was exceedingly cool. Shots by Holt and Milward were treated in a quiet way, which spoke volumes for his play. Farmer next put in a short sprint and centre to Davis, who made but a poor screw, and the ball went outside Lambie, the Scotch international obtained it from the kick-off, and Wilson missing, he ran down, and shot magnificently, this being the first time the visitors had troubled Smalley. The home team still continued to press, but weak play on the Everton right was the cause of several chances being lost. Farmer dodged his opponents in capital style, but Milward made his center. E-Rea and Lamb received great applause for a short-passing run, which was prettily checked by Ross who was in his right place, and cleared, and Milward tried a shot which went wide. Burns, the noted late Lancashire cricketer, now raced away and beat both Nidd and Ross, but his pass was not put to the best use. Milward then put in a short timely run, and passed at the proper moment to Davies, but he mulled and allowed the ball to go out. Still maintaining the pressure the Evertonians kept Niel and Stewart very busy, but their play was so good that no impression was made. At last Farmer got the best of Stewart, and shot in terrific fashion close to the goal-post, and Stirling in attempting to clear-apparently from the stand-put the ball through his goal, but upon an appeal the point was disallowed and a corner given. Pretty play by Lambie and Barbour beat Weir and Wilson, and Ross had to kick out. Milward was now prominent for an excellent shot, but this was replied to by a spendid dodge run down the right, Clarke who finished up in fine style by giving Smalley an awkward handful. This brought about half-time, and now that the visitors had the wind their combination improved, and, as they improved so Everton fell off, and for a long time their forwards play was wretched. Good combination by Lambie and Ross compelled Holt, and then Wilson to give corners, but nothing was made of them. Burns then beat Ross twice in succession, and Smalley had an anxious time, but eventually Ross lunged out, and cleared by putting over the houses. Clarke threw into goal mouth, and after some hopping and dodging about, Barbour popped on the ball and shot through thus scoring first blood for the Caledonians. The home team now woke up a little, but the defence of the Caledonians goalkeeper and backs was so good that no impression could be made, although Farmer and Milward put in several meritorious individual runs, one of Milward's shot striking the bar, and it was rather hard lines on the homesters to secure a corner just on the last minute, and as Farmer was preparing to kick the ball to have the whistle blows for time. **Teams; London Caledonians:- Stirling, goal, Stewart, and Niel, backs, Clarke, Casselton, and Smith, half-backs, Burns,**

MacAlpine, Barbour, Rea, and Lambie, forwards. Everton:
- Smalley, goal, Wilson, and Ross (captain), Weir, Holt, and
Nidd, halfbacks, Davies, Angus, Milward, Chadwick, and
Farmer, forwards.

## EVERTON 0 BURSLEM PORT VALE 1
*April 22, 1889. The Liverpool Mercury.*

This match was played on Saturday on the Everton ground
before 7,000 spectators. The home team were first to appear
and it was noticed that Ross, Waugh, and Davis were absent.
Everton lost the toss, and Port Vale played with the wind and
sun at their backs. Milward started, but Shields intercepted and
gave to Balham, who centred smartly, but Ditchfield, on the left
wing, just missed with his head. Farrar the Everton centre-half
gave a dangerous foul close to goal but Ditchfield relieved all
anxiety by shooting high over the bar. Milward then ran away
from all opponents, but in stopping to shoot was robbed by
Poulston, Ditchfield and McGuinness now ran down the centre
in nice style, but a lofty kick by Dobson temporarily relieved.
Shields, who played a grand game throughout narrowly escaping
scoring. From the kick-off Parry passed to Milward, who again
got clean away, but unfortunately overstepped the ball and fell,
and thus a good chance was lost. Parry was then noticeable for
excellent passing, both to his wing man and centre, but nothing
was made of them. Brown on several occasions losing the ball
through dallying. Ballam on the visitors right then raced away
in fine style, and secured a corner off Holt. Although placed
well, Weir cleared and gave to Milward, who in turn passed on
to Farmer, and he got away very nicely, but in attempting to
"play"with Marriott instead of going ahead he was easily robbed
by Shields, and McGunness sent the ball on the left, and Stokes
caused Smalley to fist out. McGunness, however, met the ball
and shot, but it went wide. Ditchfield then put in some tricky

play and centred and Smalley had an anxious time for shots came from Balham, McGunness and Shields the last named just grazing the bar. The visitors up to now were having all the best of the game, and if an Everton got away, his colleagues and consequently his individual efforts did not support him and were easily nipped in the bud. Parry and Milward got up, and Milward lifted the ball right into the top stand. Immediately Parry, from a pass from Chadwick, repeated the performance. The homesters were not allowed to remain at the Port Vale end very long, for the visitors forwards by quick and judicious passing, were soon round Smalley and Wilson and a regular attack was kept up for some moments and it was fortunate that Smalley was in his best humour, for he had some stinging shots to negotiate. The old saying that "Perseverance will gain its own reward" was soon exemplified. Ditchfield and Stokes by nice passing had got down in the left corner, and had drawn Dobson out when Stokes centred quickly and McGunness by a pretty overhead shot scored the first point, for the visitors. The indignant cries of their supporters somewhat roused the indifferent play of the home team, and a semblance of combination was attempted by Weir, Chadwick, and Farmer but the latter started "gallery play" and consequently the improvement went for nothing, for Poulston stepped in and made an excellent run down the centre of the field, and although challenged by four Evertonians managed to elude them all, and obtained a corner. This brought about half-time, and it was now through that the home team would make a better shape, and soon wipe the score obtained by the vistors but the play, instead of improving became worse, and it disgusted the large crowd of their enthusiastic supporters. The game eventually ended in a win for Port Vale by 1 goal to nil. **Teams; Everton:- Smalley, goal, Wilson, and Dobson (captain), backs, Weir, Farrar, and Holt half-backs, Brown, Parry, Milward, Chadwick and Farmer, forwards. Port Vale:- Broomshall goal, Marriott and Batesman, backs, Poulston, Shields, and Elston, half-backs,**

Reynolds, Balham McGuniness, Stokes and Ditchfield, forwards. Referee Mr. Walter Sugg.

## EVERTON REVIEW
*April 22, 1889. The Liverpool Mercury.*

The games on the Everton ground this Easter have been a great disappointments to the admirers of the club. The root of all the evil is the great want of combination, not only between the forwards but with the whole team. One point which must strike all throughrful persons as being altogether wrong in the continual chopping and changing of playing men out of their proper positions. Why are the reserves not called upon oftener? They won the Northwich match in a hollow fashion, and their forwards on Monday last beat the team that has been one of the hardest nuts for Bootle to crack this season. If the players and committee do not make a great change, they cannot expect to get the patronage they have hitherto to. The match on Good Friday was remarkable for the immense attendance. In the first half Everton had matters pretty well their own way, but the lazy, indifferent style of shooting lost them dozens of chances. Milward has certainly deterorated since the final introduction to the first team, and his play on Saturday was simply wretched. Brown is not class enough for a team of this standing of Everton, and it surprises more than one why he is chosen in preference to such consistent players as Keys and Briscoe. The half-backs, too, have not by any means been up to the mark of late; and Wilson through injury received in the Bootle match was only "so so" The Caledonians played a very close passing game and shot with great accuracy while the two full backs were in fine kicking form. Why Farrar, the Southport Central player was brought into the team on Saturday is a coundrum few can solve. What is the use of Mr. Stockton working up a good set of reserves with such half-backs as Pollock, C Weir, Fayer, W Jones Parry, and Chadwick, and them passed over for a stranger? With extrait de coups lacking it is not surprising that first the London Caledonians, and, then-mark it-Burslem Port Vale, should ride Everton down, even on their own ground.

Meanwhile Mr J.Rogers has sent to Mr. Frank Brettle a postcard announcing that the long looked for charity match between Bootle and Everton veterans is off, the reason being the inability to raise a team among the Bootle "Vets" What an unfortunate thing this was not found out before last Saturday week. It is rather hard on Everton who fully expected that Bootle would keep their return engagement and had by means of handbills extensively advertised the match in Everton, but it also to regretted that Stanley and Bootle Hospitals will at least be the losers of about £10 each.

To-day at Anfield Everton will try their prowess with better success, it is hoped, than of late, against the well-known Renton team, and if they are clever enough to come out of the formidable task with flying colours the bitterness of Friday and Saturday reverses will be toned down. On Wednesday Everton not content with the heavy work of late, cross over the border in order to tackle Hearts of Midlothians on the Scotchmen's native heath.

**EVERTON 2 RENTON 1**
*April 23, 1889. The Liverpool Mercury.*

The visit of the famous team to Liverpool to play Everton yesterday roused much interested and there was 12,000 spectators to greet them with a hearty cheer when they appeared in their dark blue jerseys at 2-30. Great eagerness was evinced as to what would constitute the Everton team, and it gave an immense amount of satisfaction to the greater present when it was seen that three reserves men were included in the team. Ross won the toss, and elected to play with the wind and sun. J.Campbell kicked off, and at once Keys and Briscoe got away on the right, but the ball went out. Weir met the kick off, and Chadwick tried a shot, which Hannah kicked away, and G.Campbell helped the ball onto Harvey and H.Campbell who sprinted off in splendid fashion; but Ross intercepted and sent it up field, but a foul of Weir's caused Smalley to use his hands. Holt was then noticeable for his fine tackling of the visitors forwards, and from a well judged pass Angus centered beautifully, and Keys obtained a corner off McCall. Weir put well in, and for several seconds the ball was bobbing about Lindsay in dangerous fashion, eventually Gardner punted up the field, but the home team, whose improved play was greatly appreciated, continued to have the best of matters and Briscoe and Weir both tested Lindsay with good shots. From the kick off Brown sent to Harvey, and that player again got away, but Ross overtook him and kicked into touch. Ross then saved grandly, right in the mouth of goal and by a powerful kick gave Keys possession, but the players centre was allowed to roll out on the other side. Campbell then took up a pass of Briscoe and outwitting Holt sent it to his left wing, and McNee and McCall raced along the left and centred, but Ross met the ball and kicked over the stand. Not to be so easily denied the visitors left and centre came again, and McNee by a stinging shot struck the upright. Dobson then put on a spurt and overturned Gardner, and passed judiciously to the Everton left, but Brown stepped in before Chadwick and gave the ball to J.Campbell who when pressed by Holt, sent to Harvey but Ross came away with a rush and put in a good shot which was supplemented later on by one from Briscoe. Hannah cleared the latter by a tremendous kick but Holt again spoiled the concerned effort of the visiting forwards and passed to Keys, who, when attempting to pass McCall was fouled and a free kick was awarded. Gardner cleared the free kick, but Ross coming up the right moment landed the ball back again in the goal and just as Chadwick shot through the whistle blew for a previous claim for hands. Pretty play was then shown by J.Campbell, but Dobson robbed the left wing of the pass, and a miss by McCall let in Keys. Again his centre was not put to the best. Excellent short passing was now shown by Campbell, McNee and McCall, McNee centred to the right, and Harvey after dodging Ross, scored the first goal with a magnificent oblique shot. This unexpected reverse aroused the Everton team and they put more fire into their play and forced the Scotchmen back upon their goal, and kept Lindsay, Hannah, and McCall busy. Brown showed a turn of speed, but Holt robbed him, and sent to Milward who put in a flying shot, which took Lindsay all his time to get away. Angus then put in a nice easy centre but somehow both Briscoe and Keys missed. Half-time being called. Milward kicked off and he, Chadwick and Briscoe ran through the visiting forwards and half-backs, but McCall was too good for them, and returned. The Renton forwards then replied and a similar run, and Dobson was compelled to kick out. Weir got the best of an argument with McCall and McNee and sent forward, but Lindsay ran out and kicked up the field. Farmer returned and passed beautifully to Milward but Hannah rushed in and punted up the field. Harvey dropped upon the ball and darted off, but Farmer pulled him up, and gave to Angus. Again Hannah spoiled the combination of the left wing, and then the spectators were treated to a pretty bit of passing by the Renton forwards, but they could not get any further than Ross and Dobson, who were placing in their best form. Holt obtained Dobson's pass and gave to Milward, who by the help of Briscoe and Keys made considerable headway and troubled McCall and Lindsay, who was compelled to give a corner. Weir then beat the visitors left wing, and sent to Keys, who raced off, and closed in towards goal and shot into Lindsay hands, but he only partially cleared and Briscoe was enabled to make the game equal with a good shot. This success and the hearty cheers of the spectators urged the players to greater things, and for a spell the home team kept up a regular bombardment of Lindsay's goal, but that cool player was not caught napping and treated all shots in a mastery style. Angus and Chadwick with Farmer's help built up a nice piece of combination, and Chadwick's fine shot struck the cross bar-a neat thing. Although Hannah and McCall were kicking in a most powerful style, the Everton forwards forged ahead, and directly Angus forced a corner off Hannah. This was well placed by Farmer and Milward headed in. Lindsay fisted out. But immediately a claim arose from players and umpire for a goal, as they stated Lindsay was though the goal, when he cleared and Mr Lythgoe, who was standing by the upright at once gave his decision in favour of Everton. The point was greatly appreciated by the immense assembly. But with little time being left the visitors worked hard for another point but the backs and half-backs playing a determined game, kept Smalley free from danger and when the whistle blew for time, with Everton leading by 2 goals to 1, the cheering was loud and prolonged. **Teams Renton: - Lindsay, goal, Hannah, and A. McCall, backs, Brown, Gardner and G. Campbell, half-backs Harvey, J. McCall, H. Campbell, J. Campbell, and McNee forwards. Everton: - Smalley, goal, Dobson, and Ross (captain), backs, J. Weir, Holt and Farmer half-backs, J. Keys, W. Briscoe, Milward Angus and E. Chadwick, forwards. Referee R.Lythgoe.**

**HEARTS OF MIDLOTHIAN 3 EVERTON 0**
*April 26, 1889. The Daily Post.*

Played at Edinburgh on Thursday, about 4,000 spectators being present. The play in the first half was of a retaliatory character, the forwards on the home side and the backs for the Everton doing excellent work. At half-time the teams changed ends without anything bring scored, but immediately after the restart, Taylor defeated Joliffe's charge. This success for the Hearts was followed twice afterwards and Everton lost by three goals to nil.

## EVERTON 1 WITTON 0
*April 29, 1889. The Liverpool Mercury.*

The return fixture should have been played at Blackburn but Witton preferred to again travel to Liverpool. About 6,000 spectators were present. Milward kicked off at 4-45, but sending too far forward, Isherwood had no difficulty in giving to his own forwards who ran the ball over the Everton touch line. Weir received the kick-off and gave to Keys, who raced away, and at the right moment gave to Chadwick and Angus but Smith intercepted, and by a hugh punt sent the ball to Smith jun, who shot outside the post. Milward then put in a nice run, with the assistance of Angus made good progess and Chadwick essayed a shot which Sharples threw away. Grimshaw pounced upon the ball, and then the Witton forwards showed excellent passing, and bothered Ross and Dobson considerably but Rushton relieved all anxiety by shooting over the bar. Again Milward and Briscoe tried to break through the capital defence of Smith, Frankland and Sharples but these players for a while nonplussed the efforts of the Evertonians. Eventually Keys livened up and went off at lighting speed and got well down near the Witton goal, but finished up badly by a wide shot. Weir was directly afterwards cheered for a fine save in the mouth of goal, and for a time the Visitors had the best of the matters. A foul in midfield against Witton eased the pressure and a magnificent shot by Farmer, which struck the bar, was deservedly applauded. This wakened the lethargic homesters up a little and good combination being shown by Keys and Briscoe, Milward was enabled to get in a good position but shot over. Keys made amends for this immediately by a clinking shot, which skimmed the bar. Rushton and Smith then got off and, passing Rushton centred, but Smalley cleared grandly, falling on his knees to do so. Weir then beat Higgins and Horsefall, and gave to Briscoe who in his own unique style, dodged first one and then another, and wound up with a good centre, which Angus headed in but Sharples punted out easily, and thus brought about half-time. Grimshaw restarted, and he, Higgins and Horsefield put in a very pretty passing run and compelled Dobson to kick out. The home team getting the best of the throw in enabled Farmer and Angus to get down and Milward missed an easy chance from their pass. Holt who had been doing excellent services now put in a beauty, which Sharples could only get away at the expense of a corner. Weir kicked in with excellent judgement and Briscoe headed against the bar, and another corner was obtained. Frankland and old Mike cleared this and Horsefield kept Dobson fairly busy but Weir came to the rescue and robbed them. Keys secured the ball and got off in nice style, and centred in Sharples hands but again the custodian sent clear, and it seemed as though the match must end in a draw but just about this period Keys got severely kicked in the groin, and Ross seeing Everton having so much of the game, brought him full back, sent Milward on the right and went centre forward himself, and it was not long before the Witton lads knew of his presence, and it gave immense satisfaction to the large number of spectators when, by one of his characteristic sprints he literally ran the ball through, Sharples's goal and scored the only point of the match. Shortly afterwards time was called and the match ended as above. Teams; **Witton:- Sharples, goal, Smith, and Frankland, backs, Whiteside, Iserwood, and Pickering half-backs, Ruston Grimshaw, Higgins, Smith jun, and Horsefield forwards. Everton:- Smalley, goal, Dobson and Ross (captain), Weir, Holt, and Farmer half-backs, Keys, Briscow, Milward, Chadwick, and Angus, forwards.**

### EVERTON REVIEW
*April 29, 1889. The Liverpool Mercury.*

The match at Everton on Saturday was characterized by the lethargy, which seemed to possess the players on both sides. At times there were grand points in the play but there was a great want of fire and energy. This can be accounted for perhaps by the fact that the Everton team have gone through some hard work this last week. To play five matches in nine days is more than enough for any team, and one of them entailing a journay to Edinburgh and back. In the match with Hearts of Midlothians the Evertonians had equally as much of the game as the home team. Bad shooting is the cause of their not scoring, and little indiscretion by Joliffe made them a gift of the first point. The second point was obtained from a foul in goal, and the Evertonians maintain that the ball went though without touching any one, but that the referee was not inclined to listen to their claims. Chadwick played the best back game and Weir showed up well amongst the halves. The two outside wing players seemed off colour and the forwards work devided itself among Watson Milward, and Chadwick who acquitted themselves creditably. And now for the valediction. To-morrow the official season closes, when players will be freed from the shackles of registration, and when secretaries and all who have a penchant for figures will be dabbling in statistic and striking averages. During the month of May odd games will be indulged in but they count for nothing, in an authorized sense of a club's record of a club, and will be interesting more as exhibitions games for the introduction of possible and impossible new hands. The shadow of coming events.

**EVERTON 0 BURNLEY 1**
*April 30, 1889. The Liverpool Courier.*

These teams met for the fourth time this season, at Anfield-road enclosure, last evening, and the weather being fine. There was a good attendance of spectators. On the previous matches each side had won one the remaining game being a drawn. The Burnley team has been altered considerably of late and a capital game was expectorated. Everton minus Holt, whose place at halfback was filled by C.Weir, whilst "veteran" Mike Higgins was playing forward. The visitors having kicked off an attack was at once made on the home goal, Ross relieving. The Burnley forwards returned McFettridge sending in a grand shot, which passed outside the posts. The home right next ran down, a corner kick at the other end and the danger being cleared. The homesters reached the centre line and White got the ball away in fine style. The next minute Briscoe shot wide of the Burnley posts. Smalley saved several shots in a marveluos manner, but at length Duckworth beat him with a fast shot. The centre kick brought no relief to Everton, a "foul" against Dobson looked dangerous until Ross cleared with a powerful kick in the centre, and a corner accured to Everton, but the ball was badly placed, and Keenan cleared. Burnley was next dangerous and Everton were employed in defending their goal. Ross and Dobson saved finely on several occasions. Yates made a grand dribble along the Burnley left a splendid "centre" being badly missed by Duckworth. Everton now had extremely hard lines, but the Burnley defence was magnificent, and scoring was no easy matter. The visitors forwards had several shies at the home goal which proved futile. "Hands" off Dobson pressed danger for Everton but through some misunderstanding a capital chance was lost. Cox now saved grandly and prevented an imminent goal by admirable play. Farmer sent in a splendid shot from half-back Cox again being called upon to save. Higgins also put in a bit of good play, and Everton forced a "corner" which proved futile. Half-time was called with Burnley leading by one goal to nil. Milward having restarted on behalf of Everton, a rush was made for the Burnley goal, reaching Chadwick who made a poor attempt to score. From the kick-out the visitors forwards attacked, Smalley saving finely. McFettridge shot well, the ball just passing over the bar. Burnley still kept the ball well in their opponents quarters, and Friel sent in a shot which took Smalley all the time to save. At this jucture Ross collided with the rails, and play was suspended for a time. On resuming Everton attacked "offside" play spoiling their efforts. Burnley were now having much the best of the game, their opponents however showing a solid defence. Milward almost broke through but Berry brought him up in fine style, and the Burnley forwards were again busy at the home goal. Dobson and Ross were playing a champion game however, the former clearing grandly. The home forwards at length went away with a rush, but could not score the luck being dead against them. The Evertonians were by far too slow on the ball, and were consequently repeatedly robbed. Still play was again taken in front of the visitors goal Watson with an overhead shot just topping the bar. One of the Burnley players was now hurt and had to leave the field. Smalley fisted out a shot from Hibbert over the line, and on Friel returning increased pressure was brought to bear on the Everton goal. Ross cleared, and a "foul" off Keenan gave Everton a chance, but being too slow the opportunity was lost. Everton had a further chance of equalising from a long kick by Ross but Chadwick shot yards too high. Watson dribbled well on the home right, but although Everton pressed severely and forced several corners, they failed to score, and were beaten by a goal to nil. **Teams: Burnley:- Cox, goal, Berry and White backs Friel, Keenan and McFettridge half-backs, Hibbert, Duckworth, Campbell, Crossley, and Yates, forwards. Everton: - Smalley goals, Dobson, and Ross (captain) backs, J. Weir, Farmer, and C.Weir, half-backs, Watson, Briscoe, Milward, Chadwick, and M. Higgins, forwards.**

# MAY 1889

## NEWTON HEATH 1 EVERTON 1
*May 2, 1889. The Liverpool Mercury.*

The visit of our local team to Manchester last evening attracted about 4,000 spectators, but they were greatly disappointed by the absence of Smalley, Ross, Farmer, Weir and Briscoe. Powell beat Dobson in the spin of the coin, and Parry started against the wind. Immediately Chadwick and Holt gave Brown a chance of shooting but his shot went wide. Again the visiting forwards came down and compelled Hays to fist out. Owen spoiled Milward and gave D.Doughty, who shot into Joliffe's hand. Dobson cleared and a foul off Doughty relieved danger for a while. Nidd sent to Chadwick and Milward, who executed a meritorious run and had hard lines in not scoring. Newton Heath then pressed for a spell, but Tait shot wide, and Joliffe cleared easily from Doughty. Even play now became the general order. And up to half-time neither side could claim an advantage. During the second half the Everton team had matters pretty well their own way, with the assistance of the wind, and from a good pass by Chadwick W.Wilson scored a beautiful goal. Continual pressing however did not add to the score, and it looked as if Everton would be returned victors but just on the call of time a bad miss by Dobson let in Tait, who rushed in and gave Joliffe no chance with a lighting shot, this being the only time they had passed the backs. Result a draw 1 goal each. **Teams; Everton: - Joliffe, goals, A. Chadwick, and Dobson (captain), backs, W. Wilson, Holt, F. Nidd, half-backs, Brown J. Davies Parry, E. Chadwick, and Milward, forwards. Newton Heath: - Hays, goal, Mitchell, and Powell (captain), backs, Burke, Davies, and Owen, half-backs, Tait, Gale, D. Doughty, Graig, and R. Doughty forwards. Referee T.Hulme. (Bolton).**

# EVERTON 1 NOTTS RANGERS 0
*May 6, 1889. The Liverpool Mercury.*

The Anfield enclosure was patronized on Saturday afternoon by some 5,000 spectators, who witnessed what on the whole must be described as a tame and uninteresting game, the sultry weather depriving the players of much of their usual "go" Dobson won the toss, and Geary kicked off towards Oakfield-road, some exceedingly neat passing on the part of the Notts forwards showing that the Everton defence would be severely tested. Twice, early in the game, Cook and Shaw got to close quarters, Chadwick saving well on the first occasion, and Smalley by a grand effort on the second. Parry led an attack on the Rangers goal, but several opportunities of scoring were missed, Shelton and Sharpe gave Weir and A.Chadwick no end of trouble, some of their passing runs in combination with Geary being much admired, but Smalley was safe as usual. Farmer got the leather from the visitors right wing, and the home forwards made a determined attack, which ended somewhat awkwardly, Parry in charging Toone snapping one of the goal posts. Geary again raced through the Evertonians, passing to the left wing, and a good shot was directed at Smalley, who had just cleared when he was sent spinning by Cooke. Good tackling and returns by Holt, Farmer, and Weir gave the Everton forwards many opportunities, but the defence of Smith and Topham was too good, and half-time arrived without a point being scored. The visitors attack was now somewhat weakened by a re-arrangement, Shelton taking up the halfback position and Carlin going forward. Parry restarted play, and the Evertonians were soon swarming round their the opponents goal, a well judged kick by Weir giving Parry a rare opportunity for a header. Several good chances were mulled, and Shelton relieved Wilson of the leather, Sharpe taking play to the home end. Holt cleared at a critical moment, Briscoe made a good run and centre, Toone saving finely from

Parry, Milward a minute later being unsuccessful with a fast low shot. Everton were now having much the best of the game, but hard luck attended every effort until a free kick in front of goal, when after a scrimmage Parry succeeded in getting the leather past Toone. The remainder of the game was even. Result Everton 1 goal; Notts Rangers nil. **Teams; Notts Rangers: -Toone, goal, GH. Smith, and Topham backs, W. Smith, James, and Carlin, half-backs, Shaw, Cooke, F. Geary, Sharples, and Shelton forwards. Everton: - Smalley, goal, Dobson (captain) and A. Chadwick, backs, Farmer, Holt, Weir, half-backs, Briscoe, Wilson, Parry, Milward, and E. Chadwick, forwards.**

## EVERTON 1 BOLTON WANDERERS 0
*May 6, 1889. The Liverpool Mercury.*

The re-appearance of the Bolton Wanderers as Anfield last evening, proved as popular as all their previous visits had done quite 5,000 spectators witnessing the match. The Wanderers were strongly represented, the only regular man absent being Brogan, and his place was filled by Galbraith of Bootle. Armitt assisted Everton, whilst Joliffe had charge of goal. The visitors, who invaded goal in a spirited manner, hands, opened the attack by Galbraith clearing danger at a most critical moment. Everyone backed away on the right and left and having moved up in good combination, off-side put Brisk out of court, at an easy range, and renewing the pressure another fair bid for goal, was made by Wilson centering and Armitt heading neatly. Weir made an indifferent aim on behalf of the Wanderers, and then Briscoe and Wilson passed smartly from Weir, but in an instant dangerous play by Weir had beaten Dobson, though he only shot wide. The Wanderers right wing again menaced Joliffe saving well. Play went in favour of Bolton, who kept the ball in the Everton half for considerable time. Their combination, however, was not over brilliant neither was their shooting. Dobson eased the progess with a good kick, and dashing run by the home forwards raised from Holt's pass.

Joliffe next looked like assembling to a scrimmage, by punching upwards but Dobson was at hand to clear. Going up on the left, Everton attacked well just prior to half-time. Parry making a couple of good attempts to score. Ends were changed with nothing done in the shape of goals. On resuming, Davenport and Galbraith on the one hand, and Chadwick and Armitt on the other, assumed the aggresive with the advantage going to Everton, Parry shooting strongly from a pass. Davenport and Barbour were then baulked when at close quarters and Weir and Barbour retaliated in a clever dribble, but the latter was once more foiled at the post. Turner was next disappointed in the final touch to a strong tussle in front, and Joliffe knocked out from hands. Shortly afterwards a free kick fell to Everton, Parry pushing the ball through with his hands on Dobson kicking against the bar. The ensuing play was carried on with energy and on about level terms the main features being the good combination of Chadwick, Armitt, and Parry, the heading and tackling of Holt, and the general good kicking of the Wanderers. Hands were given against Bolton a few minutes from the finish, and on Dobson placing well Armitt scored. Everton at once closed up to goal and were near increasing their lead from hands but were this time well checked, and as interesting game resulted in a victory of a goal to nil for Everton, who on the whole showed the best backs, Armitt strengthening the attack considerably. **Teams Everton: - Joliffe, goal, A. Chadwick, and Dobson, (captain), backs, Farmer, Holt, and J. Weir, half-backs, Armitt, E. Chadwick, Parry, Briscoe, and Wilson forwards Bolton Wanderers: - Harrison, goal, Jones and Doyle, backs, Roberts, Milne, and Bullough, half-backs, Turner, D. Weir, Barbour, Galbriath, and Davenport, forwards.**

## ULSTER 0 EVERTON 2
*May 13, 1889. The Liverpool Mercury.*

The Everton team paid their return visit to Belfast on Saturday last to play Ulster. A fair crowd assembled and they were pleased with the good passing at times shown by the visiting forwards. Parry started and by good combination Everton at once became the aggressors. Barry by a good run relieved the pressure but again the visiting forwards came away, and Chadwick, with a good shot scored, but off-side was given against Briscoe for playing the goalkeeper. Miller then got hold, and, helped by the shouts of the spectators kept possession of the ball until within shooting distance, but the final shot was very weak, and the ball rolled out. Up to half-time nothing was scored, but, ends being changed, the Evertonians by dint of hard forward work, put on two goals, one by Briscoe and another by Milward; and no further scoring taking place, the game resulted in Everton winning by 2 goals to nil. Smalley was the best man on the Everton side. A.Chadwick played his usual safe game, Nidd showed the best half-back form, Holt being injuried. The whole of the forwards worked well, Parry Briscoe, and Chadwick being the most prominent. **Teams Ulster:- Clusyton, goal, Elleman, and Watson backs Tienly, Rosbottom, and Reid half-backs, Gaussen, Miller, Barry, Lemon, and Small, forward. Everton: - Smalley, goal, A. Chadwick, and Dobson (captain), Weir, Holt and F. Nidd, half-backs, Parry, Briscoe, Wilson, E. Chadwick, and Milward forward.**

## EVERTON RESERVES 5 DAVEHAM 2
*May 13, 1889. The Liverpool Mercury.*

The wet weather, the attendance being only small, and the ground too slippery spoiled this match, which was played at Anfield on Saturday for good play. Everton though starting short handed, at once took up the attack, Fenn being particularly active, but Davenport's defence proved good, though the home team were very near scoring once or twice during a siege of 20 minutes. The visitors broke loose now and then, and going well on the left, the ball was shot against the bar, Stringer beating Joliffe from the rebound. Everton at once closed up to goal in good style. Keys took aim from Fenn's pass, but was checked and then Brown put in, Harbour scoring. Watson followed with a spanking shot, which Postles neatly knocked aside. Davenham then improved their position by clustering round Joliffe, who running out to clear, was nonplussed by Malanm; but just on half-time, Pollock scored a good goal, ends being changed with the record 2 each. Everton soon drew in front on resuming, Keys heading through. Watson sent the ball out of the reach of Postles a moment later, but the point was lost on appeal for a foul. The home side maintained a steady pressure from now to the finish. Watson received the ball, Fenn, and scored a fourth goal, striking the bar shortly afterwards; whilst Harbour was awarded a goal from off the post. This point was stoutly protested against by Davenham, but to no purpose and in a few minutes the game terminated, Everton winning by 5 goals to 2.

## EVERTON 6 BLACKBURN OLYMPIC 1
*May 14, 1889. The Liverpool Mercury.*

This match took place last evening at Anfield, Hunter won the toss, and for several minutes the visitors had the best of matters, and it was not long before Parker shot through. Chadwick and his old club mates Fecitt then made tracks for the opponent's goal. Beverley returned to Costley and Yates, but Costley marred a good combined run by finishing with a very poor shot, which feat he immediately repeated. Chadwick met the kick-off and sent the ball up the field to Parry, who headed past Ward, and dribbling nicely, put in a clinking shot which completely beat Hunter. Everton now lived up, and for a spell had a good look in, but tall kicking by Beverley, Ward, and Hunter kept their fortress intact. Matthews and Dewhurst then got away, and a foul by Dobson made matters look bad for Everton. A good pass, however, a little later on, enabled Fenn to score a fine goal with a low oblique shot, and he followed in a few minutes with another, which Hunter allowed to go through. Half-time arrived. At the restart the visitors certainly had the best of the opening maneuvers, and with Farmer being hurt, they had several good chances,, which were not properly utilized. The Everton forwards rallied and executed a pretty run, Chadwick finishing by shooting a splendid goal. From now to the finish the Evertonians had matters entirely their own way. Chadwick Briscoe, and Fenn each added to the score, and when time was called Everton left off winners by 6 goals to 1. **Teams Everton, Joliffe, goal, Owen, and Lloyd, backs, Wilson, Dobson (captain), and Farmer, half-backs, Fenn, Briscoe, Parry, Facitt, and Chadwick forwards. Blackburn Olympic:- Hunter (captain), goal Beverley, and Ward, backs, Astley, McOwen and Almond, half-backs, Dewhurst, Matthews, Parker, Yates, and Costley, forwards.**

## EVERTON 2 DARWEN 0
*May 20, 1889. The Liverpool Mercury.*

Although football is supposed to have given way to cricket the supporters of Everton turned up to the strength of 7,000 at Anfield, on Saturday, to welcome Darwen on their first appearance. The ground was in first class order. The visitors had their full strength, while Facitt, Almond, Bethel and Robinson substituted the home ranks. Parry started the game for Everton, and tipping the ball to the left, it was soon carried by Facitt who was awarded a fruitless corner. J.Marsden soon again had to-clear his lines with a hugh punt, and Haddon tested Smalley with two well-judged shots. After Hudden had worked a shot from Briscoe, Almond enabled his side to keep on the aggressive and Fecitt screwed across the goalmouth, where Briscoe dashed up and scored for Everton. The visitors now put in a deal of good work, but found the home defence impenetrable and it was not long before Holden knocked the ball through his own posts from a nicest-placed corner from Chadwick which brought about half-time. Changing over both teams started strongly but it was soon perceptible that the players were labouring under the heat. Both goals were visited, but no further scoring took place, which was mainly due to the fine defensive work of J.Marsden for Darwin, and Almond, Dobson, and Robinson for Everton, a pleasant game thus ending in another win for the Anfieldites by 2 goals to nil. For the losers, J.Marsden at full back was a host in himself by his clean kicking and played sterling football; Owen and Thornber were fair halves; whilst there was not much to choose between the forwards. The winning team all round played a good game, and infused some life in the first half. Dobson and Robinson were safe at back; Almond at half-back was seen at his best, and was greatly liked by the spectators, while of the forwards rank Facitt and Chadwick made good partners, Parry lacking too much after the goalkeeper to satisfy many of the patrons and Briscoe did his share of hard work. **Teams; Everton:- Smalley, goal, Robinson, and Dobson (captain), backs, Nidd, Almond, and Farmer, half-backs, Briscoe, Wilson, Parry, Chadwick, and Facitt forwards. Darwen: - Holden, goal, Marsden (j), and Leach, backs, Thornber, Owen and T. Marsden, half-backs, Hayes, W. Marsden, Haddow, Smith, and Slater, forwards.**

## BOOTLE WANDERERS 6 EVERTON RESERVES 2
*May 20, 1889. The Liverpool Mercury.*

Played at Snadfield-place the home team winning by 6 goals to 2.

## EVERTON 1 PRESTON NORTH END 3
*May 21, 1889. The Liverpool Mercury.*

The visit of North End to Anfield last evening called together a great assembly of spectators numbering about 10,000. Dewhurst started the ball, but Almond took Drummond a pass and placed to Facitt, but Chadwick missed his kick and the ball rolled out. Again the home team forced the play and this time Chadwick put in a rafting shot which Turner had some difficulty in clearing. Roused by the enthusiastic cheers of the crowd, the Everton team kept Holmes and Howarth fairly busy, but their defence was admirable. Ross jun and Dewhust put in a pretty dribble down the centre and Almond in tackling gave a corner, which proved fruitless, but not before Ross sen had put in a spinkling shot. Geary, Parry, and Wilson came away and the homesters had hard lines through Wilson's centre dropping on the crossbar while Parry paid attention to Trainor. Still having slightly the best of the argument through the good half-backs pair of Haworth Almond and Farmer, Geary obtained possession from Chadwick in midfield, and executed a brillant run; but Trainor cleared his shot, and R.Haworth sending to Ross sen, be adroitly passed to Gordon and some exceedingly pretty play was witnessed between G Howarth, Ross sen, Drummond, and Almond which eventually ended in Ross securing a corner. Dobson cleared this, but Gordon coming down in fine style prettily passed to Ross who being in a good position was enabled to score first blood for North End. Everton worked the ball up very nicely good passing being shown by Parry, Geary and Chadwick, and Parry compelled Trainor to run out to save. Half-time arrived with Everton one goal to the bad, but being in no way disheartened they continued to have equally as much of the game as the North End, but lacked the finish and judgement of that well-known team. Dewhurst when coming down the centre, saw an opening for Ross sen, who making the most of the opportunity, rushed up and scored number two for the visitors. The home team, whether through excitement or the hot face at which the game had gone on, now fell off sadly and it was not long before Ross Jun, after a splendid spirited on the right scored again, for the North End with a magnificent oblique shot. Just on the call of time Everton gamely responded to the cries of the spectators and by excellent passing brought the ball in close proximity to Trainor and Geary was enabled to send in a lighting shot, which completely beat Trainor, and made the game 3 to 1. Nothing further being added, a fast and exciting game ended as above. **Teams: Everton: - Smalley, goal, B. Robinson and Dobson (captain), backs, Howarth Almond, and Farmer half-backs, Fecitt, Parry, Geary, Chadwick, and Wilson, forwards. Preston North End: - Trainor, goal, Howarth, and Holmes, backs, Robinson, R. Kelso, and Graham, half-backs Gordon Jun. Ross, Dewhurst, Drummond, and NJ Ross (captain), forwards.**

## EVERTON 1 ACCRINGTON 0
*May 27, 1889. The Liverpool Mercury.*

About 7,000 spectators assembled at the Anfield ground to witness the last Saturday match of the season when Accrington and Everton met for the third time, the two previous games having resulted in a win for each. The home team played with the sun in their eyes during the first half and the visitors at the outset attacked rather strongly, Chippendale lifting over the bar, and Smalley saving twice smartly. Chadwick and Facitt relieved in a neat run but hands in front rendered the effort futile whilst a renewed attack by Wilson, Parry and Fenn was of no better advantage, as Chadwick shot badly. Everton continued to have the best of the game until Accrington went up in close order and forced a corner. Geary fastened on the ball quickly and ran prettily, Facitt trying a fair shot, and after Robinson had cleared danger in the goal mouth Chadwick lobbed across accurately to Fenn who lost a fine chance through slowness. Accrington replied in good formation, but before growing dangerous Farmer pulled them up effectively, and Everton looked likely of making a capture, but Geary's shot was not quite straight enough nor did Parry utilizes a pass from Farmer and Almond properly. A moment later Smalley stopped brilliantly a sharp shot from Barbour, who replied by putting just outside the post. Between now and half-time Chadwick had an opportunity of scoring but screwed far too high, and ends were changed with a clean sheet. Accrington, despite the inconvenience of the sun severely troubled Robinson and Dobson on restarting, and when the former missed his kick at a critical moment the outlook of Everton was ominous, but Dobson dashed across just in time to prevent the left wing shooting. The visitors maintained a steady pressure, their forwards showing superior combination to those of the home club, but Everton's defence was always reliable. Towards the close, Parry and Geary changed position when a marked improvement was made in the home attack, and Parry dashing through enabled Chadwick to score. Geary followed by shooting through, but a foul was ruled, and soon afterwards a spirited game resulted in a victory for Everton of 1 goal to nil. **Teams; Everton: - Smalley, goal Robinson, and Dobson (captain), backs, Farmer, Almond, and Wilson, half-backs, Parry, Fenn, F. Geary, Chadwick, and Fecitt forwards. Accrington:- McOwen, goal, Stevenson and Mclennan backs, Tattersall, Chippendale, and Pemberton half-backs, Gallocher, Bonar, Barbour Kirkham, and Lofthouse forwards.**

## EVERTON 2 BOLTON 2
*June 1, 1889. The Liverpool Mercury.*

This the last match of the season was not patronised as well as usual. About 3000 spectators were present, and they seemed well pleased at the exciting and excellent game resulted. Barbour started against the wind and sun but Geary intercepted and, Chadwick put in a good shot, which caused Harrison to use his hands. Geary then followed with another, but Robinson headed away and the visiting forwards by excellent passing gave Davenport a possible chance which Smalley cleared. Everton maintained a heavy pressure for some time and while Parry attended to Harrison, Chadwick shot through, amidst cheering. Upon the re-start Almond became very busy, and repeatedly nipped the well meant passes of Brogan, Barbour, and Weir and by judicious half-back play gave the home forwards several chances. Turner got away and centred to Brogan and with a long shot he defeated Smalley. Shortly after, half-time was called. The combination of Milward and Chadwick improved, and by Geary assistance Milward became very troublesome to Robinson and Harrison, his screw being exceedingly well judged. D. Weir and Barbour at length defeated Dobson and J. Weir and gave to Turner, who scored, but Mr. Lythgoe did not allow a strong appeal for off-side. The home team, in no way disheartened kept up the pace, and after a long period of even play Chadwick again shot through, while Geary and Parry looked after the goalkeeper. Time being shortly called, an excellent game resulted in a draw 2 goals each. **Teams. Everton:- Smalley, goal, Wilson, and Dobson (captain) backs Weir, Almond, and Farmer half-backs, Fenn Parry, Geary, Chadwick, and Milward, forwards. Bolton Wanderers: - Harrison, goal Robinson, and Kucas, backs, Bullough, Crombie and Roberts, halfbacks Davenport, Brogan, Harbour, D. Weir, and Turner forwards.**

## EVERTON FOOTBALL CLUB
*June 7, 1889. The Liverpool Daily Post.*

The annual general meeting of the above club was held last evening at the brilliant rooms of the Sandon Hotel. Mr.Councillor John Houlding was in the chair, and about two hundred members were present. The secretary report was the first item on the list and after Sir Barclay had waded through a long written speech, a resolution was adopted thanking him for his services in obtaining the passing of the rule allowing the immediate registration of Scotch and other players. The item of interest now came on-viz, the treasurer reports, and amid deep interest and attention. Mr.Wilson read his balance sheet of which, the following is an account: - Receipts-Balance in hand (June 1889 £17 3s 11d) gate receipts upto May 31, 1889. £4,328 13s 1d; members subscription, £148 4s. Amount received for advertising on boarding (Less £8 returned for infringement agreements) £18, insurance allowance (Dick and Costley) £6; total £4,511 1s.

Payments: - players wages; £1,144 14s 6d; travelling expenses £408, 17s.2d; insurance's of players £20 16s, medical expenses £18 6s; special account £60 15s; general expenses £40 12s; 6d, training expenses £23 13s 6d; trainers wages £55 15s; materials; £60 15s; 3d. Referee £48 14s; 1d; ground maintains; £970 10s 10d; groundmen's wages £37 1s; rent £150; rates and taxes £29 2s 3d; police £74 14s 1d; commission £170 5s 10d; printing and stationary £96 9s 4d; advertising £61 11s; 7d; postage and telegrams £29 18s; 7d; visiting clubs £966 18s; 6d; entertainment etc; £17 15s; deputation expenses A.Dick £5; 4s, bank interest 10s; cash in hand (banks £8 14s 6d; treasurer £5 8s 3d), £14 2d 9d; total £618 1s.

The account were certified by Messrs. R.H.Webster, and W.Henderson, but after they had been audited a bill for £38 1s 4d was presented which, when settled, will leave the club in debt to the amount of £23 18s 7d.

After several pointed and searching questions had been asked in reference to above, the Chairman stated that the balance-sheet had been subjected to a close and critical examination by reliable auditors, and therefore upon a proposition he would declare the balance sheet passed. The following officers were then elected: - President Mr J Houlding; vice president (on committee); Messrs. Barclay and Howarth, secretary Messrs; Jackson and Moyneux, treasurers; and Messrs Berry, Brockes, Fleming, Coates, Williams, Clayton, and Currier, members of the committee.

# *SEASON 1888-89*
## The Anfieldites days

**EVERTON 4 PADIHAM 1 (HT 2-0)**
SEPTEMBER 1ˢᵗ 1888
FRIENDLY MATCH
ANFIELD
GOALS FARMER (5) (3-0), THOMSON OG (2-0), CHADWOCK
(4-0), CRAVEN (89)
TEAMS
EVERTON,(2-3-5) HIGGINS, DICK (A), ROSS (NR) (Captain),
HOLT (J), DOBSON (G), WHARMBY (J), FARMER (G), WAUGH
(D), COSTLEY (J), CHADWICK (E), FARMER (G)
PADIHAM, (2-3-5) PARKS, McCRAE, HUDSON, LOFTUS,
THOMPSON, SAGAR, CREARS, BRITWISTLE, CRAVEN,
O'BRIEN, WAITE
ATT 7,000

**EVERTON 1 BLACKBURN OLYMPIC 2 (HT 0-2)**
SEPTEMBER 3ʳᵈ 1888
FRIENDLY MATCH
REFEREE H BROMNLOW
ANFIELD
GOALS HAYES (0-1) (0-2), CHADWICK (1-2)
TEAMS
EVERTON (2-3-5) JONLIFFE (C), ROSS (NR) (Captain), DICK (A),
WHARMBY (J), DOBSON (G), HOLT (J), FLEMING (G) KEYS (J),
WAUGH (D), CHADWICK (E), FARMER (G)
BLACKBURN OLYMPIC, (2-3-5) BARRETT, DARY, REDHEAD,
SALLARS, STARKIE, GIBSON, STRACHAN, HEYES, CARLISE,
HOTHWESALL, DIXON
ATT 4,000

**EVERTON 2 HALLIWELL 1 (HT 1-1)**
SEPTEMBER 5ᵗʰ 1888
FRIENDLY MATCH
REFEREE J ROGERS
ANFIELD
GOALS CHADWICK (1-0), McGUINNESS (1-1), FLEMING (2-1)
TEAMS
EVERTON, (2-3-5) JOLIFFE (C), ROSS (NR) (Captain), DOBSON

(G), WHARMBY (J), HOLT (J), DOBSON (G), DICK (A), FLEMING (G), WAUGH (D), LEWIS (W), CHADWICK (E), FARMER (G) HALLIWELL, (2-3-5) BAMBER, LUCAS, ROBB, ROBINSON, CROMBIE, McDOUGAL, TURNER, HAY, MULLEN, CROSS, McGUNNESS
ATT 2,000

## EVERTON 2 ACCRINGTON 1 (HT 0-0)
SEPTEMBER 8th 1888
ANFIELD
REFEREE JJ. BENTLEY
GOALS FLEMING (60) (2-0), HOLDEN (1-2)
TEAMS
EVERTON (2-3-5) SMALLEY (RE), DICK (A), ROSS (NR) (Captain), HOLT (J), JONES (R), DOBSON (G), FLEMING (G), WAUGH (D), LEWIS (W)(Debut, from Bangor), CHADWICK (E), FARMER (G)
ACCRINGTON (2-3-5) HORNE, STEWART, McLENNAN, Howarth, WILKINSON, PEMBERTON, LOFTHOUSE, BONAR, KIRKHAM (E), HOLDEN, CHIPPENDALE
ATT 12,000

## EVERTON 5 STANLEY 0 (HT 3-0)
SEPTEMBER 13th 1888
FRIENDLY MATCH
GOALS NOT KNOWN (30 SECONDS), FARMER (2-0) (4-0), CHADWICK (3-0)' ROSS (5-0)
TEAMS
EVERTON (2-3-5) JOLIFFE (C), DICK (A), McKINNON (A), WHARMBY (J), DOBSON (G), HOLT (J), FARMER (G), CHADWICK (E), ROSS (NR) (Captain), WAUGH (D), FLEMING (G)
STANLEY (2-3-5) ROBERTS, GRIFFITHS (F), WILSON (W), ROBERTS, MARTIN, WILSON (J), THRELLFALL, PICKSTAF, STEVENS, BROWN (W) (Future Blue), QUINE,
ATT 2,500

**EVERTON 2 NOTTS COUNTY 1 (HT 1-0)**
SEPTEMBER 15th 1888
ANFIELD
REFEREE WH JOPE
GOALS DICK (10), ROSS (2-0), MOORE (89)
TEAMS
EVERTON (2-3-5) SMALLEY (RE), DICK (A), ROSS (NR) (Captain),
HOLT (J), McKINNON (A)(Debut signed from Hearts), DOBSON
(G), FLEMING (G), WAUGH (D), LEWIS (W),CHADWICK (E),
FARMER (G)
NOTTS COUNTY (2-3-5) HOLLAND, McLEAN (J), GUTTRIDGE,
BROWN (GH), WARBURTON, SHELTON (A), WARDLE (F),
MOORE (A), JARDINE (T), HOLDEN (W), HARKER
ATT 9,000

**EVERTON 6 DERBY MIDLAND 0**
SEPTEMBER 19th 1888
FRIENDLY MATCH
ANFIELD
GOALS WATSON (20) (5-0), CHADWICK (2-0), WAUGH (3-0),
ROSS (4-0), KEYS (6-0)
TEAMS
EVERTON (2-3-5) SMALLEY (RE), ROSS (NR) (Captain),
DICK (A), WEIR (J), WARMBY, DOBSON (G), FARMER (G),
CHADWICK (E), KEYS (J), WATSON (R), WAUGH (D)
DERBY MIDLANDS (2-3-5) STORER, GILBERT, STONE (W),
SMITH (A), FLOWERS (J), ROSS (W), SMITH (G), SHANNON
(J), EVANS (G), DAFT (T), BAILEY
ATT 2,500

**ASTON VILLA 2 EVERTON 1**
SEPTEMBER 22nd 1888
PEERY BAR
REFEREE FITYZROY NORRIS
GOALS HODGETTS (4) (40), WATSON (80)
TEAMS
ASTON VILLA (2-3-5) ASHMORE, COULTON, COX , YATES,
DEVEY, DIXON, BROWN, GREEN HUNTER (Captain), ALLAN,

HODGETTS
EVERTON (2-3-5) SMALLEY (RE), DICK (A), ROSS (NR)
(Captain), WEIR (J), WARMBY (J) (Only app, Signed from Derby
County), HIGGINS (M), WAUGH (D), WATSON (R), KEYS (J)
(Only app, Signed from Derby County), CHADWICK (E), FARMER
(G)
ATT 5,000

**EVERTON 2 DERBY JUNCTION 1 (HY 0-1)**
SEPTEMBER 26th 1888
FRIENDLY MATCH
ANFIELD
GOALS HOPKINS (0-1), NOT KNOWN (1-1), POLLOCK (2-1)
TEAMS
EVERTON (2-3-5) JOLIFFE (C), DICK (A), ROSS (NR) (Captain),
WEIR (J), POLLOCK (H), HIGGINS (M), WATSON (R), WAUGH
(D), MILWARD (A), CHADWICK (E), FARMER (G)
DERBY JUNCTION (2-3-5) BROMAGE, MORLEY, HIND,
WALKER, PLACKETT' SNELSON, KENIBERLEY' SMITH,
HOUSLEY, HOPKINS, RADFORD
ATT 2,500

**BOLTON WANDERERS 6 EVERTON 2 (HT 3-2)**
SEPTEMBER 26th 1888
PIKES LANE
REFEREE T.HELME
GOALS DAVEPORT (1) (2-5), TYRER (5)(2-3), LEWIS (1-2),
,WATSON (2-2), MILNE (2-4)(2-6)
TEAMS
BOLTON WANDERERS (2-3-5) HARRISON, JONES, ROBINSON,
WEIR (R), SIMMERS, ROBERTS' DAVENPORT, BROGAN,
BARBOUR, MILNE, TYRER
EVERTON (2-3-5) SMALLEY (RE), DICK (A), ROSS (NR)
(Captain), WEIR (J), DOBSON (G), POLLOCK (H)(Debut),
WAUGH (D), WATSON (R),CHADWICK (E),LEWIS (W)(Last
apps) FARMER (G)
ATT 5,000

**EVERTON 2 ASTON VILLA 0**
OCTOBER 6th 1888
ANFIELD
REFEREE MR McINTYRE
GOALS WAUGH (42), FARMER (81)
TEAMS
EVERTON (2-3-5) SMALLEY (RE), DICK (A), ROSS (NR)
(Captain), WEIR (J), HOLT (J), FARMER (G), McKINNON (A),
WATSON (R), SUGG (FH), CHADWICK (E), WAUGH (D)
ASTON VILLA (2-3-5) WARNER, COULTON, COX, YATES,
DEVEY , DAWSON, BROWN, GREEN, HUNTER (Captain),
ALLEN, HODGETTS
ATT 12,000

**BURNLEY 3 EVERTON 0 (HT 0-0)**
OCTOBER 8th 1888
FRIENDLY MATCH
TURF MOOR
GOALS GALLACHER (0-1) (0-2), LANG (0-3)
TEAMS
BURNLEY (2-3-5) KAYS, BERRY, LANG, KEENAN, FRIEL,
ABRAMS, BRADY (A) (Future Blue), TAIT, GALLACHER,
ROLAND, YATES
EVERTON (2-3-5) SMALLEY (RE), ROSS (NJ) (Captain), DICK
(A), CHADWICK (A) HOLT (J) FARMER (G), HIGGINS (M),
CHADWICK (E) SUGG (FH), WATSON (R), McKINNON (A)
ATT 4,000

**NOTTS COUNTY 3 EVERTON 1 (HT 3-0)**
OCTOBER 13th 1888
TRENT BRIDGE
REFEREE MR MEON
GOALS JARDINE (5), DAFT (14), SMALLEY OG (44), ROSS (1-
3)
TEAMS
NOTTS COUNTY (2-3-5) HOLLAND, CURSHAM, GUTTRIDGE,
BROWN (C), SHELDON, HALL HODDER, MOORE, ALLEN,
DAFT, JARDINE

EVERTON (2-3-5) SMALLEY (RE), DICK (A), ROSS (RN) (Captain), WEIR (J), HOLT (J), FARMER (G), WATSON (R), McKINNON (A), SUGG (FH), BRISCOE (W) (Debut), CHADWICK (E)
ATT 4,000

**DERBY COUNTY 2 EVERTON 4 (HT 1-2)**
OCTOBER 20th 1888
DERBY CRICKET GROUND
REFEREE H.JOPE
GOALS COSTLEY (5) (2-0), CHATTERTON (30), McKINNON (3-1)' CHADWICK (4-1), BAKEWELL (2-4)
TEAMS
DERBY COUNTY (2-3-5) BESTWICK (TH), LATHAM, WRIGHT (LG), WILLIAMSON, HOPEWELL, ROULSTON (W), BAKEWELL, CHATTERTON, HIGGINS, PLACKETT (H), PLACKETT (L)
EVERTON (2-3-5) JOLIFFE (J), DOBSON (G), ROSS (NR) (Captain), WEIR (J), HOLT (J), FARMER (G), McKINNON (A), WATSON (R), SUGG (FH), CHADWICK (E), COSTLEY (J)
ATT 3,000

**DENTON 0 EVERTON 3**
OCTOBER 22nd 1888
FRIENDLY MATCH
GOALS
TEAMS
DELTON (2-3-5) LOWE, COOKE, SEDDON, EDWARDS, MOFFATT, CLARKE, WALTON, PLANT, DOWE, WARNOCK, SEDDON (T)
EVERTON (2-3-5) JOLIFFE (C), CHADWICK (A), ROSS (JN) (Captain), WEIR (J), FRYER (T), FARMER (G), COSTLEY (J), CHADWICJK (E), SUGG (FH), McKINNON (A), BERRY (A)
ATT 5,000

**EVERTON 6 DERBY COUNTY 2 (HT 3-1)**
OCTOBER 27th 1888
ANFIELD
REFEREE MR FAIRHURST
GOALS NEEDHAM (3)' ROSS (1-1) (5-1), McKINNON (A) (2-1)

(4-1) (6-1), WATSON (42), PLACKETT (2-6)
TEAMS
EVERTON (2-3-5) SMALLEY (RE), DOBSON (G), SUGG (NR) ,
WEIR (J), HOLT (J), FARMER (G), McKINNON (A), WATSON (R),
SUGG (FH), ROSS (NJ) (Captain), CHADWICK (E) COSTLEY (J)
DERBY COUNTY (2-3-5) MARSHALL, WILLIAMSON,
ROWISTON, HARBOUR, SELVEY, HOPEWELL, CHATTERTON,
PLACKETT (H), HIGGINS, NEEDHAM, PLACKETT (L)
ATT 8,000

**EVERTON 2 BOLTON WANDERERS 1**
NOVEMBER 3rd 1888
LEAGUE DIVISION ONE
ANFIELD
REFEREE J COOPER
GOALS BROWN (50), BROGAN (74), ROSS (84)
TEAMS
EVERTON (2-3-5) SMALLEY (RE), DICK (A), DOBSON (G),
WEIR (J), HOLT (J), FARMER (G), McKINNON (A)(Last apps),
WATSON (R), ROSS (NR) (Captain), CHADWICK (E), BROWN
(W)(Debut, Signed for Stanley)
BOLTON WANDERERS (2-3-5) GILLIAM, ROBERTS, ROBINSON,
BULLOUGH, SCOWCROFT, WEIR (D), DAVENPORT, BROGAN,
BARBOUR, MILNE, TYRER
ATT 6,000

**BLACKBURN ROVERS 3 EVERTON 0 (HT 1-0)**
NOVEMBER 10th 1888
EWOOD PARK
GOALS ALMOND (25), WALTON (0-2), DOBSON OG (0-3)
TEAMS
BLACKBURN ROVERS (2-3-5) ARTHUR, SOUTHWORTH
(Jim), FORBES, DOUGLAS, ALMOND FORREST, BERESFORD,
WALTON (N), SOUTHWORTH (J) (Future Blue), TOWNLEY,
FECITT,
EVERTON (2-3-5) SMALLEY (RE), DOBSON (G), ROSS (NR)
(Captain), WEIR (J), SUGG (FH), HOLT (J), FARMER (G),
WATSON (R), MILWARD (A)(Debut signed from Notts Rangers),

CHADWICK (E), BROWN (W)
ATT 6,000

**BURNLEY 2 EVERTON 2 (HT 2-1)**
NOVEMBER 17th 1888
TURF MOOR
GOALS GALLACHER (10), McKAY (20), WATSON (1-2),
CHADWICK (50)
TEAMS
BURNLEY (2-3-5) COX (W) (Future Blue), BERRY, LANG,
KEENAH, FRIEL, ABRAMS, BRADY (A) (Future Blue), McKAY,
McFETTERIDGE, YATES, GALLACHER
EVERTON (2-3-5) SMALLEY (RE), DOBSON (G), ROSS (NR)
(Captain), HOLT (J), SUGG (FH), FARMER (G), FLEMING (G),
WATSON (R), COSTLEY (J), CHADWICK (E), BROWN (W)
ATT 3,000

**EVERTON 3 BURNLEY 2 (HT 3-0)**
NOVEMBER 24th 1888
REFEREE S.ORMEROD
ANFIELD
REFEREE WH HOPE
GOALS CHADWICK (1-0)' COYNE (2-0)' BERRY OG (3-0)'
McKAY (1-3)' BRADY (2-3)
TEAMS
EVERTON (2-3-5) SMALLEY (RE), SUGG (FH), ROSS (NR)
(Captain), WEIR (J), HOLT (J), FARMER (G), FLEMING (G)(Last
apps), COYNE (Debut signed from Vale of Leven), DAVIES (Debut.
signed from Renton), CHADWICK (E), COSTLEY (J)
BURNLEY (2-3-5) COW (W) (Future Blue), BERRY, ABRAM,
FRIEL, KEENAN, BRADY (A) (Future Blue), McKAY,
McFETTRIDGE, GALLACHER, YATES
ATT 8,000

**WEST BROMWICH ALBION 4 EVERTON 1 (HT 3-0)**
DECEMBER 1st 1888
LEAGUE DIVISION ONE
STONEY LANE

GOALS PERRY (W) (0-1) (0-2), BASSETT (0-3), CHADWICK (E) (1-3)' HENDRY (1-4)
TEAMS
WEST BROMWICH ALBION (2-3-5) ROBERTS, WALKER, HORTON (J), BAYLISS, PERRY (C), TIMMINS, PEARSON, HENDRY, PERRY (W), WILSON, BASSETT
EVERTON (2-3-5) SMALLEY (RE), DOBSON (G)(captain), CHADWICK (A)(Debut), FARMER (G), WEIR (J), SUGG (FH),COSTLEY (J),CHADWICK (E),DAVIES (Debut signed from Chirk) ,COYNE, DAVIES (J)
ATT 7,000

**EVERTON 3 LONG EATON RANGERS 1 (HT 3-0)**
DECEMBER 8th 1888
FRIENDLY MATCH
ANFIELD
GOALS MORRIS (5), CHADWICK (2-0) (3-0), ORCHARD (1-3)
TEAMS
EVERTON (2-3-5) SMALLEY (RE), DOBSON (G)(Captain), SUGG (FH), FARMER (G), HOLT (J), WEIR (J), COSTLEY (J), CHADWICK (E), MORRIS, COYNE, DAVIES (J)
LONG EATON RANGERS (2-3-5) STUART (F), WINFIELD, WISEMAN, CLIFTON, PLACKETT, NEWTON, STUART (J), HARTS (JS), HARDY, ORCHARD, LOCKER
ATT 5,000

**BURSLEM PORT VALE 2 EVERTON 2**
DECEMBER 10th 1888
FRIENDLY MATCH
GOALS BALLAM (0-1), MORRIS (1-1), CHADWICK (E) (2-1), WEIR OG (2-2)
TEAMS
BURSLEM PORT VALE (2-3-5) MAUDSLETT, BATEMAN, SKINNER, CHADWICK, SHIELDS, ELSON, POVISON, BALHAM, RANDLE, DITCHFIELD, REYNOLDS
EVERTON (2-3-5) JOLIFFE (C), CHADWICK (A), ROSS (NR) (Captain), WEIR (J), SUGG (FH), WATSON (R), FARMER (G), ANGUS (J). MORRIS, CHADWICK (E), COSTLEY (J)
ATT 2,000

## STOKE CITY 0 EVERTON 0
DECEMBER 15th 1888
VICTORIA GROUND
TEAMS
STOKE CITY (2-3-5) ROWLEY, CLARE, UNDERWOOD, SAYER, SHUTT, SMITH, LAWTON, McSKIMMER, SLOANE, EDGE, MILARVIE
EVERTON (2-3-5) SMALLEY (RE), DOBSON (G), ROSS (NR) (Captain), WEIR (J), HOLT (J), FARMER (G), DAVIES (J), WATSON (R), MORRIS (Debut, and only apps, signed from Oswentry) , CHADWICK (E), COSTLEY (J) (Last apps)
ATT 1,500

## PRESTON NORTH END 3 EVERTON 0
DECEMBER 22nd 1888
DEEPDALE
GOALS GOODALL (5), DEWHURST (0-2), FARMER OG (0-3)
TEAMS
PRESTON NORTH END (2-3-5) TRAINER, HOWARTH (R) (Future Blue), HOLMES, ROBERTSON, RUSSELL, GRAHAM, ROSS (Jun), GORDON, GOODALL (Captain) DEWHURST, DRUMMOND
EVERTON (2-3-5) SMALLEY (RE), ROSS (JN) (Captain), DOBSON (G), FARMER (G), WEIR (J), HOLT (T) ANGUS (J), CHADWICK (W), BROWN (W), BRISCOE (W), WATSON (R)
ATT 8,000

## EVERTON 3 ULSTER 0
DECEMBER 25th 1888
FRIENDLY MATCH
ANFIELD
GOALS MILWARD (15), WEIR (2-0), JOLIFFE (75)
TEAMS
EVERTON (2-3-5) JOLIFFE (C), HIGGINS (M), ROSS (NR) (Captain), WEIR (J), POLLOCK (H), STEVENSON (G), AUGUS (J), FALL (R), MILWARD (A) WATSON (R), KEYS (J)
ULSTER (2-3-5) PINKLESTON, DOWNES, WATSON, PHILLIPS, TIERNEY, LESLIE, MILLER, MARTIN DAVIE ,COYNE
ATT 6,000

## EVERTON 0 BOOTLE 0
DECEMBER 26th 1888
FRIENDLY MATCH
ANFIELD
TEAMS
EVERTON (2-3-5) JOLIFFE (C), ROSS (NR) (Captain), DOBSON (G), FARMER (G) HOLT (J), WEIR (J), ANGUS (J), CHADWICK (E), BROWN (W), BRISCOE (W), DAVIS
BOOTLE (2-3-5) JACKSON, McFARLANE, MILLER, ALLSOP (A), HUGHES (W), CAMPBELL (W) (Future Blue), WOOD (J), GALBRAITH, JAMIESON (E), JONES, GALBRAITH (D)
ATT 16000

## ACCRINGTON 3 EVERTON 1
DECEMBER 29th 1888
THORNYHOLMES CRICKET GROUND
GOALS WATSON (1-0), BRAND (1-1), HOWARTH (1-2), NOT-KNOWN (1-3)
TEAMS
ACCRINGTON (2-3-5) HORNE (JK), McCELLAN, STEVENSON, PEMBERTON TATTERSALL HOWARTH, BRAND, KIRKHAM, BARBOUR, DONAR, LOFTHOUSE
EVERTON (2-3-5) JOLIFFE (C), DOBSON (G), ROSS (NR) (Captain), WEIR (J), SUGG (FH), PARKINSON (H)(Debut, Signed from Bell's Temparance), BRISCOE (W)(Last apps), WATSON (R), BROWN (W)(Last apps), CHADWICK (E), ANGUS (J)
ATT 2,500

## EVERTON 2 THIRD LANARKS 2 (HT 1-2)
JANUARY 1st 18889
FRIENDLY MATCH
ANFIELD
REFEREE HUGH McLNTYRE
GOALS MARSHALL (2), MILWARD (1-1), OSWALD (1-2), NOT KNOWN (2-2)
TEAMS
EVERTON (2-3-5) JOLIFFE (C), ROSS (NR) (Captain), DOBSON (G), WEIR (J), HOLT (J), FARMER (G), WATSON (R), DAVIES (J), MILWARD (A), CHADWICK (E), BROWN (W)

THIRD LANARK (2-3-5) DOWNIE, FAIRWEATHER, REA, McFARLANE, FERGUSON, THOMPSON, OSWALD (T), OSWALD (J), HANNAH, MARSHALL, JOHNSON
ATT 6,000

## EVERTON 2 CAMBUSLANG 1
JANUARY 2nd 1889
FRIENDLY MATCH
ANFIELD
GOALS CHADWICK (1-0)' GOURLAY (H) (1-1)' MILWARD (2-1)
TEAMS
EVERTON (2-3-5) JOLIFFE (C), DOBSON (G), ROSS (NR) (Captain), SUGG (FH), FARMER (G), HOLT (J), WATSON (R) MILWARD (A), AUGUS (J) DAVIES (J), CHADWICK (E),
CAMBUSLANG (2-3-5) DUNN, DOWNS, FOYETS, RUSSELL, GOURLAY (J), HENDREY, LOW, PRENDELEITH, CALDOW, GOURLAY (H), BUCHANAN
ATT 2500

## EVERTON 1 BLACKBURN ROVERS 0
JANUARY 5th 1889
FRIENDLY MATCH
ANFIELD
GOAL WATSON (25)
TEAMS
EVERTON (2-3-5) JOLIFFE (C), ROSS (NR) (Captain), DOBSON (G), FARMER (G), HOLT (J), WEIR (J), ANGUS (J), CHADWICK (E), MILWARD (A), WATSON (R) BROWN (W)
BLACKBURN ROVERS (2-3-5) McCOWAN, SOUTHWORTH (JAS), FORBES, DOUGLAS, ALMOND, FORREST, DOUGLAS, WALTON, SOUTHWORTH (J) (Future Blue) (Captain), WHITTAKER, TOWNLEY
ATT 6,000

## EVERTON 2 STOKE CITY 1 (HT 1-0)
JANUARY 12th 1889
ANFIELD
REFEREE FITZROY MORRIS
GOALS MILWARD (1-0)' DAVIES (2-0), McSKIMMER (1-2)

TEAMS
EVERTON (2-3-5) JOLIFFE (C), ROSS (Captain), DOBSON (G),
FARMER (G), HOLT (J), WEIR (J) ANGUS (J), CHADWICK (E),
WATSON (R), DAVIES (J), MILWARD (A)
STOKE CITY (2-3-5) ROWLEY (W), CLARE (T)(Captain),
UNDERWOOD (A), RAMSLEY (R), SHUTT(G), SMITH (E),
LAWTON (G), McSKIMMER (RM), HOGG (A), MILARVIE (R),
WILSON (J)
ATT 7,000

**EVERTON 0 PRESTON NORTH END 2 (HT 0-0)**
JANUARY 19th 1889
ANFIELD
REFEREE WH JOPE
GOALS ROSS (J) (55), GOODALL (0-2)
TEAMS
EVERTON (2-3-5) JOLIFFE (C), DODSON (G), ROSS (NR)
(Captain), KELSO (R)(Debut), HOLT (J), FARMER (G), DAVIES
(J), WATSON (R), MILWARD (A), CHADWICK (E), ANGUS (J)
PRESTON NORTH END (2-3-5) TRAINER, HOWARTH (R)
(Captain) (Future Blue), HOLMES, RUSSELL, GRAHAM,
GORDON, DRUMMOND, GOODALL, ROSS (Jimmy),
THOMPSON
ATT 15,000

**WOLVERHAMPTON WANDERERS 5 EVERTON 0 (HT 4-0)**
JANUARY 26th 1889
DUDLEY ROAD
GOALS WOOD (0-1) (0-2) (0-4), KNIGHT (0-3), BODRIE (0-5)
TEAMS
WOLVERHAMPTON WANDERERS (2-3-5) ROSE, BAUGH,
FLETCHER, ALLEN, LOWDER, HUNTER, WHITE, BRODIE,
WOOD, KNIGHT, WYKES
EVERTON (2-3-5) SMALLEY (RE), DOBSON (G), ROSS (NR)
(Captain), STEVENSON (G)(Debut), HOLT (J), FARMER (G),
DAVIES (J), WATSON (R), MILWARD (A), CHADWICK (E),
ANGUS (J)
ATT 3,000

**EVERTON 3 BATTLEFIELD 2 (HT 3-1)**
FEBRUARY 2nd 1889
FRIENDLY MATCH
ANFIELD
GOALS SUMMERVILLE (0-1), MILWARD (1-1), BROWN (2-1), ROSS (3-1), ELLIOTT (2-3)
TEAMS
EVERTON (2-3-5) SMALLEY (RE), ROSS (NR) (Captain), DICK (A), DOBSON (G), HOLT (J), FARMER (G), DAVIES (J), WATSON (R), MILWARD (A), CHADWICK (E), BROWN (W)
BATTLEFIELD (2-3-5) NEILL, HALL, COOK, HENDRY (T), WALKER, GOW, HECTOR, HENDRY (W),CUNNINGHAM, ELLIOTT, SOMERVILLE
ATT 5,000

**EVERTON 1 WOLVERAHAMPTON WANDERERS 2**
FEBRUARY 9th 1889
ANFIELD
REFEREE H McINTYRE
GOALS CHADWICK (E) (30), WOOD (87), KNIGHT (90)
TEAMS
EVERTON (2-3-5) SMALLEY (RE), DOBSON (G)(captain), DICK (A), FARMER (G), ROBERTS (Debut) CHADWICK (A), BROWN (W), CHADWICK (E), WATSON (R), DAVIES (J), MILWARD (A)
WOLVERHAMPRON WANDERERS (2-3-5) ROSE, BAUGH, MASON, FLETCHER, ALLEN, LOWDER, HUNTER, COOPER, WOOD, KNIGHT, WYKES
ATT 10,000
ADDITIONAL ROSS AND HOLT PLAYING FOR COUNTRY AT VICTORIA GROUND STOKE

**EVERTON 5 DUNDEE STRATHMORE 1 (HT 2-1)**
FEB 16th 1889
FRIENDLY MATCH
ANFIELD
GOALS McLAREN (0-1), ROSS (1-1) (2-1), CHADWICK (3-1), WATSON (4-1) (5-1)
TEAMS

EVERTON (2-3-5) SMALLEY (RE), DOBSON (G), DICK (A), FARMER (G), HOLT (J), WEIR (J), BROWN (W), CHADWICK (E), ROSS (NR) (Captain), WATSON (R), DAVIES (J)
DUNNDEE STRATHMORE (2-3-5) DOUGLAS, MASON, SIMPSON, LABURN, McFARLANE, STIREN, McGREGOR, DICKSON, MURRAY, McLAREN, DUNCAN
ATT 9,000

**EVERTON 0 WEST BROMWICH ALBION 1**
FEBRUARY 23rd 1889
ANFIELD
REFEREE MR COOPER
GOAL CRABTREE (48)
TEAMS
EVERTON (2-3-5) SMALLEY (RE), DICK (A)(Last apps), DOBSON (G), WEIR (J), HOLT (J), FARMER (G), DAVIES (J) WATSON (R), ROSS (HJ) (Captain), CHADWICK (E), WAUGH (D)
WEST BROMWICH ALBION (2-3-5) ROBERTS, HORTON (J), GREEN (H), HORTON (F), PERRY (G), TIMMIN, CRABTREE (W), PERRY (W), BAYLISS, PEARSON, WILSON
ATT 11,000

**SOUTHPORT CENTRE 1 EVERTON 2**
FEBRUARY 27th 1889
FRIENDLY MATCH
GOALS DAVIES (20) (2-0), MULLEN (1-2)
TEAMS
EVERTON (2-3-5) SMALLEY (RE), DICK (A), ROSS (NR) (Captain), DAVIES (J)
ADDITIONAL, NO OTHER INFORMATION TRACED

**SUNDERLAND 4 EVERTON 2**
MARCH 5th 1889
FRIENDLY MATCH
TEAMS
GOALS DAVIDSON ( ) McLACHLAN ( ) ( ), CRECKONRIDGE ( ), CHADWICK ( ), DAVIES ( )
TEAMS

SUNDERLAND (2-3-5) KIRKLEY, OLIVER, SIMPSON, McKENCHNIE, RAYLATON, GIBSON, DAVIDSON, SMITH, BRECKONRIDGE, DAVIES, McLACHLAN
EVERTON (2-3-5) JOLIFFE (C), DICK (A), ROSS (JN) (Captain), CHADWICK (A), WEIR (J) ANGUS (J), WATSON (R), DAVIES (J), MILWARD (A), BROWN (W), CHADWICK (E)

## BOOTLE 3 EVERTON 3
MARCH 9th 1889
FRIENDLY MATCH
HAWTHORN ROAD
REFEREE RP GREGSON
GOALS WOOD (0-1) MORRIS (0-2), CHADWICK (1-2)' JAMIESON (1-3), DAVIES (2-3), BROWN (3-3)
TEAMS
BOOTLE (2-3-5) JACKSON, McFARLANE, WOODS (FR), CAMPBELL (W), ALLISOP (A), HUGHES, CAMPBELL (W) (Future Blue), WOOD, GAIBRAITH (H), MORRIS (T), JAMIESON (E), HASTING (W)
EVERTON (2-3-5) SMALLEY (RE), DOBSON (G), ROSS (NR) (Captain), WEIR (J), HOLT (J), FARMER (G), DAVIES (J), WATSON (R), MILWARD (A), CHADWICK (E), BROWN (W)
ATT 7,000

## EVERTON 2 HALLIWELL 0
MARCH 16th 1889
FRIENDLY MATCH
ANFIELD
GOALS MILWARD (1-0), DAVIES (2-0)
TEAMS
EVERTON (2-3-5) JOLIFFE (C), POWELL (J), ROSS (NR) (Captain), WILSON (W), WEIR (J), NIDD (F), DAVIES (J), WATSON (R), MILWARD (A), WAUGH (D), ANGUS (J)
HALLIWELL (2-3-5) FAIRCLOUGH, LUCAS, ROBB, DERHAM, SCROWCROFT, McDOUGALL (M), CROMBIE, HAY, RUSSELL' HEWITSON, McGUINNESS
ATT 4,000

## HIGHER WALTON 3 EVERTON X1 1
MARCH 16th 1889
LANCASHIRE SENIOR CUP SEMI-FINAL
ANFIELD
REFEREE R NORRIS
GOALS MATHER (J) (25) (1-3), MATHER (W) (43), CHADWICK (1-2)
TEAMS
HIGHER WALTON (2-3-5) CHATMAN, OSE, DALY, NAYLOR (T), SPENCER, BALDWIN, MATHER (T), ODDON, MATHER (W), NAYLOR (E), NAYLOR (T)
EVERTON (2-3-5) SMALLEY (RE), DOBSON (G) (Captain), CHADWICK (A), FAYER (T), HOLT (J), FARMER (G), FLEMING (G), BRISCOE (W), BROWN (W), CHADWICK (E), COSTLEY (J)
ATT 1,500

## EVERTON 3 SOUTH SHORE 0 (HT 1-0)
MARCH 23rd 1889
FRIENDLY MATCH
ANFIELD
GOALS WILSON (1-0), WATSON (65), MOORE OG (3-0)
TEAMS
EVERTON (2-3-5) SMALLEY (RE), DOBSON (G), ROSS (NR) (Captain), WEIR (J), HOLT (J), FARMER (G), DAVIES (J), WATSON (R), CHADWICK (E), WAUGH (D), WILSON (W)
SOUTH SHORE (2-3-5) LANGLEY, GOSLING, MOORE (F), WATSON (J), SHARPLES (E), WALSH (R), HACKING (A), RICHARDS, ELSTON, ROBERTS, ELSTON, PARKINSON (A), COOKSON (H)
ATT 5,000

## EVERTON 4 SOUTHPORT CENTRAL 1 (HT 1-1)
MARCH 27th 1889
FRIENDLY MATCH
ANFIELD
GOALS WATSON (10) (2-1), FACITT (1-1)' CHADWICK (3-1), SUGG (4-1)
TEAMS
EVERTON (2-3-5) JOLIFFE (C), DOBSON (G), ROSS (NR) (Captain), WEIR (J), SUGG (FH), FARMER (G), DAVIES (J), WATSON (R),

MILWARD (A), CHADWICK (E), WAUGH (D)
SOUTHPORT CENTRAL (2-3-5) GEE, HODGKINSON, SHAW
(J), HORTON, WEIR (C), LES, HARRISON, MULLEN, FACITT,
GRAHAM, DUNCAN
ATT 1,000

## EVERTON 3 BLACKBURN ROVERS 1 (HT 1-1)
MARCH 30th 1889
REFEREE MR HELME
ANFIELD
GOALS MILWARD (10), WHITTAKER (1-1), WAUGH (46), DAVIES
(47)
TEAMS
EVERTON (2-3-5) SMALLEY (RE), WILSON (W) (Last apps) DOBSON
(G) (Captain) (Last apps signed for Southport) FARMER (G), HOLT (J),
WEIR (J), WAUGH (D last apps Retired) CHADWICK (E), MILWARD
(A), BROWN (W) (Last apps), DAVIES (J)(Last apps), BLACKBURN
ROVERS (2-3-5) ARTHUR, SOUTHWORTH (Jas), FORBES,
BARTON, DOUGLAS, FORREST, BERESTFORD, HARESNAPE,
SOUTHWORTH (J) (Future Blue), WHITTAKER, TOWNLEY
ATT 6,000

## EVERTON 8 EARLESTOWN 2 (HT 5-2)
APRIL 3rd 1889
FRIENDLY MATCH
ANFIELD
GOALS FARMER (1-0), CHAMPION OG (2-0), DAVIES (3-0) (6-2),
CHADWICK (4-0) (7-2), SHAW (W) (1-4), BROWN (5-1), MORRIS
(2-5), WAUGH (8-2)
TEAMS
EVERTON (2-3-5) JOLIFFE (C), DOBSON (G)(Captain), WILSON
(W), FARMER (G), WEIR (J), NIDD (F), DAVIES (J), WAUGH (D),
CHADWICK (W), MILWARD (A), BROWN (W)
EARLESTOWN (2-3-5) CHAMPION, GREEN, JONES, JOHNSON,
HOWELL, ALLISON, SHAW (J), SHAW (W) CONWAY, MORRIS,
SIDDELEY
ATT 500

**EVERTON 4 WITTON 1 (HT 1-0)**
APRIL 6th 1889
FRIENDLY MATCH
ANFIELD
GOALS MILWARD (1-0), FARMER (2-0)(3-1), HORSEFIELD (1-2), PARRY (89)
TEAMS
EVERTON (2-3-5) SMALLEY (RE), DOBSON (G)(Captain), WILSON (W), FARMER (G), HOLT (J), WEIR (J), DAVIES (J), PARRY (C), MILWARD (A), CHADWICK (E), WAUGH (D)
WITTON (2-3-5) SHARPLES, SMITH (J), SHORROCK, ALSTON, ISHERWOOD, PICKERING, RUSTON, SMITH (H), GRIMSHAW, HORSEFIELD, TURNER
ATT 7,000

**SOUTH SHORE 4 EVERTON 1**
APRIL 8th 1889
FRIENDLY MATCH

**EVERTON 7 NORTHWICH VICTORIA 1 (HT 6-0)**
APRIL 10th 1889
FRIENDLY MATCH
ANFIELD
REFEREE H McINTYRE
GOALS AUGUS (2) (5-0), MILWARD (10) (7-1), PARRY (3-0) (6-0), BRISCOE (4-0), LETHER (1-6)
TEAMS
EVERTON (2-3-5) JOLIFFEE (C), CHADWICK (A), POLLOCH (H), NIDD (F), WILSON (W), JONES (W), ANGUS (J), BRISCOE (W), MILWARD (A), PARRY (A), BROWN (W)
NORTHWICH VICTORIA (2-3-5) FALLOWS, MADDOCK, CROSS, HANKEY, WHITLOW, DALTON, ROWBOTTON, LEATHER, GOLDEN, UPTON, PICKERING
ATT 1,000

**EVERTON 1 BOOTLE 2 (HT 1-1)**
APRIL 13th 1889
FRIENDLY MATCH

ANFIELD
REFEREE FITZROY NORRIS
GOALS JAMIESON (3), PARRY (1-1), WOODS (J) (87)
TEAMS
EVERTON (2-3-5) SMALLEY (RE), DOBSON (G), ROSS (NR)
(Captain), WEIR (J), WILSON (W), FARMER (G), DAVIES (J), PARRY
(C), MILWARD (A), CHADWICK (E), WAUGH (D)
BOOTLE (2-3-5) JARDINE (D) (Future Blue), WOODS (F), MacFARLANE
(E), ALLSOP (A), MORRIS (T), CAMPBELL (W) (Future Blue), WOODS
(J), GALBRAITH (H), JAMIESON (E), JONES (J), HASTING (N)
ATT 10,000

## EVERTON 3 NEWTON HEATH 1 (HT 2-0)
APRIL 15th 1889
FRIENDLY MATCH
ANFIELD
GOALS ANGUS (4), BRISCOE (2-0), WILLIAMS (1-2), ROSS (3-1)
TEAMS
EVERTON (2-3-5) SMALLEY (RE), DOBSON (G), ROSS (NR) (Captain),
WEIR (J), HOLT (J), FARMER (G), BRISCOE (W), WATSON (R),
MILWARD (A), ANGUS (N), BROWN (W)
NEWTON HEATH (2-3-5) HAYS, MITCHELL, POWELL, BURKE, OWEN,
JONES, TAIT, JARRETT, WILLIAMS, DOUGHTY, GOTHERIDGE
ATT 3,500

## EVERTON 0 LONDON CALEDONIANS 1 (HT 0-0)
APRIL 19th 1889
FRIENDLY MATCH
ANFIELD
GOAL BARBOUR (0-1)
TEAMS
EVERTON (2-3-5) SMALLEY (RE), WILSON (W), ROSS (NR) (Captain),
WEIR (J), HOLT (J), NIDD (F), DAVIES (J), ANGUS (J), MILWARD (A),
CHADWICK (E), FARMER (G)
LONDON CALEDONIANS (2-3-5) STIRLING, STEWART, NEIL, CLARK,
CASSELTON, SMITH, BURNS, MacALPIN, BARBOUR, REA, LAMBIE
ATT 14,000

**EVERTON 0 BURSLEM PORT VALE 1 (HT 0-1)**
APRIL 20th 1889
FRIENDLY MATCH
ANFIELD
REFEREE MR WALTER SUGG
GOALS McGUNNESS (0-1)
TEAMS
EVERTON (2-3-5) SMALLEY (RE), WILSON (W), DOBSON (G)(Captain), WEIR (J), FARRAR, HOLT (J), BROWN (W), PARRY (C), MILWARD (A), CHADWICK (E), FARMER (G)
BURSLEM PORT VALE (2-3-5) BLLOOMSHALL, BATEMAN, MARRIOTT (T), POULSTON, SHIELD, ELSTON, REYNOLDS, BALHAM, McGUINESS, STOKES, DITCHFIELD
ATT 7,000

**EVERTON 2 RENTON 1 (HT 0-1)**
APRIL 22nd 1889
FRIENDLY MATCH
ANFIELD
REFREEE R LYTHGOE
GOALS HARVEY (0-1), BRISCOE (1-1), MILWARD (2-1)
TEAMS
EVERTON (2-3-5) SMALLEY (RE), DOBSON (G), ROSS (NR) (Captain), WEIR (J), HOLT (J), FARMER (G), KEYS (J), BRISCOW (W), MILWARD (A), ANGUS (J), CHADWICK (E)
RENTON (2-3-5) LINDLEY, HANNAH (A) (Captain) (Future Blue), McCALL (A), BROWN, GARDNER, CAMPBELL (G) HARVEY, McCALL (J), CAMPBELL (H), CAMPBELL (J), McNEE
ATT 12,000

**HEARTS 3 EVERTON 0**
APRIL 25th 1889
FRIENDLY MATCH
GOALS SCOTT ( ) ( ), TAYLOR ( )
EVERTON (2-3-5) JOLIFFE (C),DOBSON ROSS (NJ) (Captain), WEIR (J), HOLT (J), CHADWICK (A), WATSON (R), MILWARD (A) ,CHADWICK (A)
ATT 4,000

ADDITIONAL, NO OTHER INFORMATION TRACED IN LOCAL PAPERS

**EVERTON 1 WITTON 0 (HT 0-0)**
APRIL 27th 1889
FRIENDLY MATCH
ANFIELD
GOALS ROSS (1-0)
TEAMS
EVERTON (2-3-5) SMALLEY (RE), DOBSON (G), ROSS (NR) (Captain), WEIR (J), HOLT (J), FARMER (G), KEYS (J), BRISCOE (W), MILWARD (A), CHADWICK (E), ANGUS (J)
WITTON (2-3-5) SHARPLES, SMITH, FRANKLAND, WHITESIDE, ISERWOOD, PICKERING, RUSHTON, GRIMSHAW, HIGGINS, SMITH (Jun) HORSEFIELD
ATT 6,000

**EVERTON 0 BURNLEY 1 (HT 0-0)**
APRIL 29th 1889
FRIENDLY MATCH
ANFIELD
GOALS DUCKWORTH (0-1)
TEAMS
EVERTON (2-3-5) SMALLEY (RE), DOBSON (G), ROSS (NR) (Captain), WEIR (J), FARMER (G), WEIR (C), WATSON (R), BRISCOE (W), MILWARD (A), CHADWICK (E), HIGGINS (W)
BURNLEY (2-3-5) COX (W) (Future Blue), BERRY, WHITE, FRIEL, KENNAN, McFETTRIDGE, HIBBERT, DUCKWORTH, CAMPBELL, CROSSLEY, YATES
ATT 2,000

**NEWTON HEATH 1 EVERTON 1 (HT 0-0)**
MAY 1st 1889
FRIENDLY MATCH
REFEREE T HULME
GOALS WILSON (1-0)' TAIT (89)
TEAMS
NEWTON HEATH (2-3-5) HAYS, MITCHELL, POWELL (Captain),

BURKE, DAVIES, OWEN, TAIT, GALE, DOUGHTY (D), GRAIT, DOUGHTY (R)
EVERTON (2-3-5) JOLIFFE (C), CHADWICK (A), DOBSON (G) (Captain), WILSON (W), HOLT (J), NIDD (F), BROWN (W), DAVIES (J), PARRY (C), CHADWICK (E), MILWARD (A)
ATT 4,000

## EVERTON 1 NOTTS RANGERS 0 (HT 0-0)
MAY 4th 1889
FRIENDLY MATCH
ANFIELD
GOALS PARRY (1-0)
TEAMS
EVERTON (2-3-5) SMALLEY (RE), DOBSON (G) (Captain), CHADWICK (A),FARMER (G), HOLT (J), WEIR (J), BRISCOE (W), WILSON (W), PARRY (C), MILWARD (A), CHADWICK (E)
NOTTS RANGERS (2-3-5) TOONE, SMITH (GH), TOPSHAM, SMITH (W), JAMES, CARLIN, SHAW, COOKE, GEARY (F) (Future Blue), SHARPE, SHELTON
ATT 5,000

## EVERTON 1 BOLTON WANDERERS 0
MAY 6th 1889
FRIENDLY MATCH
ANFIELD
GOALS ARMITT (88)
TEAMS
EVERTON (2-3-5) JOLIFFE (C), CHADWICK (A), DOBSON (G) (Captain)' FARMER (G) HOLT (J), WEIR (J), ARMITT (T) (Police Athletic), CHADWICK (E), PARRY (C), BRISCOW (W) WILSON (W)
BOLTON WANDERERS (2-3-5) HARRISON, DOYLE (R) (Future Blue), JONES, BULLOUGH, MILNE, ROBERTS, DAVENPORT, GALBRAITH (BOOTLE), BARBOUR, WEIR (D), TURNER
ATT 5,000

**ULSTER 0 EVERTON 2 (HT 0-0)**
MAY 11th 1889
FRIENDLY MATCH
GOALS BRISCOE (1-0), MILWARD (2-0)
TEAMS
ULSTER (2-3-5) CLUSYTON, ELLEMAN, WATSON, TIENLY, ROSBOTTOM, REID, GAUSSEN, MILLER, BARRY, LEMON, SMALL, MILLER
EVERTON (2-3-5) SMALLEY (RE), DOBSON (G)(captain), CHADWICK (A), WEIR (J), HOLT (J), NIDD (F), PARRY (C), BRISCOE (W), WILSON (W), CHADWICK (E), MILWARD (A)

**EVERTON 6 BLACKBURN OLYMPIC 1 (HT 3-1)**
MAY 13th 1889
ANFIELD
GOALS PARKER (0-1), PARRY (1-1), FENN (2-1) (6-1)' CHADWICK (3-1) (5-1), BRISCOE(4-1)
TEAMS
EVERTON (2-3-5) JOLIFFE (C), OWEN, LLOYD, WILSON (W), DOBSON (G)(captain), FARMER (G), FENN, BRISCOE (W), PARRY (C), FEWITT, CHADWICK (E)
BLACKBURN OLYMPIC (2-3-5) HUNTER (Captain), BEVERLEY, WARD, ASTLEY, McOWEN, ALMOND, DEWHURST, MATTHEWS, PARKER, YATES, COSTLE

**EVERTON 2 DARWIN 0**
MAY 18th 1889
FRIENDLY MATCH
ANFIELD
GOALS BRISCOE (1-0), HOLDEN OG (44)
TEAMS
EVERTON (2-3-5) SMALLEY (RE), ROBINSON (B), DOBSON (G)(captain), NIDD (F), ALMOND, FARMER (G), BRISCOE (W), WILSON (W), PARRY (C), CHADWICK (E), FACITT
DARWIN (2-3-5) HOLDEN, MARSDEN (J), LEACH, THORNBER, OWEN, MARSDEN (T), HAYES, MARSDEN (W), HADDON, SMITH, SLATER
ATT 7,000

## EVERTON 1 PRESTON NORTH END 3 (HT 0-1)
MAY 20th 1889
FRIENDLY MATCH
ANFIELD
GOALS ROSS (NR) (0-1) (0-2) ROSS (JUN) (0-3), GEARY (1-3)
TEAMS
EVERTON (2-3-5) SMALLEY (RE), ROBINSON (B), DOBSON (G)(captain), HOWARTH (R), ALMOND, FARMER (G), FECITT, PARRY (C), GEARY (F),CHADWICK (E), WILSON (W)
PRESTON NORTH END (2-3-5) TRAINER, HOWARTH (R) (Future Blue), HOLMES, ROBINSON, KELSO (R)(Future Blue), GRAHAM, GORDON (J), ROSS (Jun), DEWHURST, DRUMMOND, ROSS (NR) (Captain)
ATT 10,000

## EVERTON 1 ACCRINGTON 0 (HT 0-0)
MAY 25th 1889
FRIENDLY MATCH
ANFIELD
GOAL CHADWICK (1-0)
TEAMS
EVERTON (2-3-5) SMALLEY (RE), ROBINSON (B), DOBSON (G)(captain), FARMER (G), ALMOND, WILSON (W), PARRY (C), FENN, GEARY (F), CHADWICK (E), FACITT
ACCRINGTON (2-3-5) McOWEN, STEVENSON, McLENNON, TATTERSALL, CHIPPENDALE, PEMBERTON, GALLACHER, BONAR, BARBOUR, KIRKHAM, LOFTHOUSE
ATT 7,000

## EVERTON 2 BOLTON WANDERERS 2 (HT 1-1)
MAY 31st 1889
FRIENDLY MATCH
ANFIELD
REFEREE MR LYTHGOE
GOALS CHADWICK (1-0) (2-2), BROGAN (1-1), TURNER (1-2)
TEAMS
EVERTON (2-3-5) SMALLEY (RE), DOBSON (G)(captain), WILSON (W), WEIR (J), ALMOND, FARMER (G), FENN, PARRY (C), GEARY

(F), CHADWICK (E), MILWARD (A)
BOLTON WANDERERS (2-3-5) HARRISON, ROBINSON, LUCAS, BULLOUGH, CROMBIE, ROBERTS, DAVENPORT, BROGAN, HARBOUR, WEIR (D), TURNER
ATT 3,000

Everton League Division One 1888-89

| No | Date | Team | Venue | Att | Score | Scorer | Games | For | Against |
|---|---|---|---|---|---|---|---|---|---|
| 1 | Sep 8 1888 | Accrington | H | 12,000 | 2-1 | Fleming (2) | 1 | 2 | 1 |
| 2 | Sep 15 1888 | Notts County | H | 9,000 | 2-1 | Dick, Ross | 2 | 4 | 2 |
| 3 | Sep 22 1888 | Aston Villa | A | 5,000 | 1-2 | Watson | 3 | 5 | 4 |
| 4 | Sep 26 1888 | Bolton Wanderers | A | 5,000 | 2-6 | Lewis, Watson | 4 | 7 | 10 |
| 5 | Oct 6 1888 | Aston Villa | H | 12,000 | 2-0 | Waugh, Farmer | 5 | 9 | 10 |
| 6 | Oct 13 1888 | Notts County | A | 4,000 | 1-3 | Ross | 6 | 10 | 13 |
| 7 | Oct 20 1888 | Derby County | A | 3,000 | 4-2 | Costley (2), McKinnon, Chadwick | 7 | 14 | 15 |
| 8 | Oct 27 1888 | Derby County | H | 8,000 | 6-2 | Ross (2), McKinnon (3), Watson | 8 | 20 | 17 |
| 9 | Nov 3 1888 | Bolton Wanderers | H | 6,000 | 2-1 | Brown, Ross | 9 | 22 | 18 |
| 10 | Nov 10 1888 | Blackburn Rovers | A | 6,000 | 0-3 | | 10 | 22 | 21 |
| 11 | Nov 17 1888 | Burnley | A | 3,000 | 2-2 | Watson, Chadwick | 11 | 24 | 23 |
| 12 | Nov 24 1888 | Burnley | H | 8000 | 3-2 | Chadwick, Coyne, Berry OG | 12 | 27 | 25 |
| 13 | Dec 1 1888 | West Bromwich Albion | A | 7,000 | 1-4 | Chadwick | 13 | 28 | 29 |
| 14 | Dec 15 1888 | Stoke City | A | 1,500 | 0-0 | | 14 | 28 | 29 |
| 15 | Dec 22 1888 | Preston North End | A | 8,000 | 0-3 | | 15 | 28 | 32 |
| 16 | Dec 29 1888 | Accrington | A | 2,500 | 1-3 | Watson | 16 | 29 | 35 |
| 17 | Jan 12 1889 | Stoke City | H | 7,000 | 2-1 | Milward, Davies | 17 | 31 | 36 |
| 18 | Jan 19 1889 | Preston North End | H | 15,000 | 0-2 | | 18 | 31 | 38 |
| 19 | Jan 26 1889 | Wolverhampton W | A | 3,000 | 0-5 | | 19 | 31 | 43 |
| 20 | Feb 9 1889 | Wolverhampton W | H | 10,000 | 1-2 | Chadwick | 20 | 32 | 45 |
| 21 | Feb 23 1889 | West Bromwich Albion | H | 11,000 | 0-1 | | 21 | 32 | 46 |
| 22 | Mar 30 1889 | Blackburn Rovers | H | 6,000 | 3-1 | Milward, Waugh, Davies | 22 | 35 | 47 |

e denotes Cap

Everton League Division One Team Selection 188-89

| Game | Keeper 1 | Back 2 | Back 3 | Half back 4 | Half back 5 | Half back 6 | Right out 7 | Right in 8 | Centre 9 | Left in 10 | Left out 11 |
|---|---|---|---|---|---|---|---|---|---|---|---|
| 1 | Smalley | Dick | Ross e | Holt | Jones | Dobson | Fleming | Waugh | Lewis | Chadwick | Farmer |
| 2 | Smalley | Dick | Ross e | Holt | McKinnon | Dobson | Fleming | Waugh | Lewis | Chadwick | Farmer |
| 3 | Smalley | Dick | Ross e | Weir | Warmby | Higgins | Waugh | Watson | Keys | Chadwick | Farmer |
| 4 | Smalley | Dick | Ross e | Weir | Dobson | Pollock | Waugh | Watson | Chadwick | Lewis | Farmer |
| 5 | Smalley | Dick | Ross e | Weir | Holt | Farmer | McKinnon | Watson | Sugg | Chadwick | Waugh |
| 6 | Smalley | Dick | Ross e | Weir | Holt | Farmer | Watson | McKinnon | Sugg | Briscoe | Chadwick |
| 7 | Joliffe | Dobson | Ross e | Weir | Holt | Farmer | McKinnon | McKinnon | Sugg | Chadwick | Costley |
| 8 | Smalley | Dobson | Sugg | Weir | Holt | Farmer | McKinnon | Watson | Ross e | Chadwick | Costley |
| 9 | Smalley | Dick | Dobson | Weir | Holt | Farmer | McKinnon | Watson | Ross e | Chadwick | Brown |
| 10 | Smalley | Dobson | Ross e | Weir | Sugg | Holt | Farmer | Watson | Milward | Chadwick | Brown |
| 11 | Smalley | Dobson | Ross e | Holt | Sugg | Farmer | Fleming | Watson | Costley | Chadwick | Brown |
| 12 | Smalley | Sugg | Ross e | Weir | Holt | Farmer | Fleming | Coyne | Davie | Chadwick | Costley |
| 13 | Smalley | Dobson e | A Chadwick | Farmer | Weir | Sugg | Costley | Chadwick | Davie | Coyle | J Davies |
| 14 | Smalley | Dobson | Ross e | Weir | Holt | Farmer | J Davies | Watson | Morris | Chadwick | Costley |
| 15 | Smalley | Ross e | Dobson | Farmer | Sugg | Holt | Angus | Chadwick | Brown | Briscoe | Watson |
| 16 | Joliffe | Ross e | Dobson | Farmer | Weir | Parkinson | Watson | Briscoe | Brown | Chadwick | Angus |
| 17 | Joliffe | Dobson | Ross e | Kelso | Holt | Farmer | Angus | Chadwick | Watson | J Davies | Milward |
| 18 | Joliffe | Dobson | Ross e | Stevenson | Holt | Farmer | J Davies | Watson | Milward | Chadwick | Angus |
| 19 | Smalley | Dobson | Dobson e | Farmer | Roberts | A Chadwick | J Davies | Watson | Milward | J Davies | Milward |
| 20 | Smalley | Dick | Dobson e | Weir | Holt | Farmer | Brown | Chadwick | Watson | J Davies | Milward |
| 21 | Smalley | Dick | Dobson | Weir | Holt | Farmer | J Davies | Watson | Ross e | Chadwick | Waugh |
| 22 | Smalley | Wilson | Dobson | Farmer | Holt | Weir | Waugh | Chadwick | Milward | Brown | J Davies |

## Everton League Appearances and goals

ANGUS (J), 5 APPS, BRISCOE (W), 3 APPS, BROWN (W) 7 APPS 1 GOAL, CHADWICK (A) 2 APPS, CHADWICK (E) 22 APPS, 5 GOALS, COSTLEY (J) 6 APPS, 2 GOALS, DAVIE 2 APPS, DAVIES (J) 8 APPS, 2 GOALS, DICK (A) 9 APPS, 1 GOAL, DOBSON 18 APPS, FARMER (G), 21 APPS, 1 GOAL, FLEMING (G) 4 APPS, 2 GOALS, HIGGINS (M) 1 APP, HOLT (J) 17 APPS, JOLIFFE 4 APPS, JONES (R) 1 APP, KELSO (R) 1 APP. KEYS (J) 1 APPS, LEWIS (W) 3 APPS, 1 GOAL. McKINNON (A), 6 APPS, 4 GOALS, MILWARD (A) 6 APPS, 2 GOALS. ROSS (JN) 19 APPS, 5 GOALS. SMALLEY (R) 18 APPS. STEVENSON (G) 1 APP. SUGG (F) 9 APPS, WHARMBY (H) 1 APP, WATSON (R) 17 APPS 5 GOALS. WAUGH (D) 7 APPS, 2 GOALS. WEIR (J) 16 APPS. WILSON (W) 1 APP. OWN GOAL 1
CAPTAINS, ROSS 19 APPS, DOBSON 3 APPS.

## Everton Friendly Matches 1888-89

| No | Date | Team | Venue | Att | Score | Scorer |
|----|------|------|-------|-----|-------|--------|
| 1 | Sep 1 1888 | Padiham | H | 7,000 | 4-1 | Farmer (2), Chadwick, Thomson OG |
| 2 | Sep 3 1888 | Blackburn Olympic | H | 4,000 | 1-2 | Chadwick |
| 3 | Sep 5 1888 | Halliwell | H | 2,000 | 2-1 | Chadwick, Fleming |
| 4 | Sep 15 1888 | Stanley | H | 2,500 | 5-0 | Chadwick, Farmer (2), Ross, Unknown 1 |
| 5 | Sep 19 1888 | Derby Midland | H | 2,500 | 6-0 | Chadwick, Watson (2), Waugh, Ross Keys |
| 6 | Sep 26 1888 | Derby Juncture | H | 2,500 | 2-1 | Pollock, 1 not known |
| 7 | Oct 8 1888 | Burnley | A | 4,000 | 0-3 | |
| 8 | Oct 22 1888 | Denton | A | 5,000 | 3-0 | Not known |
| 9 | Dec 8 1888 | Long Eaton Rangers | H | 5,000 | 3-1 | Chadwick (2), Morris |
| 10 | Dec 10 1888 | Burslem Port Vale | A | 2,000 | 2-2 | Chadwick, Morris |
| 11 | Dec 25 1888 | Ulster | H | 6,000 | 3-0 | Milward, Weir, Joliffe |
| 12 | Dec 26 1888 | Bootle | H | 16,000 | 0-0 | |
| 13 | Jan 1 1889 | Third Lanark | H | 6,000 | 2-2 | Milward, Not-known |
| 14 | Jan 2 1889 | Cambuslang | H | 2,500 | 2-1 | Chadwick, Milward |
| 15 | Jan 5 1889 | Blackburn Rovers | H | 6,000 | 1-0 | Watson |
| 16 | Feb 2 1889 | Battlefield | H | 5,000 | 3-2 | Milward, Brown, Ross |
| 17 | Feb 19 1889 | Dundee Stathmore | H | 9,000 | 5-1 | Ross (2), Chadwick Watson (2) |
| 18 | Feb 27 1889 | Southport Central | A | 500 | 2-1 | Davies (2) |
| 19 | Mar 5 1889 | Sunderland | A | - | 2-4 | Davies, Chadwick (e) |
| 20 | Mar 9 1889 | Bootle | A | 7,000 | 3-3 | Davies, Chadwick, Brown |
| 21 | Mar 16 1889 | Halliwell | H | 4,000 | 2-0 | Davies, Milward |
| 22 | Mar 19 1889 | Higher Walton (lan cup) | n | 1,500 | 1-3 | Chadwick |
| 23 | Mar 23 1889 | South Shore | H | 5,000 | 3-0 | Wilson, Watson, Moore OG |
| 24 | Mar 27 1889 | Southport Central | H | 1000 | 4-1 | Watson (2), Chadwick, Sugg |
| 25 | Apr 3 1889 | Earlestown | H | - | 8-2 | Davies (2) Chadwick (2), Brown, Morris, Waugh, Champion OG |
| 26 | Apr 6 1889 | Witton | H | 7,000 | 4-1 | Milward, Farmer (2) Parry |
| 27 | Apr 8 1889 | South Shore | A | - | 1-4 | Not known |

## Everton Friendly Matches 1888-89 Continued

| No | Date | Team | Venue | Score | Att | Scorer |
|---|---|---|---|---|---|---|
| 33 | Apr 22 1889 | Renton | H | 2-1 | 12,000 | Briscoe, Milward |
| 34 | Apr 25 1889 | Hearts Of Midlothian's | A | 0-3 | - | |
| 35 | Apr 27 1889 | Witton | H | 1-0 | 6,000 | Ross |
| 36 | Apr 29 1889 | Burnley | H | 0-1 | 2,000 | |
| 37 | May 1 1889 | Newton Heath | A | 1-1 | 4,000 | Wilson |
| 38 | May 4 1889 | Notts Rangers | H | 1-0 | 5,000 | Parry |
| 39 | May 6 1889 | Bolton Wanderers | H | 1-0 | 5,000 | Armitt |
| 40 | May 11 1889 | Ulster | A | 2-0 | 3,000 | Briscoe, Milward |
| 41 | May 13 1889 | Blackburn Olympic | H | 6-1 | - | Parry, Fenn (2), Chadwick (2), Briscoe |
| 42 | May 18 1889 | Darwen | H | 2-0 | 7,000 | Briscoe, Holden OG |
| 43 | May 20 1889 | Preston North End | H | 1-3 | 10,000 | Geary |
| 44 | May 25 1889 | Accrington | H | 1-0 | 7,000 | Chadwick |
| 45 | May 31 1889 | Bolton Wanderers | H | 2-2 | 3,000 | Chadwick (2) |

c denotes Captain

## Team selection for friendly matches 1888-89

| Game | Keeper 1 | Back 2 | Back 3 | Half back 4 | Half back 5 | Half back 6 | Right out 7 | Right in 8 | Centre 9 | Left in 10 | Left out 11 |
|---|---|---|---|---|---|---|---|---|---|---|---|
| 1 | Higgins | Dick | Ross c | Holt | Dobson | Warmby | Fleming | Waugh | Costley | Chadwick | Farmer |
| 2 | Jolliffe | Dick | Ross c | Holt | Dobson | Warmby | Fleming | Keys | Waugh | Chadwick | Farmer |
| 3 | Jolliffe | Ross c | Dobson | Warmby | Holt | Dick | Fleming | Waugh | Lewis | Chadwick | Farmer |
| 4 | Jolliffe | Dick | McKinnon | Warmby | Dobson | Holt | Farmer | Chadwick | Ross c | Waugh | Fleming |
| 5 | Smalley | Dick | Ross c | Warmby | Dobson | Weir | Farmer | Keys | Waugh | Watson | Chadwick |
| 6 | Jolliffe | Ross c | Ross c | Higgins | Pollock | Weir | Farmer | Chadwick | Milward | Waugh | Watson |
| 7 | Smalley | Ross c | Dick | A Chadwick | Holt | Farmer | Higgins | Chadwick | Sigg | Watson | McKinnon |
| 8 | Jolliffe | A Chadwick | Ross c | Weir | Fayer | Farmer | Costley | Chadwick | Sugg | McKinnon | Berry |
| 9 | Smalley | Sugg | Dobson c | Weir | Holt | Watson | Costley | Coyne | Morris | Chadwick | Costley |
| 10 | Jolliffe | A Chadwick | Ross c | Weir | Sugg | Farmer | J Davies | Angus | Morris | Chadwick | Costley |
| 11 | Jolliffe | Ross c | Higgins | Weir | Pollock | Stevenson | Angus | Falls | Milward | Watson | Keys |
| 12 | Jolliffe | Ross c | Dobson | Farmer | Holt | Weir | Angus | Chadwick | Briscoe | J Davies | Brown |
| 13 | Jolliffe | Ross c | Dobson | Weir | Holt | Farmer | Watson | J Davies | Milward | Chadwick | Brown |
| 14 | Jolliffe | Dobson | Ross c | Holt | Sigg | Farmer | Watson | Milward | Angus | Davis | Chadwick |
| 15 | Jolliffe | Ross c | Dobson | Farmer | Holt | Weir | Angus | Chadwick | Milward | Watson | Brown |
| 16 | Smalley | Dick | Ross c | Dobson | Holt | Farmer | J Davies | Watson | Milward | Chadwick | Brown |
| 17 | Smalley | Dobson | Dick | Farmer | Holt | Weir | Brown | Chadwick | Ross c | Watson | J Davies |

Team Selection for Friendly Matches 1888-89 Continued

c denotes Captain

| Game | Keeper 1 | Back 2 | Back 3 | Half back 4 | Half back 5 | Half back 6 | Right out 7 | Right in 8 | Centre 9 | Left in 10 | Left out 11 |
|---|---|---|---|---|---|---|---|---|---|---|---|
| 18 | Smalley | Dick | Ross c | - | - | - | - | - | - | - | J Davies |
| 19 | Joliffe | Dick | Ross c | A Chadwick | - | Angus | Watson | J Davies | - | Brown | Chadwick |
| 20 | Smalley | Dobson | Ross c | Weir | Weir | Farmer | J Davies | Watson | Milward | Chadwick | Brown |
| 21 | Joliffe | Powell | Ross c | Wilson | Weir | Nidd | J Davies | Watson | Milward | Waugh | Angus |
| 22 | Smalley | Dobson c | A Chadwick | Fayer | Holt | Farmer | Fleming | briscoe | Milward | Chadwick | Cosley |
| 23 | Smalley | Dobson | Ross c | Weir | Holt | Farmer | J Davies | Watson | Brown | Waugh | Wilson |
| 24 | Joliffe | Dobson | Ross c | Farmer | Stagg | Weir | Waugh | Chadwick | Chadwick | Watson | J Davies |
| 25 | Joliffe | Dobson c | Wilson | Farmer | Weir | Nidd | J Davies | Waugh | Milward | Milward | Brown |
| 26 | Smalley | Dobson c | Wilson | Farmer | Holt | Weir | J Davies | Parry | Chadwick | Chadwick | Waugh |
| 27 | - | - | - | - | - | - | - | - | Milward | - | - |
| 28 | Joliffe | A Chadwick | Pollock c | Nidd | Wilson | Jones | Brown | Parry | Milward | Briscoe | Angus |
| 29 | Smalley | Dobson | Ross c | Weir | Wilson | Farmer | J Davies | Parry | Milward | Chadwick | Waugh |
| 30 | Smalley | Dobson | Ross c | Weir | Holt | Farmer | Briscoe | Watson | Milward | Angus | Brown |
| 31 | Smalley | Wilson | Ross c | Weir | Holt | Nidd | Davis | Angus | Milward | Chadwick | Farmer |
| 32 | Smalley | Wilson | Dobson c | Weir | Farrar | Holt | Brown | Parry | Milward | Chadwick | Farmer |
| 33 | Smalley | Dobson | Ross c | Weir | Holt | Farmer | Keys | Briscoe | Milward | Angus | Chadwick |
| 34 | Joliffe | A Chadwick | - | Weir | - | - | Keys | - | Milward | Watson | Chadwick |
| 35 | Smalley | Dobson | Ross c | Weir | Holt | Farmer | Keys | Briscoe | Milward | Chadwick | Angus |
| 36 | Smalley | Dobson | Ross c | J Weir | Farmer | C Weir | Watson | Briscoe | Milward | Chadwick | Higgins |
| 37 | Joliffe | A Chadwick | Dobson c | Wilson | Holt | Nidd | Brown | J Davies | Parry | Chadwick | Milward |
| 38 | Smalley | Dobson c | A Chadwick | Farmer | Holt | Weir | Briscoe | Wilson | Parry | Milward | Chadwick |
| 39 | Joliffe | A Chadwick | Dobson c | Farmer | Holt | Weir | Armitt | Chadwick | Parry | Briscoe | Wilson |
| 40 | Smalley | A Chadwick | Dobson c | Weir | Holt | Nidd | Parry | Briscoe | Wilson | Chadwick | Milward |
| 41 | Joliffe | Owen | Lloyd | Wilson | Dobson c | Farmer | Fenn | Wilson | Parry | Facitt | Chadwick |
| 42 | Smalley | Robinson | Dobson c | Nidd | Almond | Farmer | Briscoe | Wilson | Parry | Chadwick | Facitt |
| 43 | Smalley | Robinson | Dobson c | Howarth | Almond | Farmer | Facitt | Parry | Geary | Chadwick | Wilson |
| 44 | Smalley | Robinson | Dobson c | Farmer | Almond | Wilson | Parry | Fenn | Geary | Chadwick | Facitt |
| 45 | Smalley | Wilson | Dobson c | Weir | Almond | Farmer | Fenn | Parry | Geary | Chadwick | Milward |

## Everton Reserves Matches 1888-89

| No | Date | Team | Venue | Att | Score | Scorer |
|---|---|---|---|---|---|---|
| 1 | Sep 2 1888 | Saltney | A | - | 5-1 | Harper, Keys |
| 2 | Sep 4 1888 | Bootle Reserves | A | 2,500 | 1-0 | Briscow |
| 3 | Sep 8 1888 | Spring Branch Rovers | A | - | 2-1 | |
| 4 | Sep 22 1888 | Borth Athletic | H | 2,000 | 3-0 | McKinnon, Pollock Milward |
| 5 | Oct 6 1888 | Crewe Stream Sheds | A | - | 5-1 | Keys |
| 6 | Oct13 1888 | Earlestown | H | 3,000 | 11-0 | Berry (2), Keys (2), Pollock (2), Costley, (3), Falls , Milward |
| 7 | Oct 20 1888 | Tranmere Rovers | A | 600 | 0-1 | |
| 8 | Oct 27 1888 | Bootle Reserves | A | 1,500 | 3-2 | Keys Milward, Unknown 1 |
| 9 | Nov 3 1888 | Chester Collegue | A | - | 7-2 | |
| 10 | Nov 17 1888 | Saltney | H | 2,000 | 2-0 | Jones (2) |
| 11 | Nov 24 1888 | Stoke Swifts | A | - | 0-0 | |
| 12 | Dec 1 1888 | Burslam Port Vale | H | 2,000 | 1-1 | Brown |
| 13 | Dec 8 1888 | Skelmersdale | A | - | 4-1 | Milward (3), Watson |
| 14 | Dec 15 1888 | Stoke Swifty | H | 3,000 | 3-0 | Briscoe (2), Angus. |
| 15 | Dec 22 1888 | Preston North End Res | H | 2,000 | 4-1 | Milward (3) Falls |
| 16 | Dec 29 1888 | Bootle Reserves | H | 3,000 | 1-1 | Milward |
| 17 | Jan 5 1889 | Southport Old Boys | A | - | 1-2 | Fall |
| 18 | Jan 19 1889 | Preston North End | A | - | 0-4 | |
| 19 | Jan 26 1889 | Northwich Victoria | H | 3,000 | 6-0 | Briscoe (2), Brown, (w), Taylor, Brown (r) |
| 20 | Feb 16 1889 | Tranmere Rovers | A | 1,000 | 5-1 | Milward, Brown, (2) Waugh , Briscoe |
| 21 | Mar 2 1889 | Burslam Port Vale | A | - | 4-2 | Milward (3) |
| 22 | Mar 9 1889 | Aintree Church | H | - | 3-0 | Keys (2), Briscoe |
| 23 | Mar 24 1889 | Chester Collegue | H | - | 2-1 | |
| 24 | Apr 6 1889 | Aigburth Vale | A | - | 4-3 | Weir (2) Angus, Robinson |
| 25 | Apr 13 1889 | Churchtown | A | - | 0-0 | |
| 26 | May 11 1889 | Daveham | H | - | 5-2 | Harbour (2) Pollocks, Keys, Fenn |
| 27 | May 19 1889 | Bootle Wanderers | A | - | 2-6 | Fenn, Rawstore |

## Lancashire Senior Cup

| R1 | Sep 29 1888 | Turton | H | 2,000 | 4-2 | |
| R2 | Nov 10 1888 | Padiham | H | 3,000 | 2-0 | Cookson, Costley |
| R3 | Dec 24 1888 | Blackburn Park Road | H | 4,000 | 3-2 | Jones, Harbour, Farmer |

## Team Selection for Reserve Matches 1888-89

| Game | Keeper 1 | Back 2 | Back 3 | Half back 4 | Half back 5 | Half back 6 | Right out 7 | Right in 8 | Centre 9 | Left in 10 | Left ou 11 |
|---|---|---|---|---|---|---|---|---|---|---|---|
| 1 | Jolitfe | Holdsworth | Chadwick | Parry | Pollock | W Jones | Keys | Brisoe | Harper | Cookson | Falls |
| 2 | Jolitfe | Chadwick | Higgins | Fayer | Jones | Pollock | Falls | Keys | Costley | Harper | Brisoce |
| 3 | Jolitfe | Ashcroft | Chadwick | W Jones | Pollock | Fayer | Scott | Brisoce | Costley | Cookson | R Jones |
| 4 | Jolitfe | Chadwick | Ashcroft | Parry | Pollock | W Jones | Fell | Cookson | Milward | McKinnon | Brisoce |
| 5 | Jolitfe | Chadwick | Ashcroft | W Jones | Pollock | Harbour | Keys | Brisoce | Milward | Costley | Falls |
| 6 | Jolitfe | Chadwick | Ashcroft | Fayer | Pollock | W Jones | Keys | A Berry | Milward | Costley | Falls |
| 7 | - | Chadwick | Ashcroft | Fayer | Pollock | W Jones | Keys | Dick | Milward | Berry | Fells |
| 8 | Jolitfe | Chadwick | Wharmby | Fayer | Pollock | W Jones | Keys | Brisoce | Milward | Berry | Falls |
| 9 | Jolitfe | Chadwick | - | Barbour | Pollock | W Jones | Keys | Brisoce | Milward | Berry | Falls |
| 10 | Jolitfe | Chadwick | Higgins | W Jones | Fayer | Pollock | Cookson | Harbour | Milward | Brisoce | Keys |
| 11 | Jolitfe | Chadwick | Wharmby | Parry | Fayer | W Jones | Keys | Brisoce | Milward | Costley | Harbour |
| 12 | Jolitfe | Pollock | Wharmby | W Jones | Fayer | J Parry | Brisoce | Cookson | Brown | Keys | R Jones |
| 13 | - | - | - | - | Pollock | - | Watson | Brisoce | Milward | Keys | - |
| 14 | Jolitfe | Higgins | Chadwick | W Jones | Pollock | Fayer | Brown | Angus | Brisoce | Keys | Milward |
| 15 | Jolitfe | Higgins | Chadwick | Parry | Pollock | Fayer | Falls | W Jones | Milward | Keys | Morris |
| 16 | Lindsay | Ashcroft | Higgins | Fayer | Pollock | Farmer | Keys | Harbour | Milward | R Jones | Kelly |
| 17 | - | Ashcroft | Robinson | Watson | Pollock | McGill | - | Harbour | Brisoe | R Jones | Falls |
| 18 | - | - | - | - | - | - | - | - | - | - | - |
| 19 | Jolitfe | Pollock | Chadwick | C Weir | R Jones | Fayer | W Brown | R Brown | Brisoce | Keys | A Taylor |
| 20 | Jolitfe | Chadwick | Connor | Fayer | Pollock | C Weir | Keys | Brisoce | Milward | R Brown | Waugh |
| 21 | Jolitfe | Chadwick | Pollock | Fayer | C Weir | C Weir | Keys | Brisoce | Milward | Brown | Angus |
| 22 | Jolitfe | Chadwick | Connor | C Weir | Pollock | Fayer | Angus | R Brown | Waugh | Brisoce | Keys |
| 23 | - | - | - | - | - | - | - | - | - | - | - |
| 24 | Jolitfe | - | Robinson | - | Roberts | Nidd | - | Brisoce | - | - | - |
| 25 | - | - | - | C Weir | - | - | - | - | - | - | Angus |
| 26 | Jolitfe | Fayer | Chadwick | C Weir | Pollocks | W Jones | Brisoce | Harbour | Watson | Fenn | Keys |
| 27 | - | - | - | - | - | - | - | - | - | - | - |

## Team Selection for Lancashire Senior Cup Matches 1888-89

| Game | Keeper 1 | Back 2 | Back 3 | Half back 4 | Half back 5 | Half back 6 | Right out 7 | Right in 8 | Centre 9 | Left in 10 | Left ou 11 |
|---|---|---|---|---|---|---|---|---|---|---|---|
| R1 | Jolitfe | Ashmore | Chadwick | W Jones | Hayes | Harbour | Brisoce | Fleming | Whittle | Berry | Costley |
| R2 | Jolitfe | Higgins | Chadwick | W Jones | Fayer | Parry | Harbour | Berry | Costley | Brisoce | Cookson |

## Season 1888-89 Results

| Teams | Accrington | Aston Villa | Blackburn Rovers | Bolton Wanderers | Burnley | Derby County | Everton | Notts County | Preston North End | Stoke | West Bromwich | Wolverhampton |
|---|---|---|---|---|---|---|---|---|---|---|---|---|
| Accrington Stanley | - | 1-0 | 0-2 | 2-3 | 5-1 | 6-2 | 3-1 | 1-2 | 0-0 | 2-0 | 2-1 | 4-4 |
| Aston Villa | 4-3 | - | 6-1 | 6-2 | 4-2 | 4-2 | 2-1 | 9-1 | 0-2 | 5-1 | 2-0 | 2-1 |
| Blackburn Rovers | 5-5 | 5-1 | - | 4-4 | 4-2 | 3-0 | 3-0 | 5-2 | 2-2 | 5-2 | 6-2 | 2-2 |
| Bolton Wanderers | 4-1 | 2-3 | 3-2 | - | 3-4 | 3-6 | 6-2 | 7-3 | 2-5 | 2-1 | 1-2 | 2-1 |
| Burnley | 2-2 | 4-0 | 1-7 | 4-1 | - | 1-0 | 2-2 | 1-0 | 2-2 | 2-1 | 2-0 | 0-4 |
| Derby County | 1-1 | 5-2 | 0-2 | 2-3 | 1-0 | - | 2-4 | 3-2 | 2-3 | 2-1 | 1-2 | 3-0 |
| Everton | 2-1 | 2-0 | 3-1 | 2-1 | 3-2 | 6-2 | - | 2-1 | 0-2 | 2-1 | 0-1 | 1-2 |
| Notts County | 3-3 | 2-4 | 3-3 | 0-4 | 6-1 | 3-5 | 3-1 | - | 0-7 | 0-3 | 2-1 | 3-0 |
| Preston North End | 2-0 | 1-1 | 1-0 | 3-1 | 5-2 | 5-0 | 3-0 | 4-1 | - | 7-0 | 3-0 | 5-2 |
| Stoke | 2-4 | 1-1 | 2-1 | 2-2 | 4-3 | 1-1 | 0-0 | 3-0 | 0-3 | - | 0-1 | 0-1 |
| West Bromwich Albion | 2-2 | 3-3 | 2-1 | 1-5 | 4-3 | 5-0 | 4-1 | 4-2 | 0-5 | 2-0 | - | 1-3 |
| Wolverhampton Wanderers | 4-0 | 1-1 | 2-2 | 3-2 | 4-1 | 4-1 | 5-0 | 2-1 | 0-4 | 4-1 | 2-1 | - |

## Season 1888-89 Final League Table

| Pos | Team | P | Home | | | | | Away | | | | | Pts |
|---|---|---|---|---|---|---|---|---|---|---|---|---|---|
| | | | W | D | L | F | A | W | D | L | F | A | |
| 1 | Preston North End | 22 | 10 | 1 | 0 | 39 | 7 | 8 | 3 | 0 | 35 | 8 | 40 |
| 2 | Aston Villa | 22 | 10 | 0 | 1 | 44 | 16 | 2 | 5 | 4 | 17 | 27 | 29 |
| 3 | Wolverhampton Wanderers | 22 | 8 | 2 | 1 | 30 | 14 | 4 | 2 | 5 | 20 | 23 | 28 |
| 4 | Blackburn Rovers | 22 | 7 | 4 | 0 | 44 | 22 | 3 | 2 | 6 | 22 | 23 | 26 |
| 5 | Bolton Wanderers | 22 | 6 | 0 | 5 | 35 | 30 | 4 | 2 | 5 | 28 | 29 | 22 |
| 6 | West Bromwich Albion | 22 | 6 | 2 | 3 | 25 | 24 | 4 | 0 | 7 | 15 | 31 | 22 |
| 7 | Accrington Stanley | 22 | 5 | 3 | 3 | 26 | 17 | 1 | 5 | 5 | 22 | 31 | 20 |
| 8 | Everton | 22 | 8 | 0 | 3 | 23 | 14 | 1 | 2 | 8 | 12 | 29 | 20 |
| 9 | Burnley | 22 | 6 | 3 | 2 | 21 | 19 | 1 | 0 | 10 | 21 | 43 | 17 |
| 10 | Derby County | 22 | 5 | 1 | 5 | 22 | 20 | 2 | 1 | 8 | 19 | 41 | 12 |
| 11 | Notts County | 22 | 4 | 2 | 5 | 25 | 32 | 1 | 0 | 10 | 15 | 41 | 12 |